New York Exposed :The Whitewater State
Volume 1

The whitewater guide of north flowing rivers in New York State

The drainages of Lake Ontario,

Lake Champlain,

and the Saint Lawrence River

☯A White Water Outlaw ♋ Publishing

By Dennis Squires

Both the Author and Publisher assume no responsibility for omissions, inaccuracies, errors or any other type of inconsistencies for what is printed in this book. A guide is only that, just a guide. A book, or any second hand information for that matter, will never tell you exactly what's out there. There are a lot of rivers and creeks in this state, more than one man can paddle every year. That means it has been a few years since some of these runs have been paddled/checked out. Please, if you paddle a run in this book and something has changed and/or needs to be added -- e-mail the website. Updated information will be added to the site.

This is about what Dennis experienced -- worse yet, what he thinks he remembers experiencing. High water moves rocks, small bridges and trees. So take this guidebook on your trip. Better yet, paddle these rivers with somebody who knows them. And most importantly, bring your brain -- it's worth a lot more than the best guidebook.

 Published by: A White Water Outlaw Publishing, P.O. Box 1233 Margaretville, New York 12455. Website: **www.whitewateroutlaw.com**. First edition. First printing.

Printed In Canada

Library of Congress Cataloging-in-Publication Data
Squires, Dennis
New York exposed: the whitewater state: vol. I: the whitewater guide of north flowing rivers in New York State. Dennis Squires -1st.ed.

10 9 8 7 6 5 4 3 2 1

ISBN 0-9719450-0-4

Front Cover: Tom Vickery in his backyard (Great Falls on the Black River). Photo by Julie Vickery.

Back Cover: Dennis showing you what not to do if you encounter a moose in northern New York. Photo by Ceci Mendez

Acknowledgments

Even though this is a work that I put a lot into there are several friends that helped in many ways. Many of the photographs were provided by Sally Dewes -- for that and the help she gave me to get started (and still does) word processing -- I thank her. Many thanks to Larry Quarltere -- he pulled my butt out of the fire the last minute by doing lots of scanning and proving in a variety of ways to be much more computer wise than myself. Thanks to Joshua and his company for printing the book and being so helpful every step of the way. Chris Koll jumped when I called him and sent me a treasure chest of photos -- thanks Chris. I'd like to thank Mike Duggan and Ed Huber for the use of their photos. Please Check out Ed and his website: www.splitrockvideo.com (he sells hot white water videos of the Adirondacks). Somebody had to get the front cover spot -- it went to Tom and Julie Vickery -- the photo was eye-grapping colorful, easy to write the title on and mostly importantly is an awesome photograph that begged to be seen by.... millions. My friend Lee Schaller helped with typing and word processing. Beth Sherr helped with e-mailing and word processing. Thanks to Dan Sherr for your belief and support in this project (and for honoring my tires). Buddy Mike Feldman helped with his profound wisdom and did the introduction to the book. Many thanks to Jody Dixon for proof reading and editing and offering extra profound advice. I have included a few of Mike and Jody's pictures as well. I want to thank Chester Shew for his help with scanning. Thanks to Edna Herman and her daughter Karen Straut for coming to help with computer stuff whenever I got stuck. I especially want to thank my mom, I really appreciate that ever-nurturing way that she has about her -- she is my greatest role model. Thank you everybody -- I'd offer to kiss you all but I think I already have…except for Chester, Chris, Tom and Mike…no, that's not right…there was that time that Mike and I……………man I wish I could have used that photo, but his wife would kill me.

Dedication

A very special dedication goes out to Lucie Squires. She was my grandmother and much loved. The intensity of fear she felt for water was transformed in me into an intense love of the water. I'm sure she still shudders whenever I say the word "Waterfall."

Introduction*

There are a lot of boaters that claim to be water logged, pruned and permanently wrinkled from having paddled incessantly all over the globe. What many don't realize is that there are paddling destinations a lot closer to home. Rivers and creeks that many of us cannot even take for granted because we don't even know they exist. My dog-eared Delorme Map of New York State is my "secret creek" index. Many of us have such a book, as does Dennis. It contains notes on runs that have been compiled over the years, some of which were successful, some turned out to be exquisite gems and others are best left unmentioned. Dennis would come over to my house and start the game of "I've got a creek." He would open his ratty Delorme and offer a coy hint such as, "It doesn't have much of a watershed…" I would immediately counter with, "Hmmm, uh-huh, did I mention this ducky run I've been scouting?" And on it would go until the wee hours… of 9 pm. Dennis ALWAYS won. Not only would he know the run I was describing he would predict the optimal flows months in advance, even in a drought year. I would of course try to guess his "secret creek" run and be off by a whole planet, usually Uranus.

Dennis has done his studies, Doctoral level. This is the most comprehensive regional guidebook I've read and amazingly Dennis has paddled virtually every run listed. Very few boaters realize the wealth of whitewater rivers and creeks that the Adirondack Mountain Region offers.

The initial purpose of this guide, as Dennis professes, was to focus on the steep creeks of New York State. My 'old school' mores objected to such a notion as to put down in writing all the logistics of the creek runs. Part of the challenge of paddling these out of the way gems was to research and plan the trips. Many winter nights were spent scanning topo maps, counting the contour lines, checking the headwaters and ardently anticipating the spring thaw. Hey, there I go again. OK, ardently anticipating the January thaw. For it is far easier to drag a boat over snow to that out of the way put-in, than to drag-carry-curse over rocks-stumps and through hordes of black flies. Anyone that deserved to paddle deserved to pay the price. But, that was more than a few years ago. Old School, New School, the line blurs as new technology, techniques and perspectives are assimilated into our sport. Actually if I adhered to the Old School I would have missed a lot of great paddling days. Days when I soloed some great runs on the verge of categorizing them as 'epic adventures.' This practice of solo boating is a common thread Dennis and I share.

The first time I saw Dennis was a foreshadowing of what was to become a symbiotic and kindred relationship we share today. Back in the late-1980's I was guiding a raft down the Indian River on a day when the bus traffic was thick. We were just out of the Gooley Steps where the roar of the water lets up enough to allow you to hear the curses and screaming of a run gone very wet. Standing near waist deep in the middle of the river was a boater, sans boat, supported by his paddle. As raft after raft passed this hapless new boater each guide would scream, "Don't stand up in the river!!!" Dennis was cursing just as loud, "I'll stand up in any!@ #%# river I want!!!" As I floated past I thought to myself, "He'll be a helluva' boater someday...if he lives." It took a few years before our paths would cross again.

Just a few years ago Dennis and I were paddling on a nearby creek (the location is up to Dennis to reveal). Now if Dennis had listened to all those raft guides so many years ago back on the Indian River he would have been screwed at that moment. With the exception of one other drop, we had been boat scouting our way downstream. We were at the lead in for an easy class V waterfall that needs to be scouted from shore. The catch was that the easy class IV lead-in had, well -- become easy to us. It's a common phenomenon, you paddle a difficult section enough times and you become a little... relaxed. Dennis peeled out and headed downstream as I watched from the eddy. The creek constricts to about half its width and descends 50 yards to the last available eddy to get out and scout from. It's steep enough here -- where you can just see the must-make eddy as the water drops over a ledge. A second after Dennis drops over the horizon line, and where I should see him eddy out, I see his bow slowly come up and flip over backwards. I'd already started down before his boat is completely over, but by the time I'm there Dennis is already out of his boat. Dennis is standing waist deep and hanging on to the small submerged tree that had caught his boat and flipped him over -- momentarily pinning him upside down underwater and forcing a wet exit. I watch his water filled boat disappears over the waterfall, just a short 20 feet away. The look on Dennis' face brings back memories from the Indian River and I have to suppress the urge to say, "Hey, don't stand up in the river." It was the least I could do.

This book will bring the reader a life's worth of joyful creek'n and river running. Use it with care. It is not a substitute for experience and skill. Don't boat alone, always have air bags in your boat and never...ever...stand up in moving water.

Mike Feldman
February 2002

*(Authors' note) I got to read this introduction about one month before the book went to the printer. All I could think was "Hey -- I work on this book for several months (and years of research) and Mike gets to go first? And then came a comforting thought -- "Thank God the river tends to be more fair than the rest of life."

Foreword

As anybody who saw that American Whitewater issue (Sept./Oct.2000) might suspect, and everybody who paddles here knows -- New York is an incredible place to paddle -- and it's getting better. It's getting better because the weather pattern has been changing here for years. The winters and springs both seem to be getting warmer.

This project started off as a steep creek only book. But then I decided to make it more complete by adding a number of class 1, 2 and 3 runs. This is my attempt to create THE comprehensive whitewater guidebook(s) for New York State. The number of runs grew and grew as this undertaking unfolded and this turned into Book 1. It covers the northern part (north flowing rivers) of the state. Book 2 will be out later in 2002. The decision was made to divide all the information into two books because I didn't want to write (or publish) a 450-page guidebook.

You'll also notice after studying both books that there is a personal bias towards the eastern 2/3 of the state -- especially the Adirondacks. Yes, I hear that there is some whitewater in the western part of the state. Which is why in future editions I'd be glad to have someone who lives out that way enlighten me (man, I could just imagine a 550 page guidebook). So please feel free to send me: photo, stories, descriptions and dirty limericks (but, no underpants -- please).

I hope you find the information in this book to be complete and helpful. I always thought I could spell -- that is until I discovered the cursed spell checker (but what do I know, I always used to think I was funny too). I wanted to write this book, as I would speak -- but that might not be readable (or printable) -- so I've only left in a few of the slang words. What the hell does an outlaw care about being proper anyway? It's also my wish to entertain and perhaps surprise you a bit. Hopefully, I won't cross over your line too far, too many times. It's just that, little dennis didn't stay in therapy long enough, and sometimes gets out of control -- "Wanna come out and play?"

Dennis Squires
April 2002

P.S. Just in case you were wondering -- there are three reasons why I used a somewhat small font size for this book: the first reason is that I wanted to get as much stuff packed into a handy size book as I could, secondly I didn't want a thick book that would be hard to see over when it's sliding around on your dashboard and the most important reason is...I don't want you reading this while you're driving down the road -- so but it back on the dashboard!

TABLE OF CONTENTS

Surfing the Web/Finding the Holy Grail

http://wwwdnyalb.er.usgs.gov/rt-cgi/gen_tbl_pg - This is for current water levels in c.f.s. (cubic feet per second) and in feet. **We use this more than anything** else: just type **usgs (United States Geological Survey)** into your search engine -- then click on real-time water data and then click N.Y. -- next click on current stream flow conditions -- when you find the river you want -- click on the station number and you'll see a graph that answers all your questions (for example; should I leave work early or call in sick and **blow off work totally**.)

http://tgsv.nws.noaa.gov/er/nerfc/gis_maps - This shows other watersheds and their gauges in feet. You'll see: Colton, Edwards, and Chasm Falls -- which are all way up north and aren't on the U.S.G.S. page.

http://www.nae.usace.army.mil/waterres/htdocs/index. - This is from the Corp. of Engineers (this shows some other things that have releases on them).

www.accuweather.com - This gives weather radar/rain forecast and **rain amounts.** Knowing where it just got done raining several inches will let you know (because you have this book and a Gazetteer) what's going to be running in that area **even before it shows up on the gauges listed here.** The gauges tend to be on bigger rivers and/or farther downstream than many of the hardest runs described here. So consider the lag time, little steep creeks may peak almost as soon as it quits raining; while rivers that are bigger and have the best runs a long ways below their headwaters (like the Independence) can take as long as 24 hours to peak.

Waterline

This is a free remote dial-up service that allows access to water level information from any telephone at any time. This is especially useful to paddlers without access to the Internet or those who are on the road, driving from river to river. This service is accessed by dialing: **800-452-1737**

You can interrupt any spoken message at will by entering a new site code. For more information and codes for other areas, call Waterline Customer Service at **800-945-3376** or **visit Waterline on the Web** at: **www.h2oline.com.** This site is also the place to go for the info/dates about the **new releases in N.Y**. starting in 2002. If you don't pre-register with Orion Power for the releases they will be **canceled.**

Even as this book is going to print several new gauges are being added to this list for N.Y. **Your phone calls mean that more sites will be added in the future.** This is a great resource. **Make lots of calls they like it!** Please support the sponsors (they pay for this service) whose messages are played at the beginning of your call. Gauges sites in the U.S. are in trouble; help yourself -- call this number and use that website.

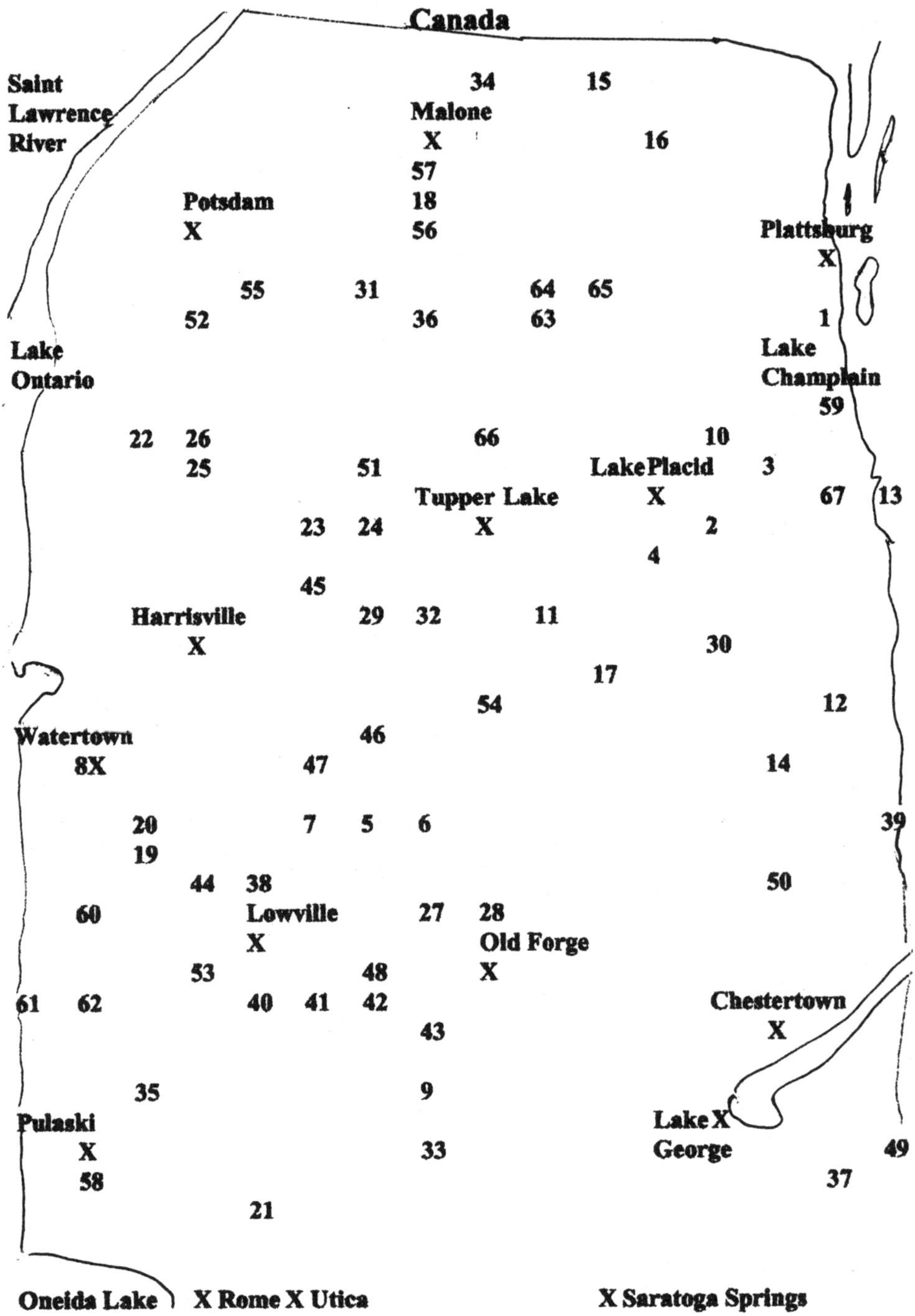
Canada
Saint Lawrence River
34
15
Malone
X
16
57
18
Potsdam
X
56
Plattsburg
X
55
31
64
65
52
36
63
1
Lake Ontario
Lake Champlain
59
22
26
66
10
25
51
Lake Placid
3
Tupper Lake
X
67
13
23
24
X
2
4
45
Harrisville
29
32
11
X
30
17
54
12
Watertown
46
8X
47
14
20
7
5
6
39
19
44
38
50
60
Lowville
27
28
X
Old Forge
53
48
X
61
62
40
41
42
Chestertown
43
X
35
9
Pulaski
Lake X George
X
33
49
58
37
21
Oneida Lake
X Rome X Utica
X Saratoga Springs

Master List of Rivers

1. Ausable-Chasm
2. Ausable-East
3. Ausable-West
4. Ausable-Upper
5. Beaver-Eagle
6. Beaver-Moshier
7. Beaver-Taylorville
8. Black
9. Black-Upper
10. Black Brook
11. Bog
12. Boquet-Upper
13. Boquet-Steele Woods
14. Boquet-South
15. Chateaugay
16. Chazy
17. Cold
18. Deer
19. Deer-New Boston
20. Deer-Copenhagen
21. Fish
22. Grass-Lampson Falls
23. Grass-Twin Falls
24. Grass-Upper
25. Grass-Middle
26. Grass-North
27. Independence
28. Independence-Upper
29. Jenny
30. Johns
31. Lake Ozonia Outlet
32. Little
33. Little Black Brook
34. Little Trout
35. Mad
36. Meachem
37. Mettawee
38. Mill-Lowville
39. Mill-Port Henry
40. Moose-Bottom
41. Moose-Lower
42. Moose-Middle
43. Moose-South
44. Negro(No)
45. Oswegatchie-Fine
46. Oswegatchie-Middle
47. Oswegatchie-West
48. Otter
49. Poultney
50. Putnam
51. Raquette-Piercefield
52. Raquette-Colton
53. Roaring Brook
54. Round Lake Outlet
55. St. Regis-Parishville
56. St. Regis-Silver Staircase
57. Salmon-Malone
58. Salmon-Pulaski
59. Salmon-Schuyler Falls
60. Sandy
61. Sandy South
62. Sandy South-Lorraine Gulf
63. Saranac
64. Saranac-High Falls
65. Saranac-Moody Falls
66. Saranac-Permanent
67. The Branch

How to get the most from the book

This section is to help you get the most from the information in this book. Each of the river descriptions contains the following sections.

RIVER: This tells the name of the river and the branch or section being described. The number of stars (*) shows the quality of the run. The more stars, the better. A five star (*****) run is Nirvana! The: scenery, the challenge of the run, and how much (or little) it runs, or how unique goes into this rating. Johns Brook is a *****!!!!!

SCENERY: Seems kind of obvious doesn't it?

ACCESS: This is the part of the run that is farthest from the road. This could be a long ways from help. The distance indicated is as the crow flies and since I'm assuming that you're not a crow and not able to fly, this probably isn't much help. What may actually be out there in the woods, I don't know -- I spend my time on the river -- not running through the bushes looking for hiking trails. The many exceptions to that statement are contained within this book. **Access distance is drawn from maps and is not an opinion.**

CLASS: I'm using the standard rating system of AMERICAN WHITEWATER. Many factors influence this rating (and yours) other than what's listed here: air and water temperature, strainers, and how you're feeling on any given day. High water moves trees and rocks. This guide is written for (due to the author's limited mental capacity) and assumes that you are going to paddle within your abilities and present skill level (this is especially true if the run is rated class 4 or higher). Wherever you're at -- keep paddling -- there's lots of stuff in here for everybody!

LENGTH: This is the approximate river distance of the section being paddled. If the shuttle (driving) distance is much different it will be mentioned, otherwise it won't.

AVERAGE GRADIENT: It's just that, the approximate average (written in feet per mile) over the length of the run. If a section is particularly steep it will be noted.

GAUGE: There are 19 USGS gauges that may be referred to:

1. Crown Point on Putnam Creek.
2. Granville on the Mettawee.
3. Parishville on the West Saint Regis
4. Harrisville on the Oswegatchie
5. Plattsburgh on the Saranac
6. Coldbrook on the Esopus
7. Hope on the Sacandaga
8. McKeever on the Moose
9. North Creek on the Hudson

10. Ausable (Forks) on the Ausable
11. Donattsbugh on the Independence
12. Perry Mills on the Great Chazy
13. Phoenicia on the Stony Clove
14. Watertown on the Black
15. Boonville on the Black
16. East Ausable on the East Ausable
17. Colton on the Raquette
18. Edwards on the Grass
19. Chasm Falls on the Salmon

WATER LEVEL: This is additional information beyond a gauge reading: such as how fast a river may rise and fall, how long it stays up, or if a dam affects the flow.

BEST BETTING TIME: An educated guess, as to when there is at least a 71.7% chance that you'll have water for the run in a year of somewhat average snow and rain (there's something to paddle most months of the year -- most years every month offers something). Yes -- I could have called this the season, like other guidebooks do -- boring!

OTHER LOCAL RUNS: You'll see the closest, easy run and hard run listed; with your Gazetteer and this guide you'll quickly find more.

BOOGIE TIME: This is the approximate percentage of the run (for example 80% means being able to stay in the boat 8 out of 10 miles -- without getting out to scout from shore) that was boat scouted on **MY** first trip down the described run. This number assumes the boater is used to and comfortable with boat scouting (and that you are doing something equal to your present skill level.) Scouting from the boat is much quicker than from shore and a useful skill to learn. Some of us love to boogie down the river, to go-go-go. But by all means -- when in doubt, get out and look. Remember the ability to boof/ski jump and catch tiny eddies every time is an invaluable skill for a steep creek boater.

TIME TO DO FIRST RUN: I'm assuming that there will be a group of three boaters. Especially on class 4 (and harder) runs you should add about one half to a full hour for each additional person for a three hour run (if you are paddling with Derek multiply everything by two). Realize that paddling with a big crowd presents certain problems; many of the harder runs have few eddies, and those few eddies are often only big enough for one boater (i.e. -- you can't fit five cars in a one car garage). The other problem is that if it takes a long time to do a run people will get cold, maybe too cold.

FIRST KNOWN DESCENT: The odds are that if my friends and I didn't do it first, we don't know who did. So please inform me if you know who did, I'd love to know.

RAFT: Almost every run described in this guide has never been rafted. Many however, are doable. It should be added though that I had a certain, what you might call, reputation, as a raft guide. For example, after guiding on the Penobscot for a summer -- the bad boys from Boston used to show up on Saturdays and ask for the guide (me) that would make them swim and bleed. The grizzly crews that mooned all the other raft companies on the way to the put-in would also be, automatically, told to get in my boat. This is stated here for your benefit -- if it says this is an exciting raft trip in the description -- **IT IS!**

DUCKY: You can paddle a heavy-duty inflatable kayak/ducky on almost anything. This is here mostly so that you'll be aware of runs where a ducky may be a good option, or even the preferred craft.

FOOD AND GAS: The closest places are listed. In the Adirondacks small towns often close up early, by 8 or 9 p.m., even earlier in the off-tourist (spring paddling) season. You have been warned: if you wind up doing a lot of driving after dark …… **told you so.**

CAMPING: Paddlers have been known to be cheap…thrifty…ya that's what I mean …thrifty…so I've listed nearby free camping that I know about. If nothing is close I list paid camping or inexpensive motels, which even Dennis appreciates when it's cold and snowing at night.

PAGE IN THE GAZETTEER: This is the NEW YORK STATE ATLAS AND GAZETTEER BY DELORME. If you want to find anything in New York use this. When we first started boating friends and I called this the 'Boaters Bible'. It's located in convenience stores and bookstores everywhere. DeLorme can be reached at (207)- 846-7000 or their website is www.delorme.com.

COUNTY: This lists the county/counties the described section flows through.

CLOSEST RIVER STORE: I trust you'll appreciate this extra listing. It's a last minute addition just for you. If there are two stores close by I'll list both.

DIRECTIONS: I refuse to further explain this.

DESCRIPTION/HAZARDS: You'll find that the harder the run the less description it tends to get. That's because this is only a report of what I found when I paddled it. The belief here is that experienced paddlers want the challenge of doing it themselves, and not being led by the hand. Hazards as they existed the last time the river was paddled will be noted. Remember things can change a lot after high water moves them around.

NOTES: Here's room for your notes, doodles, corrections and words of wisdom. If you feel there's something I really need to know e-mail me (and yes, there are questions that are too stupid to answer -- but I'll try).

MAPS: The maps in this book are: hand-drawn, simple, readable, and usable. The author believes that the main purpose of maps in a guidebook is to show you the location of the put-in and take-out, along with the roads you'll need to know. That means no fancy maps. It also means you won't get maps that you can't read or use. **Bring your Gazetteer** (I wish they would pay me a dollar for every time I said that……no such luck)

CARTOONS: These are the first ones I've ever done. Hopefully the humor will outshine the artistic content. I apologize if you need a magnifying glass to read a couple of them, remember this is my first book/feeble writing attempt; there has been so much to learn and the book is late going to the printer and it's May and Johns Brook is running and I NEED To GET ON THE RIVER. My basic belief (and lifestyle) is that humor, marching to your own drummer and having big brass ones is the only way to go!

PHOTOGRAPHS: There were a lot of photographs to choose from. Finding the very best/most appropriate ones and deciding how many to put in the book was a very tough choice to make. Fortunately we are all blessed by the fact that the author paddles with people that like to take photos and are really good at it.

ADVERTISING: You will find some ads within this book. This has been done with the intention of helping out everyone involved in this project. Knowing where/who has boating gear, gas, food, beer, camping…can only make things easier for everybody.

You may notice that within the book some of the ads don't have borders around them; and none of the cartoons have borders/boxes around them. This outlaw (who happens to love *The Treasure of the Sierra Madre)* has strong feelings about borders…"Borders? I don't need no stinking borders!"

River Classification

Class 1: Moving water with few riffles and small waves, obvious and clear lines with few or no obstacles.

Class 2: Easy rapids with waves up to three feet and clear, wide channels that are obvious without scouting. Some maneuvering is required around obvious obstructions.

Class 3: Rapids with: large, sometimes irregular waves (capable of swamping an open boat), narrow channels, rocks, and holes that often require complex maneuvering. Scouting from shore may be needcd.

Class 4: Long, turbulent rapids with powerful holes, waves and constricted passages that often require precise, expert maneuvering. Scouting from shore is often necessary, and conditions make rescue difficult. All boaters in canoes and kayaks should be able to Eskimo roll. This is considered a must for anyone paddling any of the class 4 (or harder) rivers in this book.

Class 5: Extremely difficult, long and very violent rapids with highly congested routes, which almost always must be scouted from shore. Rescue conditions are difficult and there is significant risk to life in the event of a mishap. The ability to Eskimo roll is mandatory for all paddlers.

Class 6: Generally considered unrunnable; difficulties of class 5 pushed to the extreme of navigability, with irregular currents and horrendous holes. This is almost impossible and very dangerous. For teams of experts only, after close study and with all precautions taken.

Flood

A flood run on Catskill Creek the week before Christmas of 2000 inspired this page.

If you think you just have to paddle something at flood levels, first read William Nealy's "*Kayak,*" and then only do it on a river you'd risk your life on -- after first thinking about how much your loved ones mean to you … (you know, those people you always blow off to go paddle).

We had only made it a little over a mile when we all regrouped in the trees. The group consensus (I wanted to go on) was to get off the river.

Why did we get off? Well, it could have had something to do with the fact that the river was high when we got there -- and then it proceeded to rise another 2 feet while we ran shuttle and got dressed. Perhaps the fact that there was never more than 50 feet (.3 of a second) between the trees and telephone poles going by should have given us a clue. Staying together also proved to be a major problem (i.e. fog, hyper speed, debris, unknown mega holes, lack of eddies.... etc.). If you're going to be out there in conditions like that a small group seems better.

The fog was so thick.............................. it was so thick that you could only see 60' -- which isn't much time to deal with big holes you've never seen before. Almost immediately 3 people flipped in big holes and a big hunk of wood whacked Sally in the helmet before she was able to roll (as always she still managed). There were few eddies to be found and they were usually behind logjams and up in the trees outside the banks. Don't even ask about the eddy walls and fences.

Rivers at flood are dangerous. They don't read or act like they're supposed to. Even on a creek/river that you know well everything will be different. Rapids that are always there will be gone. There will be rapids that were never there before. If you have to paddle this kind of monster -- you'll probably want to **wait until right after the peak has passed** (then you don't have to keep looking behind you: looking for trees, ice bergs and gas tanks that are evil and wish only to crush and destroy everything in their path). Waiting for the peak to pass is also a **good rule of thumb for high water** (but not flooding) **runs on any river**. After rivers peak: the wood is hung up (and you can usually see it), all the wood isn't moving with/behind/barreling down on you…and you'll be able to enjoy the illusion of being under control. When in doubt, keep your butt off the river and encourage your brain dead friends to do the same.

Years ago I learned about flood rivers when I was paddling some part of the Westfield River in Massachusetts with my buddy Peter. I was having a great time surfing a big bouncy hole when he started yelling at me. Yeah! Yeah! Why was he yelling so loudly (?) I was the one having the big fun surf. After I got out of the hole and paddled into the eddy he told me. The end of a submerged 30' tree had hit the river bottom and stood up and toppled back over -- end over end. It had been 10'-20' away from (behind) me when it happened. I never even saw it coming -- or going.

And then there was that first trip down the Boquet.......................

Safety

If you are new to: New York, its springtime cold weather, or the potential remoteness of the Adirondacks, there are a few things to consider in order to be safe.

Here are three things you probably haven't thought about: Exostosis, where's the sun and whose land is it anyway?

Exostosis is when your ear canal slowly grows shut and you can't hear anymore -- it sucks! There are several people that I personally know of (besides me) that this is happening to. Keep that cold water out of your ears with a really good helmet liner/skullcap. If your ear canal is closing then get a surfers earplug (you can still hear with one of those).

There are a lot of runs in this book that flow in a westerly direction, which means that you have the same challenge that I found on rivers in California. The sun will be in your eyes if you get a late start. An early start gets you: on the river ahead of the bugs, off the river before the sun is sinking, back in town before everything closes and gives you more time to celebrate with abandon (not too much abandon, you've got to get up and paddle tomorrow).

There is public land and private/posted land in northern New York. I try to ask permission before walking through posted land. Sometimes I don't find anybody to ask and they find me after I get off the river -- they usually aren't happy. Being patient and diplomatic almost always works. It is a fact that in N.Y. you can portage/scout a river if you have a legal put-in and take-out. That doesn't mean that the angry landowner and his friend, the local sheriff, know the law. Laws change all the time, so be nice and don't travel as a horde of naked screaming thrill seekers (at least wear a towel). "Creek Week," which takes place in April, is a chance to stay on good terms with the locals.

We're supposed to purify the water before we drink it -- so they tell me (could you ever figure out who the hell they, are?) I'd suggest learning the paddle and hand signals of AMERICAN WHITEWATER. Coming up with some of your own signals for special situations and knowing your paddling partners may save somebody's life. Study possible rescue routes and how to get to the road. On some of these runs you are many miles from help. Having a map and compass never hurts.

One challenge of boating creeks in New York is the weather. Often when water levels are good the weather just plain sucks. Listen to weather reports and learn how to stay warm. For clothing we use only synthetic materials and dress in layers. We wear dry suits, have helmet liners, and wear pogies or neoprene gloves in extreme cold weather. Bring extra food and clothes in a dry bag. Bring a throw bag (learn how to use it) and learn river rescue. At least one member of the party should carry a breakdown paddle and a saw.

It would probably increase your safety and fun factor if you: pick me up in your large, cushy, shuttle vehicle, supply quality munchies, drive me to the river, carry my boat (carrying me is pushing it I suppose), put my lunch (which you made with TLC) in your boat, blow warm air on my hands (or toes) if they are cold and take me out to dinner afterward, buying good wine and believing all of my stories while encouraging me to tell you more. I would, of course, provide this service for only a small charge.

River:	**Ausable Chasm****(Keesville)**
Scenery:	Great
Class:	IV-V
Access:	.6-mile (it's sheer walled in the chasm)
Length:	3.5 miles (the chasm itself is only .8 mile)
Average gradient:	Over 300'/mile in the chasm
Gauge:	Ausable gauge should be 500cfs as a minimum
Water levels:	750cfs is ideal and 1000cfs would start making scary holes. This river takes a while to peak -- but it rises fast.
Best betting time:	Late May and periods in the summer and fall
Other local runs:	Salmon (III-V)* / East Ausable / Lower (I-III)**
Boogie time:	Scout the entire chasm before getting in
Time to do first run:	2 hours (after scouting)
First known descent:	Mike Duggan and Pete Iscaro in the late 90's
Raft:	Not a good idea…. although I….
Ducky:	Yes -- at lower levels you'd have a blast
Food and gas:	Keesville
Camping:	Campgrounds close to the chasm
Page in the Gazetteer:	103
County:	Clinton
Closest river store:	Adirondack Lakes and Trails in Saranac Lake

Directions: Just off of Route 9 (north of Keesville) is a small road on your right that goes down into the NYSEG power plant (in front of Rainbow Falls). The put-in is behind that plant -- which as I write this is not yet a legal put-in. It's an easy put-in. I was involved in the first test study on this section and I can tell you there will be legal access at some point -- hopefully soon. Actually the landowner of the tourist area in the chasm seemed to be the biggest sticking point. But anyway, to find the take-out bridge drive north about 3 miles on Route 9. If you can't find it don't ever call me and want me to go boating.

Descriptions/hazards: (This is based on my one run down through here during the test study in 2001.) Just above the put-in is Rainbow Falls; it's 50'+ and nasty looking (V+) -- I know somebody will run it (Tao?).

The first drop happens quickly after the put-in pool, in fact everything will happen quickly for the next .8 miles. Going way right off the big horseshoe shaped ledge works fine. The next ledge is long and drops more than you thought that it was going to, when you scouted it earlier (right? -- come on say I'm right). Around the next corner you'll run a ledge that has a nastier hole at the bottom than you thought -- paddle dam it! Next up is a big pile of rocks that we all elected to run on the left side. Big pushy water moves you at express speed down into the corner. You could catch the eddy on the right side like we did. All the current slams into the corner at a scary speed. Don't underestimate it. Around this corner you get to breathe (about twice) before you're into the next drop. This drop is class IV-ish and funnels you into the hole. At 750cfs we found this hole was much friendlier than it looked (a couple of guys hit the right side with a lot of angle and flushed right through). When Mike and Pete did the first descent here the level was higher and they both had a long, scary, double surf/trashing/ thrashing in this hole. At 1000 cfs run it on the left side -- any higher and all bets are off. The river eases up below here and you'll be out of the gorge before you know it. As you exit from the walls the river splits around an island. Go left and **you'll find a couple of holes that are a slice of heaven.** All I can tell you is that the holes were a load of fun at 750 cfs and they would be even better with more water (but with more water the gorge will be too high). There's an access road of some sort on the right side of the river at the head of the island. I don't know if it's posted (probably), but it would make things mighty easy to play here. These holes are worth driving to, in and of their selves. The long class I paddle down to the Route 9 Bridge would be too bony below 500 cfs. But the chasm would still be fun.

Notes
1
2
3
4
5

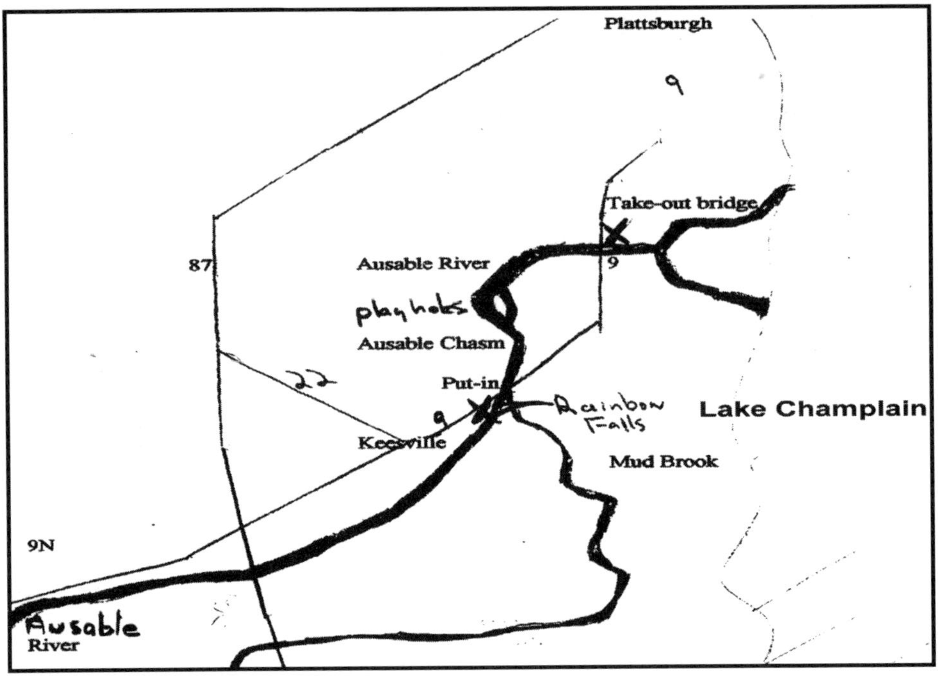
Plattsburgh
9
Take-out bridge
87
Ausable River
9
play holes
Ausable Chasm
22
Put-in
9
Rainbow Falls
Lake Champlain
Keeseville
Mud Brook
9N
Ausable
River

Leland Davis entering (first descent) High Falls Gorge. Photo by Mike Duggan.

River:	**East Branch of the Ausable*** (Keene)**
Scenery:	Good
Class:	III-V
Access:	.2-miles
Length:	2.5 miles
Average gradient:	70'/mile (Champagne Falls/gorge is 165'/mile)
Gauge:	East Branch Ausable should be 3.6' or more
Water level:	This comes up faster and drops slower than other runs in the area
Best betting time:	April and early May
Other local runs:	Johns Brook (V)*****/ East Ausable / Lower (I-III)**
Boogie time:	75% -- scout Hulls Falls and Champagne Falls
Time to do first run:	2+ hours
First known descent:	??
Raft:	Yes -- if it's over 4.2' and with a very good crew
Ducky:	Yes -- you could probably go as low as 3.4'
Food and gas:	Keene
Camping:	Split Rock Falls and there's the very reasonable Brookside Motor Inn in the middle of Upper Jay -- the more people you have the better the deal it is
Page in the Gazetteer:	96
County:	Essex
Closest river store:	Adirondack Lakes and Trails in Saranac Lake

Directions: Take-out just above the Route 73 Bridge in Keene. It's common to park on Grist Mill Road on the north side of the river. To get to the put-in you must drive south on Hulls Falls Road. Drive down 2 miles and park at the bridge. The rapid you're looking at is Hulls Falls. The upstream right side is the only one that isn't posted. The opposite downstream side is posted but obviously gets used.

Description/hazards: Hulls Falls isn't as nasty as it looks -- as long as you're right side up and on line coming off the last part. Just downstream you'll find two class IV rocky little drops that are boat scout-able. Then it calms down for a bit and you'll pass under a closed bridge. Enjoy the next 7 minutes down to Champagne Falls. When the horizon becomes obvious -- get out and scout on the left side. This section is great fun and the main reason that you're here. You can always portage on the left if need be. Around the corner you have two river wide ledges (that become **terminal holes** at high water -- don't run this section when the water is high). Below the holes is a short class IV-IV+ gorge that has a great boof in the middle. There's a little bit of class III+ and then it tapers off down to Keene.

2a. Kenne to Upper Jay: (I-III)**/6.5 miles: Even though this run is next to the road, it's still a nice section of easy water to paddle. You'll notice that it's gotten to be a good size (wide) river at this point. I remember it being mostly class I and II with a couple of class III's. And you can take out close to that great motel in Upper Jay. If you like it easy keep going -- it's about 12 miles to Au Sable Forks, almost all class I and easy class II. You'll find a couple of class III's and a big surprise in Jay. **Jay Falls** (which can be easily portaged on the right side) **is a class IV-V-ledge drop that has several moves in it**. It's even a lot of **fun most of the summer** -- it doesn't take much water.

And just in case you're wondering -- don't bother checking out Clifford Brook. The brook is probably the only thing in the state I wouldn't do again; it has more wood in it than the surrounding forest.

P.S. Kenne Valley to Hulls Falls: (I-II)** This is a nice canoe run -- you can even start above Kenne Valley if you want to (it runs next to route 73). You can take-out at the Route 73 Bridge, just below the bridge on the left, or on the left above Hull's Falls (you don't want to run the falls (V) in a canoe). Spruce Hill Brook enters on the right side -- just above the hard bend to the left that marks the approach to the falls, you had better be hightailing it for river left.

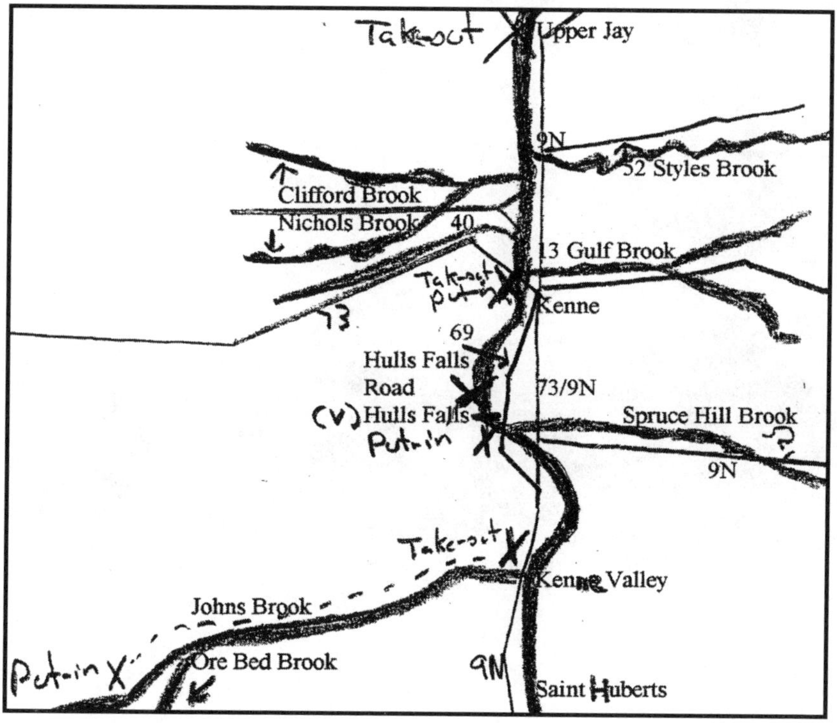

Notes

1

2

3

4

5

Ed Huber running Hulls Falls. Photo by Mike Duggan.

River:	**West Branch of the Ausable***(Lake Placid)**
Scenery:	Good/impressive/awesome
Class:	IV-VI
Access:	.4-mile (and access within High Falls Gorge is awful)
Length:	6.5 miles
Average gradient:	70'/mile / High Falls Gorge (VI) is 1100'/mile and The Flume (V-VI) is 600'/mile
Gauge:	The Ausable should be 800cfs or more/1600cfs is nice
Water Level:	This is a run to do when it's low-medium. If this is too high there are lots of other good runs close at hand.
Best betting time:	April-early May
Other local runs:	East Ausable (III-V)***/ East Ausable/ Lower (I-III)**
Boogie time:	30% -- there's a lot of scouting and walking to do, and High Falls Gorge to stare at
Time to do first run:	4-5 hours
First known descent:	?
Raft:	Yes -- if it's high -- but stop above High Falls Gorge
Ducky:	Yes
Food and gas:	Lake Placid
Camping:	Ray Brook or Wilmington Campgrounds or the Brookside Motor Inn in Upper Jay
Page in the Gazetteer:	96
County:	Essex
Closest river store:	Adirondack Lakes and Trails in Saranac Lake

Directions: Put-in at the Conservation Monument at Route 86. The option you might consider for a take-out is just above High Falls Gorge at the big parking lot. The other option for take-out (which means walking around High Falls Gorge) is at the Route 73 Bridge a little east of Whiteface Ski Center. The Flume is located here (at the Route 73 Bridge) -- you may want to get out on the left before the bridge, maybe.

Description/hazards: Starting at the monument you'll do some drops that are class III-IV with some class II in between before the river thinks of getting really serious. When the river starts to look steep either get ready for serious boogie boating or get out and look. It's hard to walk here so it's best to scout this before getting in the water. You can park at the pull off just before the tight curvy part of the road. The next few hundred yards are class IV/IV+, if it's not too high (if it's high, this piece through here is class V or more). You'll find the river then calms before the end of the earth appears. You're now at the head of High Falls Gorge (class VI). If it's summer and the tourist store is open you will have to walk around this (I would anyway!). If not, it has been portaged on the left. You can legally portage on the right side; just climb down the steep bank after the fence. The gorge was run in 2000 -- with no lack of excitement! If you're still in the game after the gorge you'll find a runnable drop and then a big one that you'll probably walk (unless the gorge wasn't enough for you…you tough person…you.) The short nasty rapid that comes next (in a short gorge) is class V-ish and doable. As you come around the next corner you'll be going under the bridge to Whiteface Ski Center. You'll be busy for the next several minutes, with class IV stuff before arriving at The Flume. There are trails here, use them. This is class V+/VI boating. You can get out above the bridge or downstream in a few hundred yards, after walking around The Flume. It is fun to run Demon Falls at the end of the day (while thinking of that fisherman) -- just get back in on the right below The Flume (dynamic entry style).

Extra: It's flat water from Demon Falls down to the Wilmington Dam. There is a put-in on the left side just below the dam -- right in town.

From Wilmington all the way to Au Sable Forks is 11 miles and much of it is posted. You'll find the first 7 miles are class II and easy class III. At higher levels this isn't an ideal canoe run because the river is big here -- the steepest parts can be big and pushy class III-III+. At about 7.5 miles the river gets even steeper -- and stays that way for a mile. This ends in a pool above a dam in the hamlet of Rome -- portage on the right (?) or take-out by walking up the steep nasty trail on the right. This take-out is found by driving down the road from Au Sable Forks into Rome and parking close to the water tower. If you stay on the river you'll find that it's 1.25 mile down to the take-out at the Forge St. Bridge. **The first part of this is class IV** when you've got good water. As you careen downstream the river will ease to class III and then class II, down to the bridge in Rome.

The next 13.5 miles is nice canoeing. Except for a couple of short class III's this is all easy -- until just above Keesville. At the edge of town a **series of class II-III ledges** starts a short white water run that includes 2 drops. Both the drops are ledges and should be scouted (the bigger one is an **18' falls**). Get out on the left before Rainbow Falls (the big dam above it would probably make it obvious).

Note: High Falls Gorge may be the biggest thing that's been run/survived in this state (Jesse Sharpe didn't survive Niagara Falls). I have no desire to do it myself. The run is a stunt run and had injuries and near disasters on the one descent. You can read all about it in AMERICAN WHITEWATER.

The poor fisherman screamed and threw his fishing pole into the water. But then, you'd freak out too if a brightly colored demon from hell dropped out of the sky and tried to take off your head. In reality it was just little ole' me boofing the last drop/falls. I had scouted the drop earlier in the day when nobody had been around. The poor guy had been enjoying the day in a beautiful and quiet place. And then out of nowhere this thing flies off a waterfall and skips on the water and bounces right at him. It took him a while to regain his pole -- but he still hadn't regained his manly dignity as the demon paddled away, after all he had screamed in a very unmanly fashion.

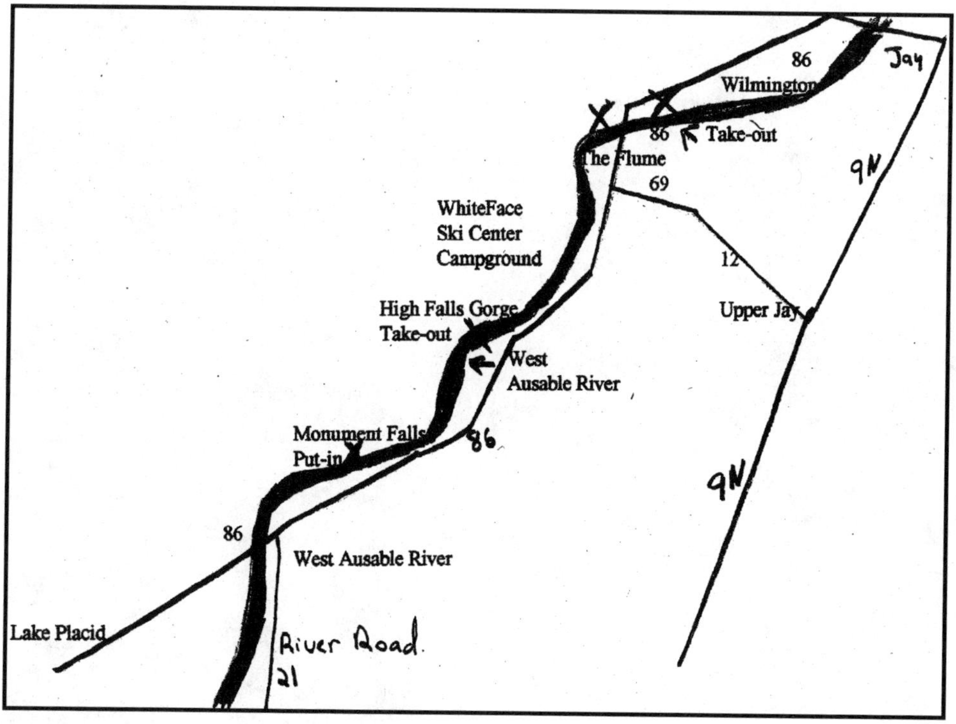
86
Jay
Wilmington
86
Take-out
The Flume
69
9N
WhiteFace
Ski Center
Campground
12
Upper Jay
High Falls Gorge
Take-out
West
Ausable River
Monument Falls
Put-in
86
9N
86
West Ausable River
Lake Placid
River Road
21

Notes
1
2
3
4
5

B.J. Johnson at the top of the fourth drop (High Falls Gorge.) Photo by Mike Duggan.

River:	**West Ausable/Upper***(Lake Placid)**
Scenery:	Good
Class:	II-III+
Access:	1-3 miles
Length:	5 miles
Average gradient:	70'/mile
Gauge:	The Ausable should be 1800cfs or more
Water level:	This can be run at a wide range of flows
Best betting time:	April-early May
Other local runs:	West Ausable (IV-VI)*** / East Ausable/ Lower (I-III)**
Boogie time:	99%
Time to do first run:	2 hours
First known descent:	?
Raft:	No -- it's small and woodsy in the upper part
Ducky:	Yes
Food and gas:	Lake Placid
Camping:	State land all around or the Brookside Motor Inn in Upper Jay
Page in the Gazetteer:	96
County:	Essex
Closest river store:	Adirondack Lakes and Trails in Saranac Lake

Directions: Turn off of Route 73 and drive up Heart Lake / Adk.Loj Road -- you can get in where you cross the river (it's about 6 miles up the road). For the higher put-in just turn left on South Meadow Road (if it's open and passable). Drive up .75 mile and then walk down to the river. To find the take-out drive back down to Route 73 and take a left; park at the pull-off that is just upstream of the bridge by the ski jumps.

Description/hazards: If you use the higher put-in you'll find the first 1.5 miles to be small, woodsy and class I-II. The best stuff starts below the lower put-in. You'll find class II and easy III until a short section of III+. The cool thing that comes next is the head-on collision that Indian Pass Brook makes where it enters the Ausable. From here down the run is class I to easy III all the way down to the take-out by the ski jumps at Route 73. I'll mention that South Meadow Brook is rumored to be class III-IV and it's a walk-in.

Notes

1

2

3

4

5

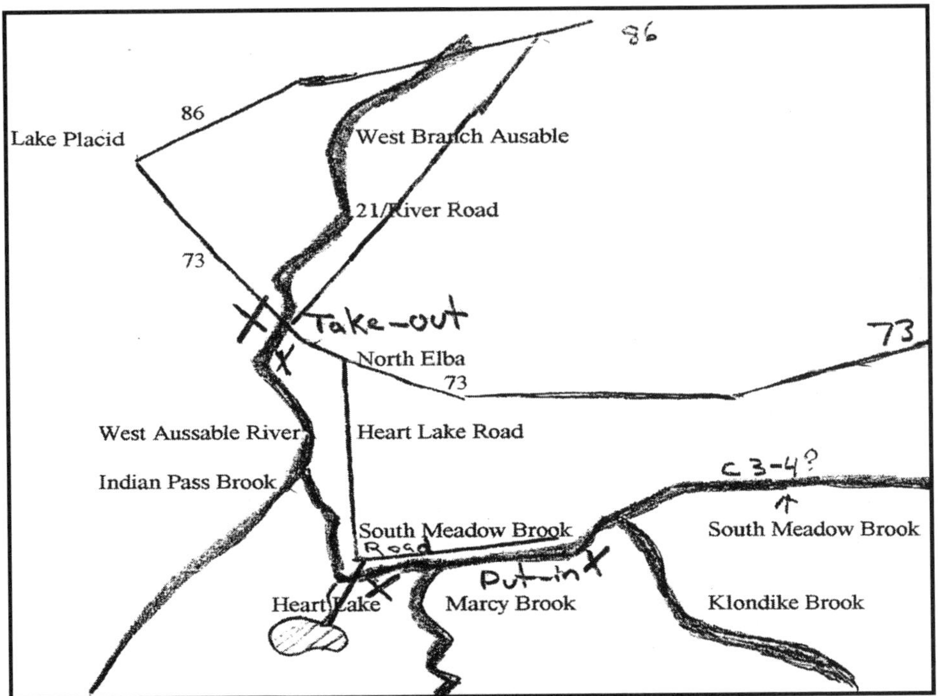
86
86
Lake Placid
West Branch Ausable
21/River Road
73
Take-out
73
North Elba
73
West Aussable River
Heart Lake Road
Indian Pass Brook
c 3-4?
South Meadow Brook
South Meadow Brook
Road
Put-in
Heart Lake
Marcy Brook
Klondike Brook

River:	**Beaver/Eagle****/(Belfort)**
Scenery:	Good/very good
Class:	V
Access:	500 feet
Length:	.4 mile
Average gradient:	460'/mile
Gauge:	Fall releases of 200cfs
Water level:	Check in AMERICAN WHITEWATER -- there is often a very minimal flow that makes for a fun ducky run on a warm day.
Best betting time:	Sept. releases and spring spillover
Other local runs:	Moshier (IV-V-)****/Taylorville (IV-IV+)*** / Moose-Middle (II-III-IV-)***
Boogie time:	0% -- yes, that's right **0%**. Scout everything first.
Time to do first run:	30 minutes (depending on your heart rate)
First known descent:	?
Raft:	Yes -- if you're brave (I wouldn't do it without a wetsuit)
Ducky:	Yes -- in fact there is often a base flow
Food and gas:	Groghan or Lowville
Camping:	At Taylorville put-in or Moshier take-out
Page in the Gazetteer:	85
County:	Lewis
Closest river store:	White Water Challengers in Old Forge & Mountain Man in Inlet & Old Forge

Directions: There is a spur road that turns off of Soft Maple Road and runs along this section and makes for easy viewing and access. Starting out of Lowville on the Number 4 Road is usually easiest. The put-in and the take-out have the same parking spot (you're carrying your boat back up to your car). Just follow the boaters ahead of you.

Description/hazards: It's possible to run part of the dam to start off the trip. After the dam you only have moments until all hell breaks loose. The first drop can be pretty much braced down: **Quick:** grab an eddy-peel out-punch/sneak the hole-paddle and pray-(you will get water in your face off the left side and never even see the next 20' of horizon lost-but keep paddling anyway-there's still a hole at the bottom whether you can see it or not)-**if** you make it through right side up, paddle into the eddy and hoot and holler and smile a lot and shake your head up and down at everybody else in the eddy and on shore-head downstream-miss the rocks-start paddling harder and aim left- (damn how did you get pushed to the right against that rock and why is that eddy trying so hard to suck you back into the hole at the bottom of the drop?)-O.K. it took a couple of tries but you're off that damn rock and away from the hole (even though that guy came down almost on your head and beat you with his paddle on the way by)-punch that-yeah!-No big deal-eddy out-peel out-what is that crap ahead of you-just keep paddling-man it's rocky at the top of the falls, more than you realized from shore, try to boof-come on boof?/!#$-damn that boof sucked!-Oh well, guess you had better go over and talk to everybody and look cool even though that boof sucked-maybe nobody noticed-damn what a rush. Do you want'a go back up top and do it again?

Like everybody else my first reaction to seeing the Eagle section was "Holy Shit." But after watching a few guys run down I did it myself and found it to be forgiving and huge fun! Over the last several years many people have survived this natural wonder, even crash pad Karl who ran it all backwards on a fifty-dollar bet.

The ugliest thing I've seen was the rafters from California. The raft flipped over sideways part way down the biggest drop and the guys got banged and bloodied (despite having wetsuits on) on the shallow ramp/slide/falls/thing. The amount of testosterone that they had been exuding before seemed to diminish somewhat.

Notes

1

2

3

4

5

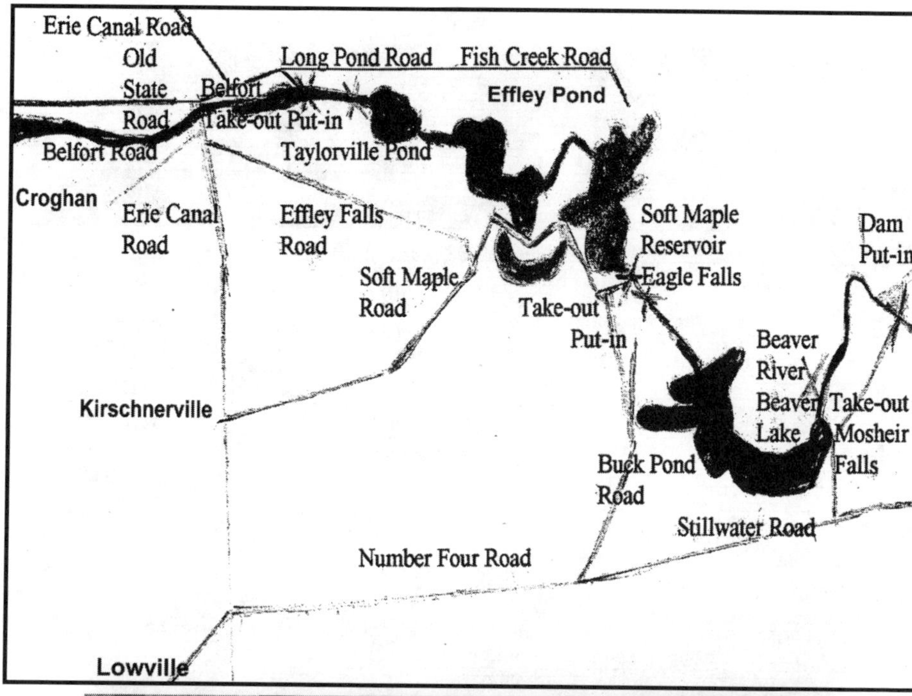

Mike Duggan flying down the eagle section. Photo by Bernie Wooten.

River:	**Beaver/ Moshier****(Belfort)**
Scenery:	Very good
Class:	IV-V-
Access:	.5-miles
Length:	2.4 miles
Average gradient:	90'/mile
Gauge:	We're still trying to figure out how the Stillwater Reservoir pool level indicates spillover
Water level:	The fall release level of 400cfs is fine (check with AW)
Best betting time:	Fall releases and possible spring spillover
Other local runs:	See the Eagle and Taylorville sections
Boogie time:	75% -- scout the first two horizon lines and the last section
Time for first run:	2-3 hours
First known descent:	?
Raft:	Yes -- but it's going to be really tight at the end
Ducky:	Yes
Food and gas:	Grogan or Lowville
Camping:	At the take-out
Page in Gazetteer:	85
County:	Herkimer
Closest river store:	White Water Challengers in Old Forge & Mountain Man in Inlet & Old Forge

Directions: The take-out is at Moshier Falls powerhouse (at the Herkimer/Lewis county line). A "Beaver River Canoe Route " sign marks the turn off of Stillwater Road. Be forewarned that the Stillwater Road to the east is slow dirt for many miles -- so you're better off coming in from Lowville on the Number Four Road. There's a locked gate at the powerhouse which is only open during releases so if you're trying your luck some time other than fall releases you'll have to walk 2 miles up the road (but then, if this is running naturally there are many other things to do.)

Description/hazards: Unless you like starting your day with a class VI rapid you'll probably skip the first…thing. The bottom half of this one has been run on the left. The rumor is that, somebody ran this whole thing starting from the top in 2001 -- God bless them! For the sane boater the action starts at a 12' falls, which makes for a great picture. And to make it even better there is an awesome fun boof on the far right. Most people run this drop multiple times! Almost immediately you'll come to the next scout. **Do NOT** underestimate the hole. You want to run this left or left center. Be ready. You'll come to another hole in 30' and then have to negotiate the rocky drop below that. Now take a breather and enjoy the next 1mile. You'll be floating mighty pretty water and boat scouting rapids no harder than easy class IV.

Now you've done it! You've arrived at the star attraction of the day. The next couple of hundred yards are pushing towards class V. This scary/wonderful thing is 4 drops all pushed back to back. Make sure you get down the first part right side up or you will wind up having a bad day. You can always cheat towards the right a little bit. The second part features a nasty hole with a strong eddy feeding the right side. I once spent too much time there, upside down…arrgghh! And please boof far left at the next hunk -- it will make your day much nicer than Derek's was the day he went through here upside down (this ended with him going to the Utica hospital for his third time in the 90's). Get it together and punch the left side of the hole at the last section. Now go back and do it again. And again! Hundreds of boaters will be thronged along the banks, for hours; they are there only to watch you, so do it right!

We had looked forward to this day for several months. This was the first time that we were going to get a chance to run this section of the river. My friends and I managed to get down to the first rapid ahead of everybody else and we had a great time running it -- multiple times, on both sides of the river.

When we got out to scout the second drop, I thought it looked incredibly easy. How wrong I was...I decided to go for the more exciting line, out in the middle of the river. You couldn't imagine my surprise when my boat stopped cold at the bottom and I got pulled back into the hole! At first, I was amused. But, after spending the better part of a minute or more trying to get out, I started to worry a little bit. At some point, I realized that I was not going to come out with my boat and I bailed. I still didn't come out of the hole. The falls were landing on my head and bouncing me against the rocks on the bottom, like a basketball. That was when the thought went through my head, "I'm going to die in a stupid Class III (?) hole." I started to swallow water and my head wasn't coming to the surface. At about that point, my amphibian/survival brain kicked in and I tried doing something else...anything else. The only thing I hadn't tried before was swimming to the right, into the worst part of it. Just before the point of passing out, I felt myself get ripped out of the bottom of the hole. Of course, the excitement wasn't over yet because there was a nasty, Class IV ledge-drop in about 40 feet. With the amphibian/survival brain still fully engaged, I barely managed to get a handhold and pull myself up on the edge of the river, right at the top of the drop. At about that point, my buddy Jim came running up and asked if I was okay. I then spit out some more water and mumbled something about how I'd probably live. He said, "Jeez, I saw it all through my camera. The timer said that you were under for almost a whole minute and I never even saw your head come up."

Never take a Class III (?) hole for granted.

Notes

1

2

3

4

5

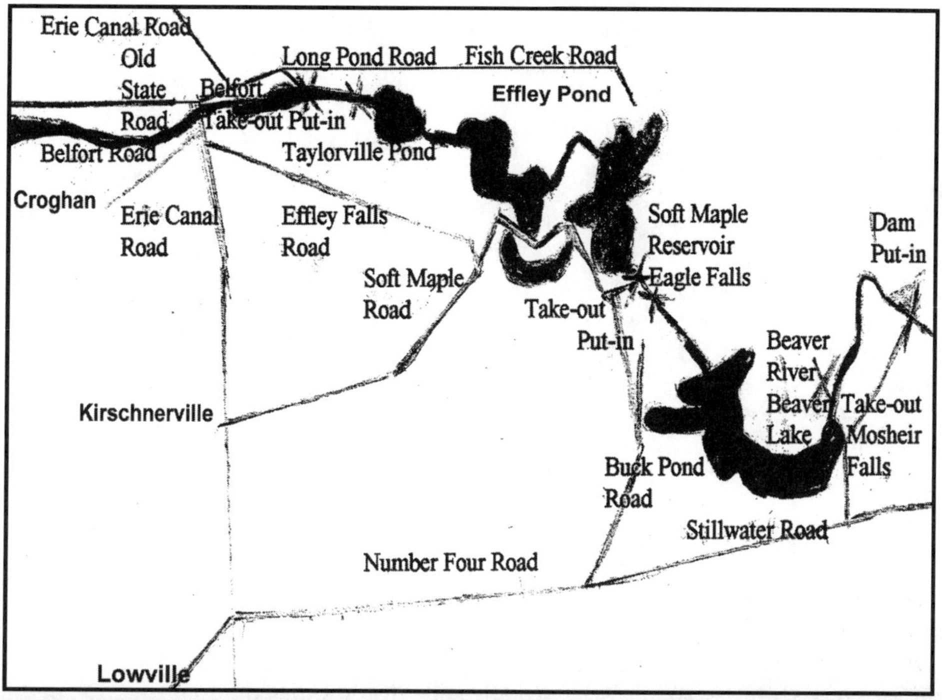

Mike Feldman in the middle of the bottom Moshier. Photo by Jody Dixon.

River:	**Beaver/Taylorville***(Belfort)**
Scenery:	Very good
Class:	IV
Access:	600 feet
Length:	1 mile
Average gradient:	120'/mile
Gauge:	Only at the dam
Water level:	The 400cfs release is fine (during 5 days in Sept.)
Best betting time:	Fall releases and spillover (how does the Stillwater reservoir pool level indicate spilling downstream?)
Other local runs:	Eagle(V)****/Moshier(IV-V-)****/Moose-Mid(II-III,IV-)***
Boogie time:	60% -- this whole run is nothing but horizon lines!
Time to do first run:	1-2 hours
First known descent:	?
Raft:	Maybe -- a 12'er would be fun with a very good crew and the knowledge that all the kayakers you're running over hate you
Ducky:	Yes
Food and gas:	Groghan or Lowville
Camping:	At the put-in
Page in the Gazetteer:	85
County:	Lewis
Closest river store:	White Water Challengers in Old Forge & Mountain Man in Inlet & Old Forge

Directions: Come out of Lowville on the Number 4 Road and turn left on Erie Canal Road. Just as you cross the bridge and come into Belfort turn right and then right again. From there it should be obvious -- if it isn't I hope you don't try boogie boating while we're on the same river. Follow the guy ahead of you -- the shuttle is less than a mile.

Description/hazards: If anybody ever cuts out the tree you can start at the dam and run the nasty, rampy undercut drop to start your day off. Otherwise slide in below; eddy hop, paddle like hell to the left to stay out of the big nasty hole, grab a few moments - go screaming down a big slide-breathe, fly/eddy hop down a very rocky drop, walk up the drop next to the one you just did and run it a few times-breathe, decide which line you want to mess with at the next one (the right side likes to flip you against the wall), surf a little-boof a small falls-bounce over rocks and hang out and wurf (yes, wurf) a while at the small hole, now go get your car and go to another section that's releasing.

Bits and pieces: People are doing moonlight runs again tonight... Jeez Steve -- how many stitches did it take to close that hole in your forehead? ... Did you hear about those guys running the big slide on Thermarest pads last night? Man! -- Did you see Laurel come all the way down the big slide upside down? ... WATCH OUT for that first hole, it's REALLY bad.

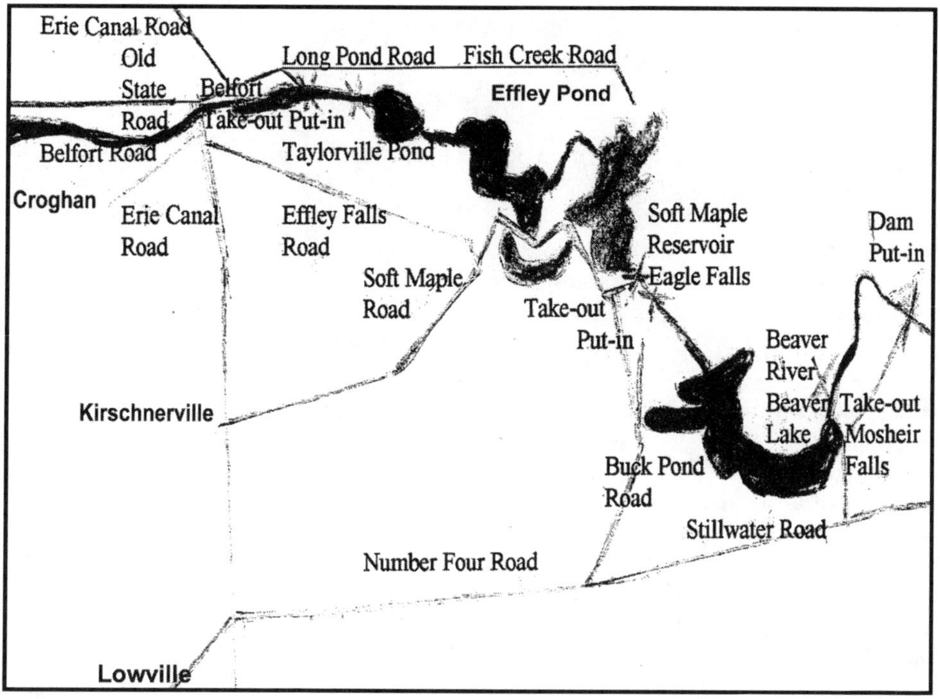

Notes

1
2
3
4
5

Buy Book 2

River:	**Black***(Watertown)**
Scenery:	Horrible/good
Class:	III-IV-V
Access:	.6-mile
Length:	8 miles (or **park and play** at Hole Brother's)
Average gradient:	30'/mile
Gauge:	Watertown
Water level:	1000cfs is low 2000-4000cfs is great and more water makes it scarier and scarier.
Best betting time:	April and early May -- this will be high (often 8000cfs or more). Check the Internet or call (Glen Park Hydro) 518-788-4960 to ask for a release (this runs all summer and fall).
Other local runs:	Deer/New Boston (II-III)** / Deer/Copenhagen (II-V)*
Boogie time:	90% -- look at Knife's Edge and Rocket Ride
Time to do first run:	3+ hours
First known descent:	? In the 70's
Raft:	Yes -- commercial river trips
Ducky:	Yes
Food and gas:	Watertown
Camping:	Down by Lake Ontario (don't expect to get any sleep)
Page in the Gazetteer:	83/91
County:	Jefferson
Closest river store:	T.I. Adventures in Clayton

Directions: Put-in off of Newell Street at A.R.O.'s raft headquarters. To find the take-out drive west on Coffen St. When you get to 12 go north and take the first left as you cross the bridge, drive down into Brownsville and park at the big parking lot on your left. This take-out is immediately below the bridge in Brownsville.

Description/hazards: There's a class III-III+ curve to start your day. Right below is some decent surfing and below the next bridge is Hole Brothers. At most levels this is a great **park and play spot** (rodeos have been held here). You can find this spot easy enough -- it's right behind Hudson River Rafting. The next notable is Knife's Edge. Follow somebody or stay left at the first two ledges and then left center at the third. You'd be better off following someone with a clue. And stay away from that horrible nasty undercut cliff at the bottom left side of this drop. At the dam you can portage or run the falls as the water starts to come up (the nice people at the dam are giving you water). Enjoy the gorge and beware the re-bar at the Rocket Ride (the old concrete dam). All the way down the run you don't want to touch the walls or the rocks -- they're infested with an incredibly sharp nasty type of rock known as Churt -- which will slice flesh with very little pressure. Stay right side up.

Extra! There is an awesome **park and play spot** for front surfing/flat spins that almost always seems to be running. The spot is just off route 3 just east of Watertown. There is a small park there where you can park and then paddle upstream a few hundred yards - - and play until you drop -- at which point you can drift down to your car -- I hope you brought a friend to carry your boat back to your car.

There is talk of changing this wave to a world-class hole (just say no) and having the 2005 World Championships here. This would be in addition to the big whitewater festival that is held here by American Whitewater every July. The Black River is the only class 3-4 run in the state that you know is going to run every single day of the summer.

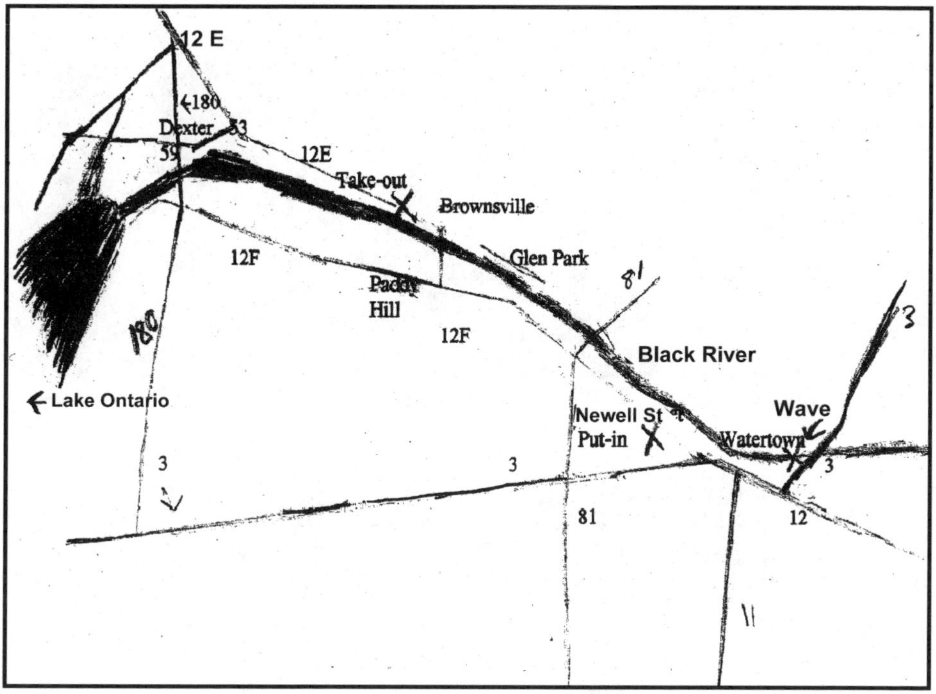

Notes
1
2
3
4
5

Tom Vickery in the middle of Poopchute (high water). Photo by Julie Vickery.

River:	Black River/Upper**(Hawkinsville)
Scenery:	Good
Class:	II-III
Access:	.5-mile
Length:	6 miles
Average gradient:	40'/mile
Gauge:	Black at Boonville should be 5.5' or higher
Water levels:	Big waves and holes at high water -- stays up a long time
Best betting time:	April-early June
Other local runs:	Moose / Bottom (IV+/V)**** / Moose / Middle (II-III-IV-)***
Boogie time:	100% -- after the dam that is
Time for first run:	1-2 hours
First known descent:	?
Raft:	Yes -- when it's on the high side
Ducky:	Yes
Food and gas:	Boonville
Camping:	On state land just north of the Moose River/Boonville Road
Page in Gazetteer:	77/85
County:	Oneida/Lewis
Closest river store:	Northern Outfitters in Utica & White Water Challengers in Old Forge & Mountain Man in Inlet & Old Forge

Directions: Put-in right below the low head dam in Hawkinsville. To get to the bottom just drive up the Pines Road in Hawkinsville. When you get to Moose River Road go straight across and it becomes Joslin Road. Go a couple of miles and take-out where Joslin crosses the river.

Description/hazards: Get in below the dam. Don't be a knucklehead like my pal Chris (he thought the hole didn't look bad and decided to run it). It was bad. The run is straightforward and can be boat scouted all the way down. There's even a bit of playing to do. If it's high (over 7') some of the waves get several feet high and make for **big fast surfing.** Unfortunately most of these have to be caught on the way down. This comes up and stays up (often) -- making this a good intermediate run.

Extra! If somebody is looking to paddle a long easy (I-II+, IV) run -- just start way up towards North Lake. The only real drop is just below the bridge at Enos (IV-IV+).

Notes

1

2

3

4

5

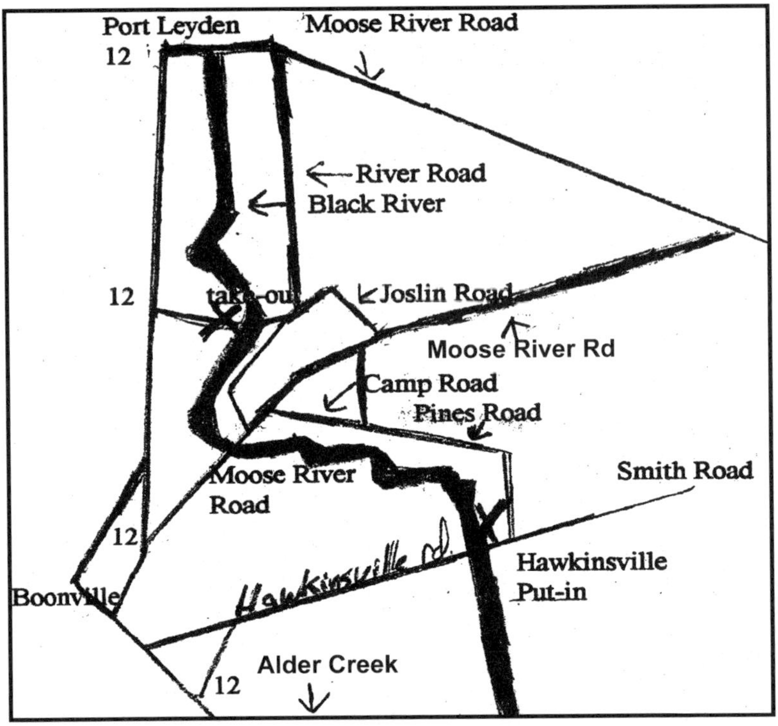

The long lost fourth stooge has finally been found – in the Adirondacks

River:	**Black Brook**(Black Brook)**
Scenery:	Fair/good
Class:	III-IV+
Access:	.4-mile
Length:	2.7 miles
Average gradient:	80'/mile
Gauge:	East Ausable should be 3.97' or more
Water levels:	High water puts you in the trees, so the run will be exponentially more dangerous.
Best betting time:	April-mid-May
Other local runs:	East Ausable (III-V)*** / East Ausable/ Lower (I-III)**
Boogie time:	90% -- at least scout the hard drop by the road
Time for first run:	2+ hours
First known descent:	?
Raft:	No
Ducky:	Yes
Food and gas:	Au Sable Forks
Ducky:	Yes
Camping:	Campgrounds in Wilmington or Taylor Pond or the Brookside Motor Inn in Upper Jay.
Page in Gazetteer:	96
County:	Clinton/Essex
Closest river store:	Adirondack Lakes and Trails in Saranac Lake

Directions: Take-out at the Route 12/Wilmington Road Bridge. For the put-in head north up Route 12, and take a left at the T. The bridge in town is the put-in. This run has been done by only a few, as far as I know.

Description/hazards: The run starts right in the hamlet of Black Brook, so you can't expect too much in the way of gorgeous vistas. The brook is fairly small (that's why it's called a brook) and flows through a lot of trees when it's high, so beware. In some places there are fewer eddies than you may like. The hard drop that you can scout from the road isn't too far below town but isn't easy to see as it starts on a bend in the brook. The nicest part is the section below that. You can sort of see it from the road, and it's class III+ at medium water. Looking up from the take-out you may see a strainer, note it, there are likely to be more.

Notes

1

2

3

4

5

Why do you think this is called Black Brook?
maybe when the sun comes up we'll find out
I hate paddlin with guys that always have to start early

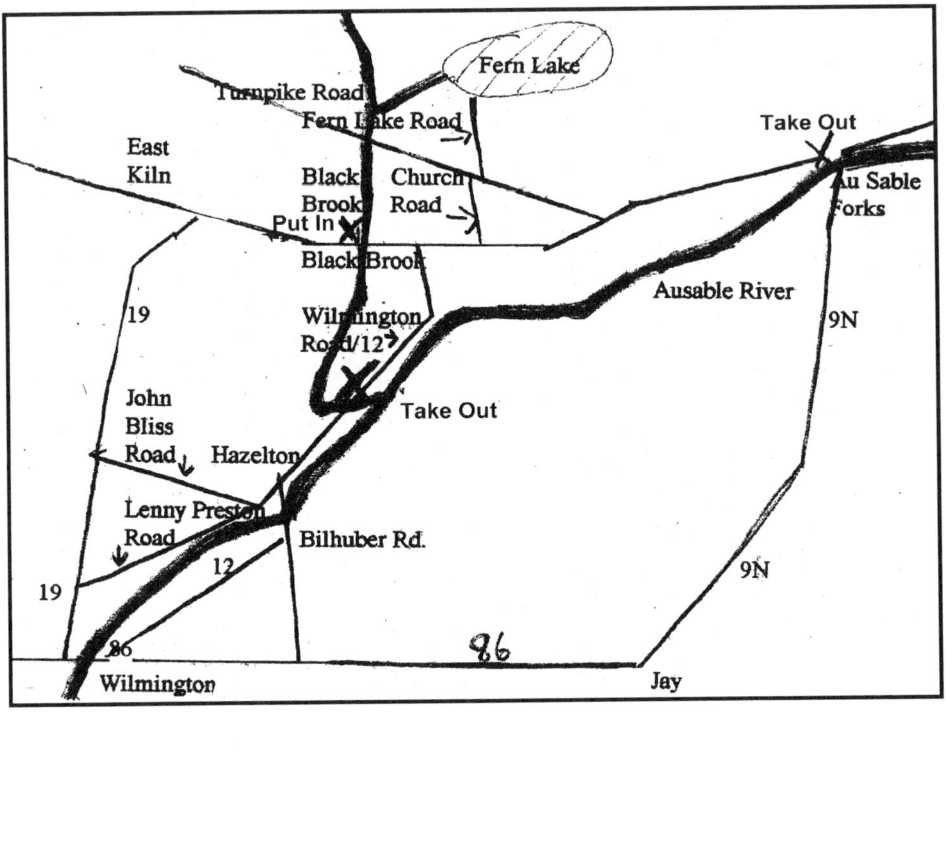

Fern Lake
Turnpike Road
Fern Lake Road
Take Out
East Kiln
Black Brook
Church Road
Au Sable Forks
Put In
Black Brook
Ausable River
19
Wilmington Road/12
9N
John Bliss Road
Take Out
Hazelton
Lenny Preston Road
Bilhuber Rd.
12
9N
19
86
86
Wilmington
Jay

River	Bog**(Tupper Lake)
Scenery:	Good
Class:	I-V (mostly class I-III)
Access:	3+ miles
Length:	7 miles
Average gradient:	25'/mile
Gauge:	Will most likely be up if the Hudson is 4' or more
Water level:	This has a big and slow moving watershed -- it stays up a long time, especially in late spring-early summer. Save this run for when other things are too low.
Best betting time:	April-May
Other local runs:	Round Lake Outlet (IV-V)*** / Grass/Upper (I-III, V)***
Boogie time:	90%
Time to do first run:	3+ hours
First known descent:	??
Raft:	Yes -- if it's a fairly high level
Ducky:	Yes
Food and gas:	Tupper Lake and Long Lake
Camping:	State land by the put-in or down Route 30 at Lake Eaton
Page in the Gazetteer:	94/95
County:	St. Lawrence
Closest river store:	Adirondack Lakes and Trails in Saranac Lake

Directions: Turn off of Route 30 just south of Tupper Lake and head west on Route 421. It takes about 1 minute to get to the take-out bridge. Check out the drop above and the drop below the bridge. These are 2 of the 4 hard ones on this section. Please realize that Round Lake Outlet stays up longer, so the water that you're looking at here may be mostly from the Outlet (especially early summer). Keep driving up this road, and as you pass Horseshoe Pond you'll notice the turn on the left that takes you down to the put-in.

Description/hazards: There's a short and rocky drop right below the dam. After that you'll find miles of easy water mixed with some stretches of class II-II+. Get out to scout some significant ledges (about 1 mile down), and get ready for the big drop of the day, a class V ledge falls. Passing under a bridge is your only warning that it's coming. Yes, this falls (called Pa's Falls) is exciting to run. It's easy for 1.5 miles and then you'll find a long stretch of class II-III that ends where the outlet for Round Lake* joins in. The going is easy until you get to the drop above the take-out bridge. Beware of the hydraulic. And please, check carefully the line for the last drop -- it's a dozzy (if anybody knows the right way to spell this please tell me.) It would make a great picture if somebody takes the shot from their boat at the bottom, out on the lake.

(*) As of late 2000 the Nature Conservancy has bought much of the land around Round Pond Outlet. You may still find posted signs that no longer apply.

If you thought this was going to be another story about Dennis getting munched on the river you'd be wrong! I got munched after I got off the river. Just west of the take-out (while checking out a future camping spot) I found myself hung up -- the right side of the car hanging over the bank. What to do -- except start digging under the car? As this progressed the side was jacked up and flat stones where placed under the tires to level the car. In the meantime it should be mentioned that today was the day that the annual black fly horde first appeared and found a hot juicy meal. Agh1##***Damn!?###!!! After a few hours of being dined on, digging, jacking and piling stones, the time was at hand. There would be only one attempt to drive off the stones. Failure would mean rolling over down the hill (since I'm here writing about it you probably figured out that I made it). Man, talk about anti--climatic.

Lessons for the day; carry a good jack, carry a strong shovel, keep a winch/come-a-long in the car and remind yourself that the only good reason to be in the Adirondacks during bug season is to be on the river -- paddling.

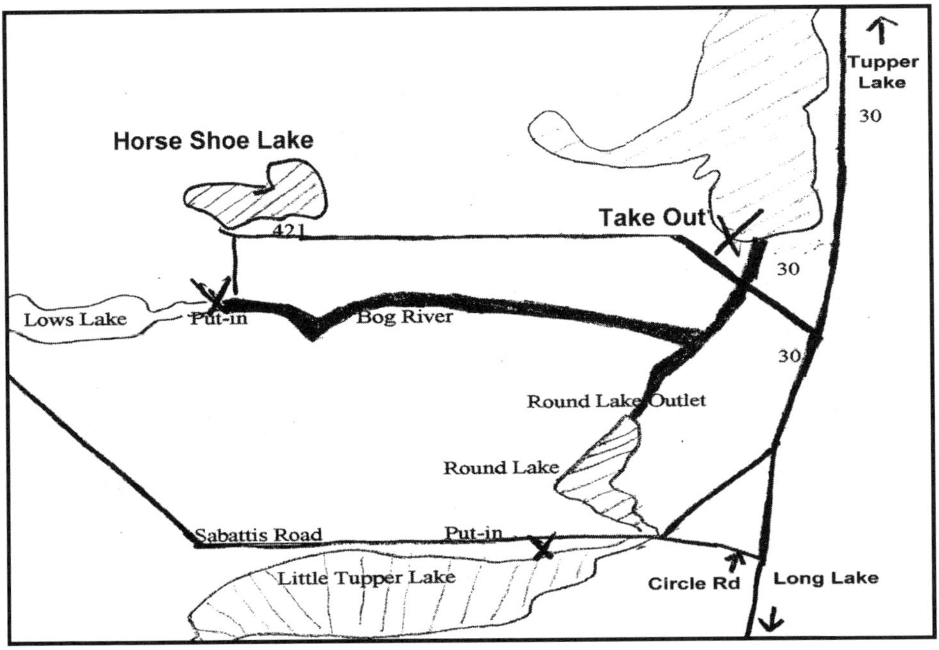

Notes

1

2

3

4

5

Jody flies the highest because she grunts the loudest. Photo by John Szumoski.

River:	**North Fork Boquet***** (Elizabethtown)**
Scenery:	Very good
Class:	IV-V
Access:	.25-mile
Length:	3 miles
Average gradient:	140'/mile / steepest section is 280'/mile.
Gauge:	E. Ausable at 4.2' or more / Hudson (North Creek) 7' or more
Water level:	It doesn't take much water to paddle this -- and it's flashy -- up and down quickly.
Best betting time:	April (snowmelt plus rain)
Other local runs:	Johns Brook (V)***** / Boquet/ Steel Woods (II-III)**
Boogie time:	80% -- if you're a good boat scouter/probe unit
Time to do first run:	3 hours
First known descent:	Dennis did a run on this in the early 90's
Raft:	No -- it's too tight in there
Ducky:	Yes -- this is a great low water run
Food and gas:	Keene Valley / Noonmark Diner
Camping:	Split Rock Falls
Page in the Gazetteer:	96/97
County:	Essex
Closest river store:	Adirondack Lakes and Trails in Saranac Lake

Directions: As you drive north on Route 73 you'll come to Malfunction Junction--bear right on Route 9 towards Elizabethtown. Just as you cross the bridge pull off on the right side. This is the take-out and the incredible Split Rock Falls. To find the put-in -- drive back up Route 73 past Malfunction Junction and start up the long hill. As you cross the river (the second bridge that is -- the first one is the South Branch) you can pull off on the right or left. Be sure to stop and gawk at the top drops!

Description/hazards: If you started above Route 73 you found some serious class V. The drops just above and just below the bridge have been run. However there are consequences. The shoebox is the drop 150 yards below the bridge. The launch is tight (hold the paddle vertical), the landing is shallow on the left (I broke my boat there) and the hole immediately after is very nasty. Only do this drop with safety (to pull your sorry as… out of the hole) and with the knowledge that Dennis is not doing it again (scratch that). Then things calm down to class IV for a while. Note that a good put-in for the sane members of the group is down the steep bank right below the shoebox. If anything looks iffy get out and look. The section that starts just above and keeps going past the South Branch confluence is incredibly rocky. At this point you'll be paddling over and through medium sizes boulders -- if you love rocky runs you'll want to marry this one. In the middle of an easy stretch along the road, you'll cross under a bridge. Relax for a few minutes. The rocks will start getting bigger and the river will be getting steeper. Enjoy! This all goes on for a glorious length of time. As you see a huge boulder in the middle -- get out! Immediately below is Andy's hole. At lower water levels is can be run on the far left -- any place else and this hole could be your last surf. The portage is high up on the right side. The whole section here is class V at high water. Andy's hole is named for a guy by the name of Andy (why imagine that) -- who almost drowned in this hole while his partner watched, helpless. At higher water this hole has a horribly flat backwash and doing safety is very, very, tough. In a few hundred yards you'll arrive a Split Rocks Falls -- get out above or below, your choice. The falls are usually run at low water levels. If you go for it expect to go way deep in the first drop and perhaps wind up running the second drop backwards (you won't be the first). Also know that the gorge below starts off with an unrunnable slide/permanent tree. You could do a short section below that but it's short and very hard to climb down to.

In 2001 we figured out that the last 1-mile above Split Rock is a great bone run. Just start at the little footbridge next to Route 9 a little over a mile upstream of Split Rock. If it looks like there's barely enough water to get down this wide stretch of the river, you're all set. The gorge downstream is much like a low water run on the best parts of the Upper Yough -- all packed in together. The East.Ausable gauge will probably be reading around 3.8'. This run can rise very quickly if it's raining (into the class V zone) -- it also drops pretty quickly (just enough time for a great paddle).

Blurb! There is supposed to be a class III-IV run on the North Boquet, up by Reber. I haven't done it or know who has. If you feel like exploring -- let me know what you find.

I'd apologize, but then, this is a tale worth telling. It was just after Thanksgiving and there were several inches of snow on the ground, and it was raining...hard. So it seemed like a good idea to see what was around to boat that hadn't been done before. So I snagged my friend Joyce for shuttle duty and we headed over to the Boquet. The river was high and rising as I scouted it for the first time. My plan was to start at the bottom and work upstream since it was bank full and debris was most likely moving at this level. When I finally got to the top, the water was so high that I actually got in on a small tributary. A thick blanket of fog settled in making it even more sporting. With the level and the fog I can say honestly that it was the only run I've been scared on in my entire misspent career. There were no eddies and the biggest boulders were now ugly pourovers. The speed of the current only seemed to magnify the lack of visibility. I was out of control and I knew it. As the river got even more continuous and steeper the chaos factor increased dramatically. There, just above what is now called Andy's hole (that's better than Dennis' Demise) was a...tree! Trying to get out without an eddy I managed to lose my paddle and barely hang onto the boat. Next I went running down the river after the paddle, to no avail. There would be no more boating that day.

Believe it or not, the next day I found it! It had wedged itself in a tree in a place easy to see. It had swum over a mile on its own over Split Rock Falls and the gorge below. IT had done class V-VI and come home to me! Kinda' makes ya' think Old Yella' doesn't it?

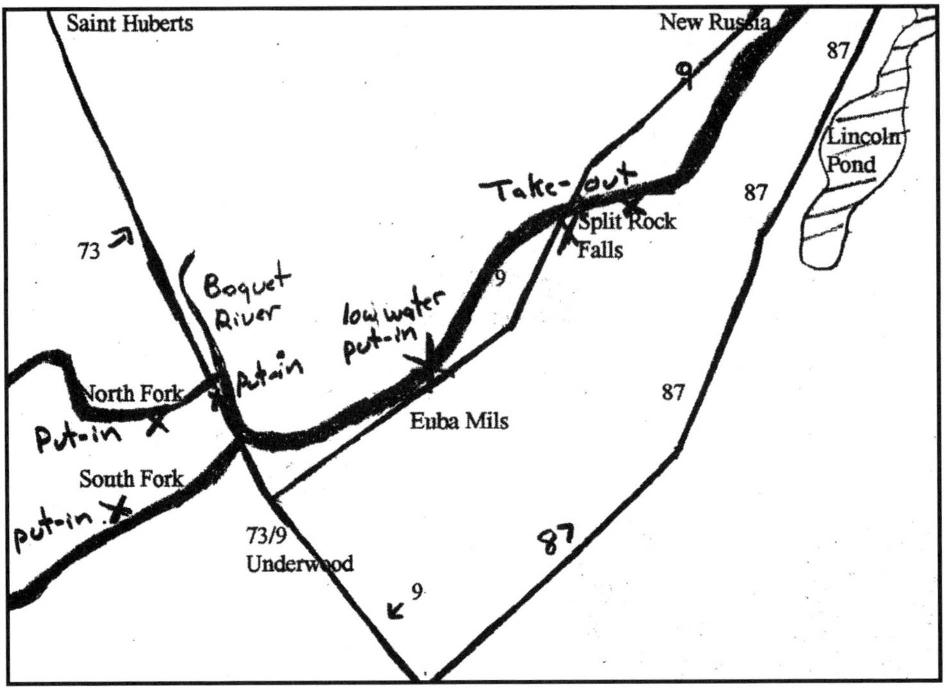

Notes

1

2

3

4

5

Buy Dennis breakfast

River	**Boquet/Steel Woods***(Elizabethtown)**
Scenery:	Very nice
Class:	II-III
Access:	.75-mile
Length:	6 miles
Average gradient:	30'/mile
Gauge:	3.6' at East Ausable is minimal / 4.0' is good
Water level:	The waves get up to 3 or 4 feet and are good fun at fairly high levels (4' and over)
Best betting time:	April-early May
Other local runs:	Boquet (IV-V)*****/ East Ausable/ Lower (II-III)**
Boogie time:	100%
Time to do first run:	3 hours
First known descent:	?
Raft:	Yes -- over 4'
Ducky:	Yes
Food and gas:	Elizabethtown
Camping:	Split Rock Falls
Page in the Gazetteer:	96
County:	Essex
Closest river store:	Adirondack Lakes and Trails in Saranac Lake

Directions: The put-in is on Route 8 a little downstream of E-Town. The normal (what's that?) put-in is at the dam. For the take-out, go back into town and head north on Route 9. In 4+ miles you want to turn right on Steel Woods Road. Stay on that until it T's with another road -- in just a minute you'll see the river on your side. You can just park and take-out down by the last drop.

Description/hazards: At most levels you can surf the hole/waves at the small dam. The first few miles below are class I and take you into a really remote neck of the woods. The rapids will start to build gradually -- until it feels like you're on a little roller coaster ride. At higher level this is a lot of fun. These rapids are mostly waves and even though they go on for a while they are over with too soon. Things calm down and stay remote until you pass under the high bridge. Around the next corner is the drop of the day (III+/IV) and the take-out.

Notes

1

2

3

4

5

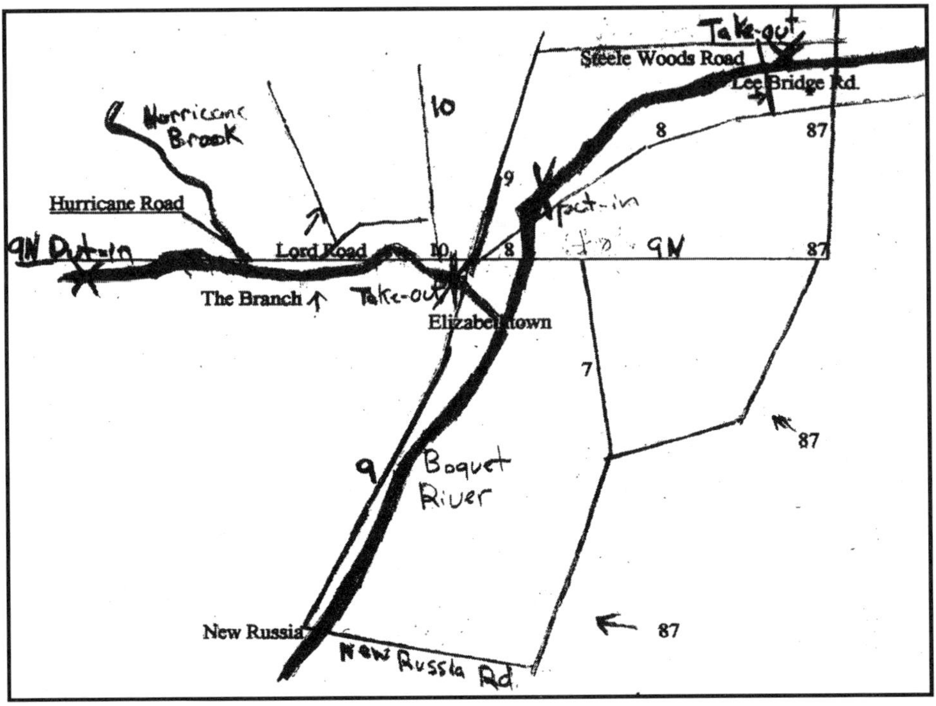

Mike Duggan going over falls #2 at Split Rock. Photo by Pete Iscaro.

River:	**South Branch of the Boquet*(Keene Valley)**
Scenery:	Very Good
Class:	II-V
Access:	Miles from the road
Length:	3+ miles/ if you can't walk that far go paddle the North Boquet
Average Gradient:	110'/mile
Gauge:	East Ausable will be at least 4.5’, maybe more
Water levels:	If this is high enough to do everything will be running
Best betting time:	Mid to late April
Other local runs:	John's Brook (V) ***** / East Ausable/Lower (l-lll)**
Boogie time:	80% -- there are drops and slides if you walk in far enough
Time to do first run:	5 hours or more -- depending on how far you walk in
First known descent:	Mike Duggan and friends in the mid 90's
Raft:	No
Ducky:	Yes
Food and gas:	Keene Valley
Camping:	Split Rock Falls
Page in the Gazetteer:	96
County:	Essex
Closest river store:	Adirondack Lakes and Trails in Saranac Lake

Directions: Get off of I-87 at exit 30 and head towards Lake Placid. When Route 73 splits off to the right you want to continue to the left for about .5-mile. Just before you cross over the South Branch, pull in and park on the left (west) side.

Description/hazards: If it looks high enough to boat at the Route 73 Bridge, it is. As you start your long walk, (oh, by the way, this is a hike in), you'll notice that this bottom stretch is class III+/lV. As you walk up there is some decent stuff for a little ways (lll-lV) -- and then it starts to flatten. The trail will disappear. A pattern will form; just as you're ready to stop, because you haven't seen much for a while -- you'll see something that looks promising. A handful of those somethings will look pretty cool. If you hike up far enough you'll get an awesome view of South Dix, and you'll see the slides. They're huge. Will you run them?

This run may be worth doing once. The problem is that only minutes away the North Boquet and John's Brook will be running. So unless you've run the NB & JB so much that you've grown bored, or you're just into S & M, I'd personally head for the NB or JB myself (and stop and eat a BP & J). Go hike South Dix and the slides, after.

Notes

1

2

3

4

5

Still reading that cool new guidebook, babe?
there is so much stuff in here honey, I still haven't read about all the branches of the grass yet!!

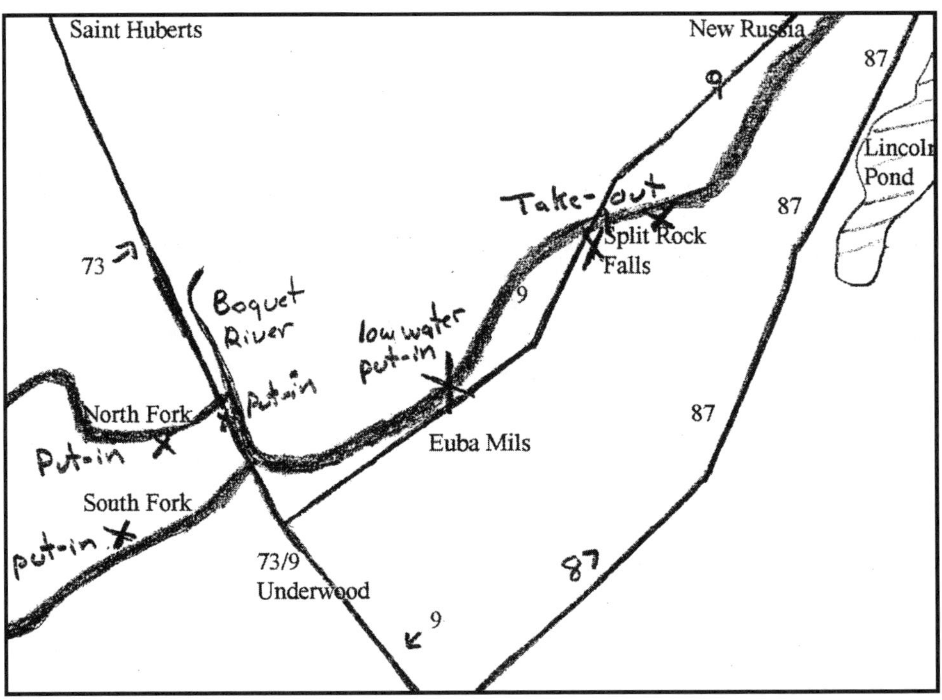
Saint Huberts
New Russia
87
9
Lincoln Pond
Take-out
87
Split Rock Falls
73
Boquet River
9
low water put-in
put-in
North Fork
Put-in
87
Euba Mils
South Fork
put-in
73/9
Underwood
87
9

River:	**Chateaugay**(Chateaugay)**
Scenery:	It's a very nice!
Class:	III-V, Vl
Access:	sheer walls
Length:	2 miles or 8-10 miles
Average gradient:	120'/mile (not counting dams and 120' waterfalls)
Gauge:	The Chazy at 4.0' is about minimum/ 4.5' is fine
Water level:	Ledges in high water mean unpleasant hydraulics. They may even let some water out in the fall -- it seems to run Oct.-Nov.
Best betting time:	April-mid May
Other local runs:	Chazy (III-V)** / Salmon / Malone (II-III, IV-)***
Boogie time:	60% -- scout those horizon lines!
Time to do first run:	2 hours (for the short run) or 5 hours (for the whole run)
First known descent:	?
Raft:	Yes -- but only to High Falls, with no portaging possible
Ducky:	Yes
Food and gas:	Chateaugay
Camping:	High Falls Campground
Page in the Gazetteer:	101/102
County:	Franklin
Closest river store:	Adirondack Lakes and Trails in Saranac Lake

Directions: The take-out is legal at Sam Cook Road in Cook's Mill at the bridge. There's another possibility a few miles above (the next bridge upstream), but it's posted (ask?). To put-in go past Route 11 and find Chase Lake Road, the spot you're looking for is where the power lines cross over (downstream of the Lower Chateaugay Lake). Park here and walk a few minutes to the river.

Description/hazards: You can do the 2 miles down to High Falls as a shorter trip if you want. The 2 miles are fairly quick and has lots of excitement concentrated in a short run. You'll quickly find yourself running class IV ledges. There's an S-turn and shallow landings below many of these ledges…all day long. You can largely eddy hop down through the gorge. **When you get to a big horizon line get out and look at this slide**. The previous sentence is all that we were given as a description (before our first trip) for the drop called No Scout. In reality you want to get out before you see this horizon line. If you wait until you see the drop you're running the drop -- like it or not. To spot this section (are you paying attention?): about 1.5 miles down from the put-in things will suddenly narrow down, speed up and start to take a hard bend to the left. Get out on the right side well before the bend. At high water there's no way to scout this and you just stay right, paddle hard and pray even harder. You'll find some more ledges and then a house on the left. About .4-mile below here the water backs up behind High Falls (120'), you might want to get out here. Or for a longer run get back in after walking around the falls. You'll find class III-IV and arrive at the tunnel. This is 200' long and deserves a look (it's dark in there!). Next you'll need to walk around the 60’ dam. And paddle the deep class III-IV chasm. At the end you'll see the higher take-out I mentioned in the directions. There's also a monster-ish 300 yd. long slide (class V) that deserves a look. Right down the middle baby! You can walk back up to the bridge above this drop and take-out. To be legal and nice you could take-out down at Sam Cook Bridge.

One side of my brain was saying, "Rob said there's nothing more than class IV above High Falls." The other side (which I usually automatically listen to) was asking, "What the hell are you doing, Dennis?" As I paddled around the corner I got to live that fear that paddlers dread may come true some day. At the top of the drop all I saw was two exploding piles of water -- one after the other -- and a huge drop behind that. "Oh God it's a 50' waterfall." Knowing that I was committed I went into survival mode (despite my stories I really don't like that mode of paddling.) The water was low so I went for the middle of the drop -- paddling hard and hoping that I wouldn't break my back and/or legs. After the water cleared (from my eyes) from the second exploding pile of water I was relieved to see it wasn't a vertical falls. I wasn't too crazy about the water pillowing off the big rock at the bottom and feeding back into the big hole in the center. As I got there I caught the edge of the ledge coming off the left side and ski jumped the hole and skipped off the boil -- right into the eddy on the right side. I was all wound up -- I don't run drops like that out of control. And Sally was right behind me!

Have you ever tried to move quickly when you're crawling over green slime? The water was shallow and thick with the slime. I was trying to pull/push the boat up on the ledge, get myself up, and pull out the throw bag all at the same time. I had the pedal to the metal and wasn't moving. In the midst of all this inept fumbling I was thinking Sally was right behind me. ....uck!....uck!.....Fu....I kept yelling it over and over in my desperation. By the time I finally got it all together and the rope out I realized that Sally wasn't coming. Thank God she was smart enough not to follow me (as I'm writing this I think I see a pattern forming).

Notes

1

2

3

4

5

When you meet Dennis give him a hug (or a dollar)

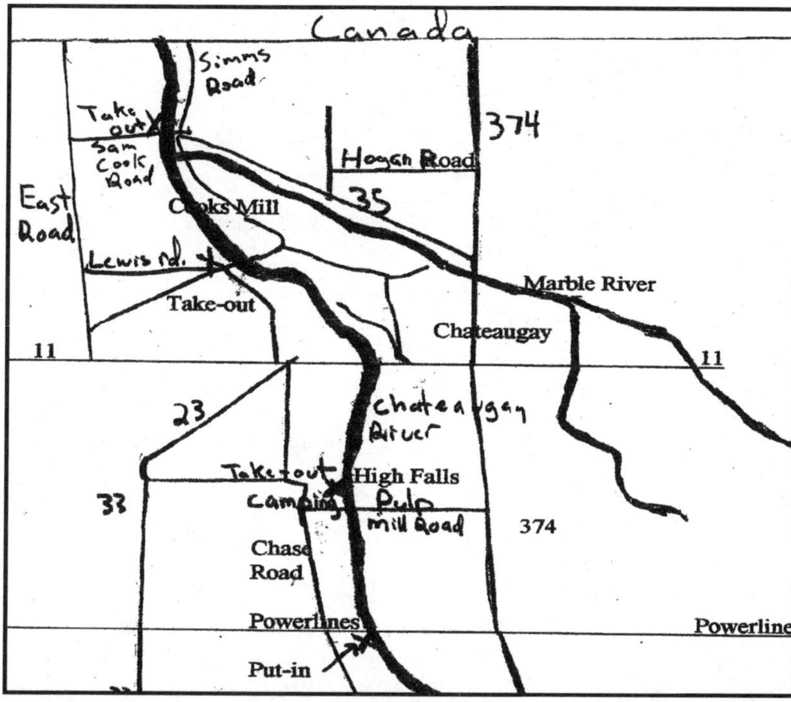

Derek Snyder coming out of the tunnel on the Chateaugay. Photo by Dennis Squires

River:	**Chazy (Great) River**(Mooers Forks)**
Scenery:	Good
Class:	III-V
Access:	1-mile
Length:	8 miles
Average gradient:	45'/mile
Gauge:	800cfs on the Great Chazy is minimum (1500 is nice)
Water level:	Above 1800cfs the hole below the big slide is class 5+
Best betting time:	April-mid May
Other local runs:	Chateaugy (III-V, VI)** / North Chazy (III)**
Boogie time:	90% -- scout the big slide and Woods Falls
Time to do first run:	3+ hours
First known descent:	?
Raft:	Yes -- and you'll have your hands full
Ducky:	Yes
Food and gas:	Mooer's Forks
Camping:	You're guess is as good as mine
Page in the Gazetteer:	103
County:	Clinton
Closest river store:	Adirondack Lakes and Trails in Saranac Lake

Direction: Just south of Altona you'll find that the Woods Falls Road crosses over the river, this is the put-in. Park only where it doesn't say you can't (I guess that means you can). To get to the take-out, drive north on Woods Falls Road. You can take-out at Woods Falls, or 1.5 miles beyond that (where the river is next to the road), or at Emery Road, which is 1.6 miles farther yet.

Description/hazards: The rapid above the bridge looks kind of exciting doesn't it? The rapid around the first corner will sneak up on you and eat you alive at high water (the hole is ravenous and the next section which comes at you fast will pull you deeper into it than a full grown Sperm Whale. What I'm trying to say is scout before you get in the boat -- especially if it's high. The hole at the end of the Sperm Whale would not be a nice place to be (meaning it won't poop you out for a long time). This is the crux of the whole run. Below here are easy sections alternating with some good class IV stuff. Scout Woods Falls. If you go down to a lower take-out (worth doing if you've got the time) you'll find a couple of more points of interest. These points of interest consist of a handful of class III-IV slidey ledge type things. You'll even find a little something to **surf.**

Extra! There is a long class III type run on the North Branch of this river. It's close to the road, small, prone to wood and rocky. It could make a decent intermediate/advanced run. I say this because even though it's class III, it is tight and woodsy -- which will mean very few eddies to escape the strainers. The river drops 310' from Ellenburg Depot to Gero Road There's another 200' of drop down to Mooer's Forks (this section is flatter). Just in case you've heard about the section above Miners Lake -- don't paddle it. It's got class III stuff on it -- but it's on the Indian reservation and they will absolutely not let you paddle this stretch of river.

I had been out-voted and over-ruled. Damn -- I wanted to go to...Oh it doesn't matter. We drove to Woods Falls first and checked it out. There was a lot of water. The seven of us drove up top and hopped in (after not parking where we shouldn't -- so I guess it was O.K.). I was feeling my oats so I took off around the corner and chose to run the drop without scouting. As I started over the drop I realized that perhaps there had been a slight misjudgment made. God -- the hole looked big and hungry. The probe did its job and fed the river gods well. When I finally got out and rolled up, a single glance downstream had me eddying out and giving frantic paddle signals upstream. Everybody made the eddy (barely) even M. who had been paddling with internal injuries (I don't know how he managed to roll -- I guess he really is a hero -- too bad I didn't spell out his name). After seeing the next drop some of the troop walked off and the rest foraged on. The river proved to be easy except for occasional nice big ledgey drops. You could boat scout everything, except Woods Falls. Get out and look. From here down it's mostly easy with just two goodies left.

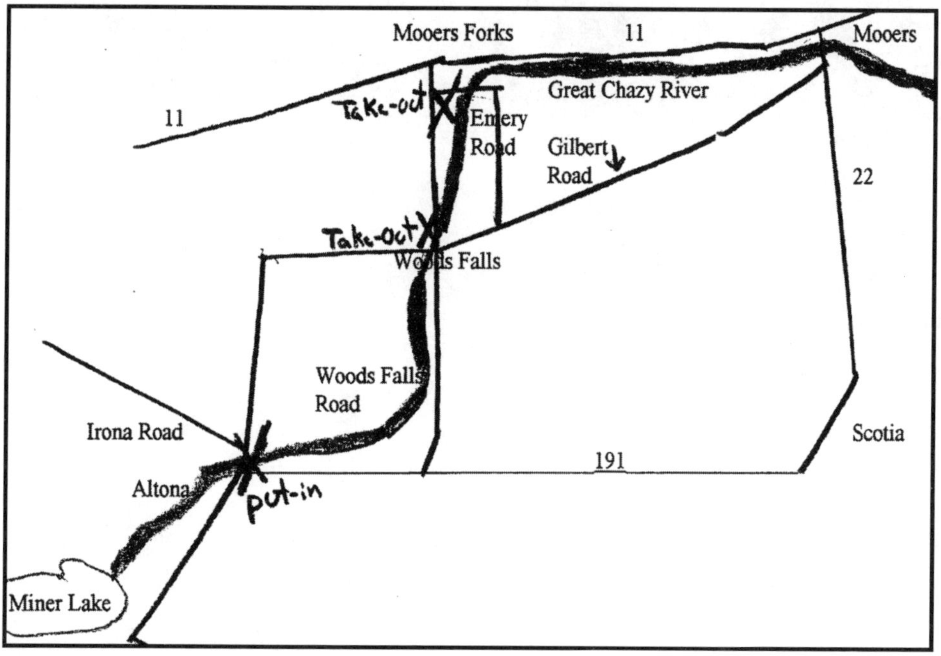

Dennis will tell his stories to anybody that will listen. Photo by Ceci Mendez.

Notes
1
2
3
4
5

Touch Dennis' booties, I dare you

River:	**Cold**(Long Lake)**
Scenery:	Very good
Class:	II-V
Access:	Many miles
Length:	24+ miles
Average gradient:	48'/mile (not counting the flat water at the end)
Gauge:	Hudson should be at least 6.0'
Water level:	It's a long walk if you don't find enough water at the put-in
Best betting time:	April-late May
Other local runs:	Round Lake Outlet (IV-V)*** / Bog (I-V)**
Boogie time:	95% -- and there is a lot of flat water
Time to do first run:	1-2 days
First known descent:	Don Morris in the early 90's?
Raft:	No
Ducky:	Yes
Food and gas:	Long Lake/Newcomb
Camping:	Various spots (state land) along the river
Page in the Gazetteer:	96/95/87
County:	Essex/Hamilton
Closest river store:	Adirondack Lakes and Trails in Saranac Lake

Directions: Take-out at the beach in Long Lake. The other possible take-out is at Axton Landing, the state has a boat launch and parking area there. To find the put-in, drive east on Route 28N through the village of Newcomb. About 6 or 7 miles after Newcomb you'll want to turn left on Route 2 (Boreas Road). In a few minutes you'll go left again and head north on Route 25 towards the Iron Works by Henderson Lake. Drive up as far as you can and park. The actual place the real trip begins is the outflow of Duck Hole (which is 5 miles north by northwest from where you're parked). I should point out that paddling on the lakes between you and the put-in is a no-no (which is too bad because if you could paddle across, the hike would only be 2.5 miles and would eliminate much of the uphill hiking).

Description/hazards: You're hiking in the high peaks area of the Adirondacks-- enjoy! No sniveling about having to carry your boat -- be a man (have you ever noticed that it takes more work not to offend people)… guess I'm just plain lazy. You first have to decide if you want to do this as an overnight trip (carrying extra gear), or as a 16-hour one-day trip (more if you're not pushing along all day long). The first 1.5 miles is the hardest of the whole trip; don't you just love getting up way early, driving in the dark, hiking for miles with your boat and extra gear, getting munched by bugs (the earlier you start the less you'll get munched), and then running the hardest drops as soon as you get in? You'll be paddling class IV for over a mile until it pushes toward the class V zone for 2-3 hundred yards. Then you pass into a steep gorge for 2 miles and get to paddle class II and III. Next up is 2 miles of marsh (check out the old cabin towards the end). In the next 6 miles there are 2 drops of note: Millers Falls (IV+/V-), which is by a lean-to and a 4' drop which ends in a big pool. It's now 4 miles of easy water down to the Raquette River. From here take a left and paddle several miles south to the Village of Long Lake. You could head north instead and get out at Axton Landing, but it's 4 miles longer and the shuttle is 40 minutes longer. The good side of this option is that you'll be going downstream on the Raquette and moving with the river (and the wind would probably be in your face paddling south on the lake). You'll also get to paddle Raquette Falls (but you'll never get there before dark if you do this as a one-day trip). It's 20 miles below the Duck Hole put-in to the head of the falls. The falls are over a mile long: the first drop is IV+/V, there's a long stretch of class III, a class IV drop and then the big nasty ledge with a horrible hole that you really want to look at. There is a big meadow with lots of camping here on the right side. Things will slowly calm down until it flattens for the last 6-7 miles down to Axton Landing. The take-out spot you're looking for is at an angle behind your right shoulder -- don't paddle by the take-out.

The take-out

Notes

1

2

3

4

5

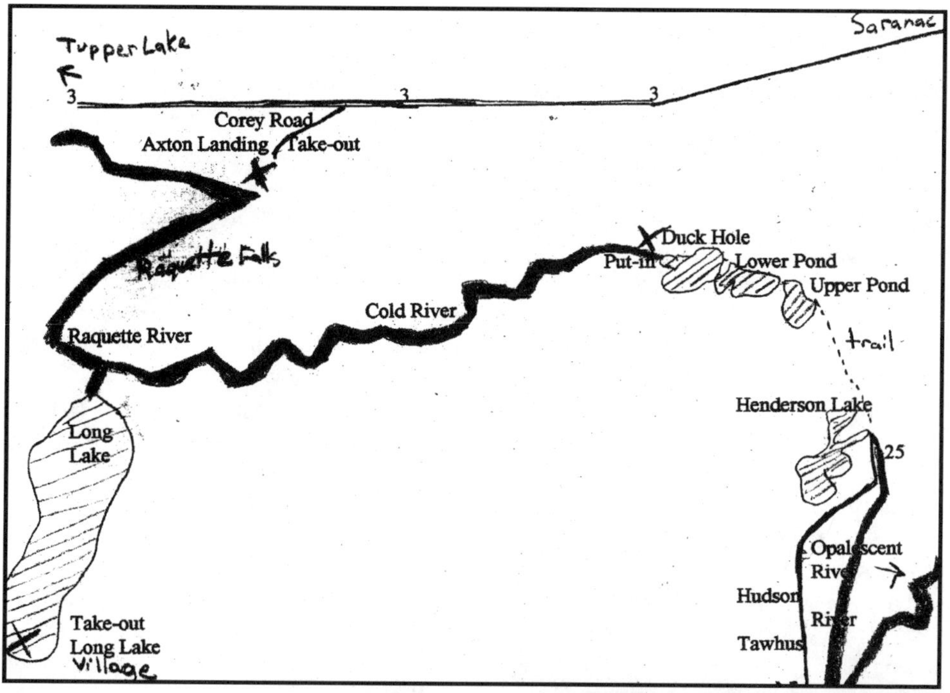

Raquette Falls at low water. Photo by Sally Dewes.

River:	**Deer River****(Dickinson Center)**
Scenery:	Good
Class:	IV-V
Access:	1-mile
Length:	5 or more miles
Average gradient:	80'/mile.
Gauge:	Parishville: 700cfs and rising or 1100cfs and dropping is O.K.
Water level:	There is no gauge on the Deer River. Checking the river at the take-out in Dickinson Center will tell the story. Look at the bridge in town and realize that the run is the narrowest at this point. If it looks like a lot of water watch out for holes and trees.
Best betting time:	April and early May
Other local runs:	Lake Ozonia Outlet (IV-V)***/ West St. Regis (III-IV+, VI)***(may be a better bet if the Deer is low -- it's got a much bigger watershed) / Salmon / Malone (I-III, IV-)**
Boogie time:	75%-80%
Time to do first run:	3-4 hours
First known descent:	????
Raft:	Probably not -- although a small one at high water might be possible -- with a couple of walk-a-rounds
Ducky:	Yes -- watch out for ledge holes -- they get beefy
Food and gas:	Dickinson Center or St. Regis Falls
Camping:	At the put-in
Page in the Gazetteer:	101
County:	Franklin
Closest river store:	Wear on Earth in Potsdam.

Directions: Take-out where the river leaves the road a few hundred yards downstream of the Route 5 Bridge in Dickinson Center (I ask permission to park at a nearby house). The put-in is about 5 miles up the road where the bridge (Conservation Rd.?) goes over the Deer. There is also a great place to camp on state land at the put-in.

Description/hazards: It is possible to start higher but it's mostly flat water. The bridge above Reynoldston Road (which is several miles upstream of the suggested put-in) is where you'll find High Falls (V) with a class IV+ ledge above that and about 3 miles above that is some class IV-V for a short distance. These are great rapids but add at least 10 miles to the day, almost all-flat water.

From the normal put-in it's only a few minutes until you start hitting the ledges. This part of the river has many class IV-ish ledges that are great fun. You usually get multiple options of which drop to run. After the river starts to narrow you'll find things are getting steeper and rockier and if it's high you'll discover that you just blundered into the first class V section. Trees like to park across the river here (it's exciting to have to do log jumps the last second) -- stay alert. This all goes on for a few hundred yards and ends in a 15' falls. We normally run left at the falls and scout the drop immediately below. After that things very gradually ease off and turn flat for a while. But coming into the last half mile of the run (which is in town) things get humping. It's good to look at this part when doing shuttle in the morning. This has holes, trees and feels much like running a gauntlet at high water. Stay in your boat. **No swimming allowed!**

"God it's high." Tony is expressing intelligent concern. I'm thinking I want to do it anyway. But then Tony slept in a real bed in a motel last night, he's probably thinking clearer. Geez, if I wasn't a guide/paddling nomad (bum) I could perhaps some day make clear-headed decisions too. Because then I'd eat home cooked meals and sleep inside. Tony says, "If somebody swims you'll lose your equipment and have to save your own butt." We decide to go paddle something else. (See the Lake Ozonia description).

We are back 2 hours later. The water is still high but down about 4 inches. "Let's do it." The decision is mutual this time.

Short of being an otter splashing with total abandon this is the best way to experience a day in this world. Like two otters crossing back and forth we playfully make our way down the river. Time seems to stop. I often wonder if this is the most real, most whole thing I'll ever experience in this bag of skin.

What we find is some big holes and big fun. As usual the stretch above the falls is upon us before we see it coming. I'm thinking to myself, "Man, this is cranking, this is nasty -- this is fun!" When I get there -- Tony is standing at the top of the falls ready to do safety.

I get slowed down in the hole at the base of the falls -- so Tony is now explaining how that won't happen in his boat. I find it hard not to laugh when Tony gets stopped and then tries to get out of the hole but I'm ready with the rope. What Tony does next surprises (and slightly amazes me) -- "What the hell kind of a stroke was that?" He comes right out of the hole and he's off to the next drop. He doesn't need to wait for me since we're not setting safety here, even though some other river guide calls it a class VI drop. Man -- I sure hope that somebody writes the guide for N.Y. that everybody can trust. Oh ya' that's right...this is it!

Extra: There's class II-II+ if you continue down below town to Route 11B. You can even keep going down to Lawrenceville and enjoy sections that drop up to 60'/mile (II-III?). If you paddle on as far as North Lawrenceville, the river still averages 40'/mile. The river is wide here so I can't imagine that it's any more than class I-II -- good canoe country.

Notes

1

2

3

4

5

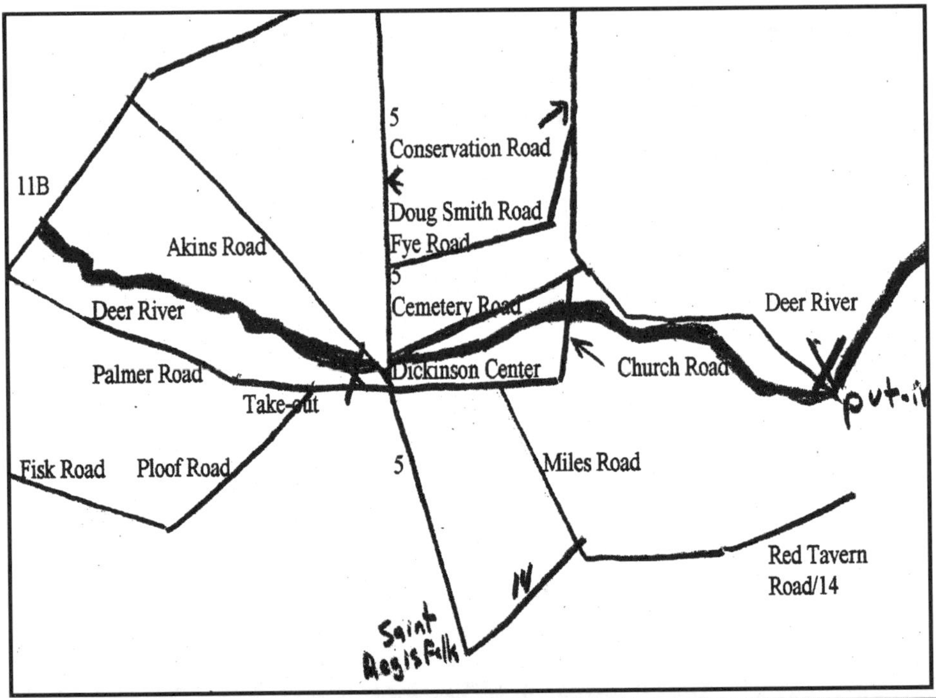

Sally Dewes approaching Deer Falls. Photo by Dennis.

River:	**Deer**(New Boston)**
Scenery:	Good
Class:	III
Access:	1-mile
Length:	10.5 mile
Average gradient:	35'/mile
Gauge:	The Fish will have to be at least 2.5', call (800-249-4112) and tell Brad to paddle more. Even though this looks to be a long ways from the Fish, it actually drains the center of the Tug Hill Plateau, as does the Fish.
Water levels:	This can be run at a very wide range of flows
Best betting time:	Late March-early May
Other local runs:	Black (III-V)*** / Mill / Lowville (IV-V)***
Boogie time:	99% -- stop and **hug a tree**
Time to do first run:	2-3 hours
First known descent:	?
Rafts:	Yes -- if it's fairly high
Ducky:	Yes
Food and gas:	Copenhagen or Carthage
Camping:	Campground off of Route 26 north of Lowville
Page in the Gazetteer:	84
County:	Lewis
Closest river store:	T. I. Adventures in Clayton

Directions: Put-in at New Boston, close to the Route 177 Bridge. To find the take-out, drive north on the River Road (it's right there at the bridge) -- right into Copenhagen. Simple enough, eh? You can get out on river left just as you're getting into town. **DO NOT PADDLE ANY FARTHER**, the next drop is not runnable, and there's no way out just above it.

Description/hazards: Even at this upper put-in the Deer is rather wide. The views are wide open, and the rapids are easy to see coming. The rapids are spaced out, and consist of waves and some ledges. The only real concern might be the hydraulics below some of the ledges at higher flows. Have a mellow day. Get out in Copenhagen well above the huge, inescapable, inaccessible and unrunnable (get the picture, yet?), **High Falls.**

Notes

1

2

3

4

5

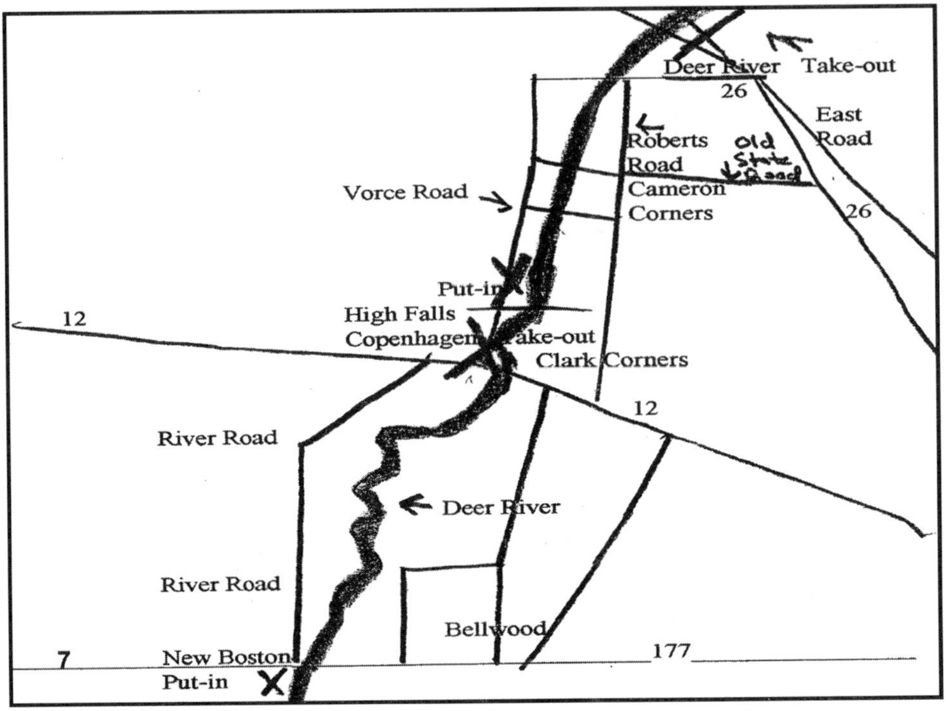

The good news is that the bugs don't come out everyday. Photo by Sally Dewes.

River:	**Deer*(Copenhagen)**
Scenery:	Good
Class:	I-V
Access:	.65-mile
Length:	3-4 mile
Average gradient:	40'/mile
Gauge:	The Fish will probably have to be at least 3'. The power station at High Falls steals much of the water just above this section, so call 800-249-4112 (for the level) and tell Brad he's doing a great job. Though this looks to be far from the Fish, it actually drains the center of the Tug Hill Plateau, as does the Fish.
Water levels:	You can't often find enough water to do this run
Best betting time:	Late March-early May
Other local runs:	Black (III-V)*** / Mill/ Lowville (IV-V)***
Boogie time:	60% -- scout the drops
Time to do first run:	2+ hours
First known descent:	?
Raft:	Probably isn't worth the trouble
Ducky:	Yes
Food and gas:	Carthage or Copenhagen
Camping:	Sleepy Hollow Campground on Route 26
Page in the Gazetteer:	84
County:	Lewis
Closest river store:	T. I. Adventures in Clayton

Directions: Put-in on the River Road, which is on the west side of the river. You're parking about 1.5 mile north of the middle of Copenhagen. Basically, you're getting in as soon as you can below High Falls. The take-out is found by driving down (north) on the River Road about 4 miles into Deer River. You could take-out at the Route 812 Bridge or the one upstream.

Description/hazards: At the put-in the Deer is rather wide, and it stays that way. This section only has a handful of drops, but they're good ones. The drops are big, wide and plenty rocky. The scenery is fair to good. This is a mellow run to do if you're in the area, you'll even find a fair amount of good easy surfing as you go. This is a run that I think is more fun with a play boat -- it is mostly class 11-11+. Getting in can be a little tricky, just like finding enough water can be. If you should paddle this, you'll find that the views are pretty big and wide too -- that's because you're on top of the Tug Hill Plateau. The plateau is a unique landform; it differs greatly from the geology of, say, the western Adirondacks, which are right next door. That means solid rock and lots of ledges, and more solid rock.

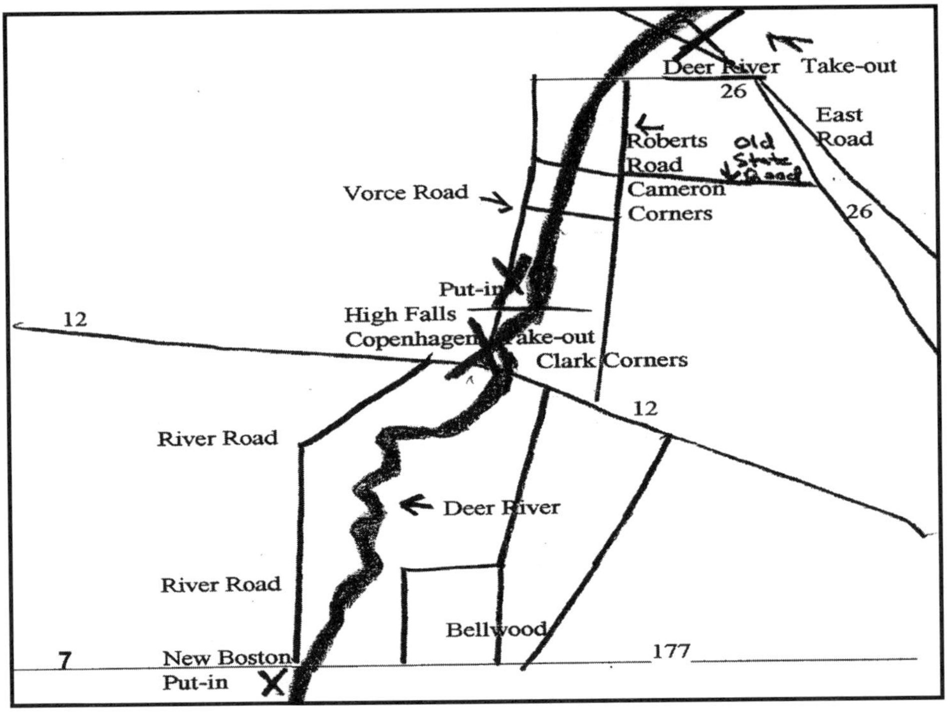

Notes

1
2
3
4
5

Ask Dennis to tell you stories -- while you buy the drinks

River:	**Fish Creek*****(Taberg)**
Scenery:	Very Good
Class:	III-III+ (up to IV at 6' or more)
Access:	1-mile and lots of sheer walls
Length:	4 or 8 miles
Average gradient:	65'/mile
Gauge:	Call Brad at Northern Outfitters (800-249-4112) 1.5' is minimal / 3' is great / 3.5'- 4' is perfect / 6' is high
Water level:	At high levels this is a powerful and continuous run. Swimming is a dangerous choice.
Best betting time:	Ice out (which sometimes happens as early as February) until early May
Other local runs:	Mad (III+/IV, VI)** / Black / Upper (II-III)**
Boogie time:	97% -- walk the dam at the mid point of the full run
Time to do first run:	All day / either put-in (surf until you can't grip your paddle)
First known descent:	?
Raft:	Yes -- above 3.25' for the lower half and 3.6' for the upper half
Ducky:	Yes -- great low water surfing
Food and gas:	Taberg or Rome
Camping:	Delta Lake Campground
Page in the Gazetteer:	76
County:	Oneida
Closest river store:	Northern Outfitters in Utica & Syracuse

Directions: Take-out on Blossvale Road about .5-mile below the center of Taberg. There's a grassy pull off and stairs that lead right into the water. For the put-in: drive back into town, take a left on Main St., a right on Coal Hill and then a right on Palmer Road, take a left on Boyd and drive a little ways (until the hard bend), park on the right side across from the gate that says City of Rome water supply. You've got to walk about 10 minutes down the gated road and get in below the dam. For the top put-in don't turn on Palmer -- rather stay on Coal Hill for several miles and take a right at the T. You'll cross the river and park and walk down on the right side. This is Point Rock.

Description/hazards: Starting at Point Rock you get to see the incredibly scenic upper gorge. This area is class II-III (III-III+ if it's high). There are several waterfalls coming in off the sides that are must-see. One point nine (1.9') feet is minimal for this part, which has mostly a cobblestone bottom and some good surfing waves. There is one gnarly hole, right in the wave train, about 2.5 miles down. About 4-4.5 miles from the start is a short pool -- right above a 16' dam that has a hydraulic that is inescapable. At higher levels you can't mess around here. The take-out is 20' above the dam on the left--immediately after the sheer wall ends on the left side. The current is fast here so at high water-stay loose-stay relaxed-stay calm-and **get the hell out!**

From the dam down (the lower put-in) the river is a bit harder. There's tons of surfing on this lower half. The river now has ledges that form fantastic holes -- this is in addition to all the front surfing spots. You could easily spend all day just on the last 4 miles here. Some people even **park and play at the take-out;** there seems to be great surfing there at a wide range of levels. You could even get in at Palmer Bridge if you've only got a couple of hours. The last 3 miles of this run has several big bad holes at high water -- remember that, even though you'll be in an exhausted surf-drunk daze.

Extra: There is an upper section that is class ll-lll at most levels. However the walk down the bank to the river (river right) approaches class V. This run starts up at the really big dam off of Swancott Road – 2.5' is minimal (3.5' would be much better).

NEWS FLASH: Fish Creek in upper New York State has the best white water play ground to be found anywhere in the U.S. Someone who should know makes this claim. He's the author of a new river guide for the state of N.Y. Mr. Squires has paddled rivers from Maine to California -- over 160 rivers in fact. When finally reached for comment (coming out of the woods in the dark and dragging his kayak), Mr. Squires' only comment was "We got lotsa' rain...............everything high...did 3 rivers today...damn tired.... food...need food..."

Notes

1

2

3

4

5

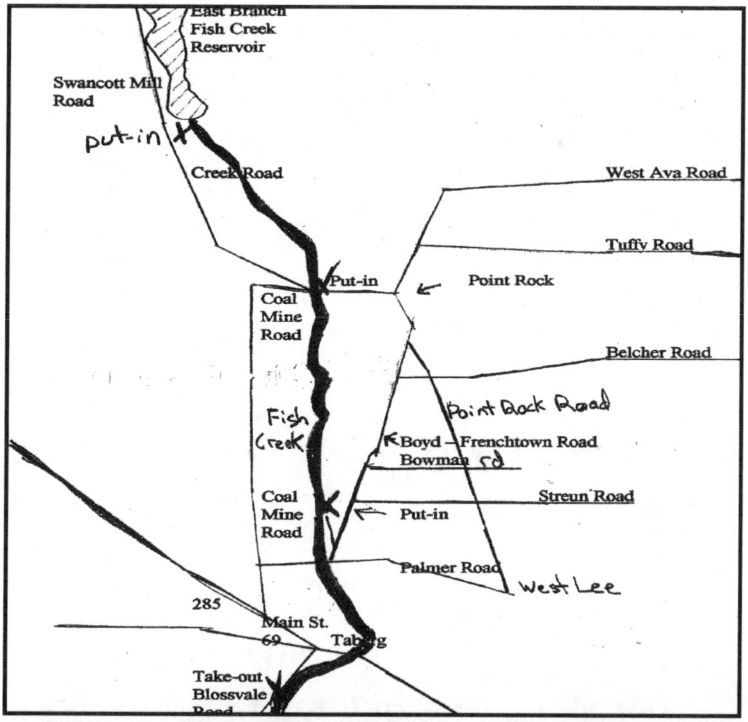

Everybody loves the Fish. Photo by Sally Dewes.

River: **Grass/Lampson Falls*** (Degrasse)**
Scenery: Very good
Class: III-V
Access: 2-miles
Length: 6-8 miles
Average gradient: 60'/mile
Gauge: Harrisville at 800cfs and rising (or 900 and dropping) is fine; 1600cfs is high (still O.K., but the holes will keep getting even nastier as the water level goes even higher.)
Water level: This entire river holds water a long time because it has a large swampy watershed -- it's still worth doing when the Harrisville gauge has dropped to 800cfs or less.
Best betting time: Early April (after ice-out) -- mid May
Other local runs: Grass / Middle (III-III+, V+)*** / Grass / Twin Falls (IV-V+)*****
Boogie time: 80% -- you'll need to scout some of the drops
Time to do first run: 3 hours for the 6 mile run and 4 hours for the 8-mile run
First known descent: ?????
Raft: Yes -- above 1200 cfs
Ducky: Yes
Food and gas: Degrasse or Russell (it isn't fancy but it'll do)
Camping: On state land about 1 mile south of Degrasse on Route 27 (you'll see a big sign on your right/west side) -- or just east of Russell on state land.
Page in the Gazetteer: 93
County: St. Lawrence
Closest river store: Wear on Earth in Potsdam

Directions: There is a small yellow-on-brown state sign about 4 miles north of Degrasse (1mile past the little landing strip on the west side of the road), this is the put-in. Just walk in about 12 minutes with your boat. You come right to the river at the head of Lampson Falls. The easiest way to find the take-out is to head north on Clare Road and take a left at the 4-way intersection. When you get to Russell drive over the bridge and take a left. There's a small ballpark on your right side -- it's a good place to get out. If you really need to not paddle the last 2.5 miles of class I-II, there's another take-out. Drive back out of Russell the way you came in. About 2 miles east of town is a small one-lane dirt road that may have a state sign (yellow-on-brown) on it. The sign will say Donnerville State Forest. Drive a few miles and take the right-hand turn when the choice presents itself. If you get lucky and actually find the river, you'll be at the confluence with the North Branch. Be sure to flag the take-out so you don't paddle by it. Unless you really wanted to use the lower take-out and run miles back to your car in the dark -- in the woods…stumbling all the way (and cursing -- ya -- here would be a lot of cursing).

Description/hazards: Unless you like a whole lot of excitement to start off a trip, it's suggested that you start below Lampson (50'+) Falls. This is beautiful spot to just hang for a minute and gaze at the falls. Immediately below you'll find a **play spot**. It's usually mild -- but it can be fun if you've got a decent level. The first drop is a funnel of water that'll get you in the right frame of mind. The next one has an ugly hole at the end of a long funneling ramp. You can do some **wild rodeo moves** in there -- if you want to or not (I was 2 for 4 on missing this hole on my first 4 trips). The **hole and wave behind that nasty one is great**. The hole is a spot that's **worth playing** for a while. It's just quick water down to the big drop below. Paddle hard and don't mistake the nasty factor of how strong that eddy is that feeds the hole at the bottom of the drop. If the water's high enough you can run that little drop just above this one -- that one over there on the right. Be sure to clear the sweet looking itsy-bitsy hole -- it ain't so sweet. The following drop has an angled ledge hole that shouldn't be underestimated -- it's eaten a few boaters. Quick scouting the rest of the horizon lines would be a good idea. You can go left or right at the one with an island. The next to the last big one gives you three choices at most levels. Way left is coolest. Right center is the most photographic.

That dagger RPM sure got me in a lot of trouble (because it was so good and so predictable). The summer of '96 it rained a lot and I ran everything in the RPM.

I'm three quarters of the way down the face of Lampson Falls and stuck up against a piece of the falls. The run had gone well -- at least up until now. The hole at the top, that would end life, as we know it, had been skirted. The boat skimmed over the edge of the right side -- right into the eddy in the middle. Fine so far. Coming slowly out of the eddy to get my bearing went fine. I came sliding down that steep smooth part in the middle -- just as planned. Then the boat turned sideways (which was intended, since where I scouted from it was impossible to tell if this was piton country). The boat side-slipped about 4 feet and stopped dead as the edge of the boat impacted what felt like a curb sticking up, right at water level. Now I'm stuck a dozen feet from the bottom -- looking at a nasty rock jutting up below me and getting a good look at the hole. I'm not happy. If I wiggle and push to the side maybe, maybe I'll miss that nasty thing. "Shit" (I glance off the side) -- "God"(looking at the hole) -- "Damn" -- "Damn" -- "No you don't." It just took me several attempts to escape the boil line. Every time I paused (thinking I was out) it would tug me back towards it. Don't think I'll do that again.

Notes

1

2

3

4

5

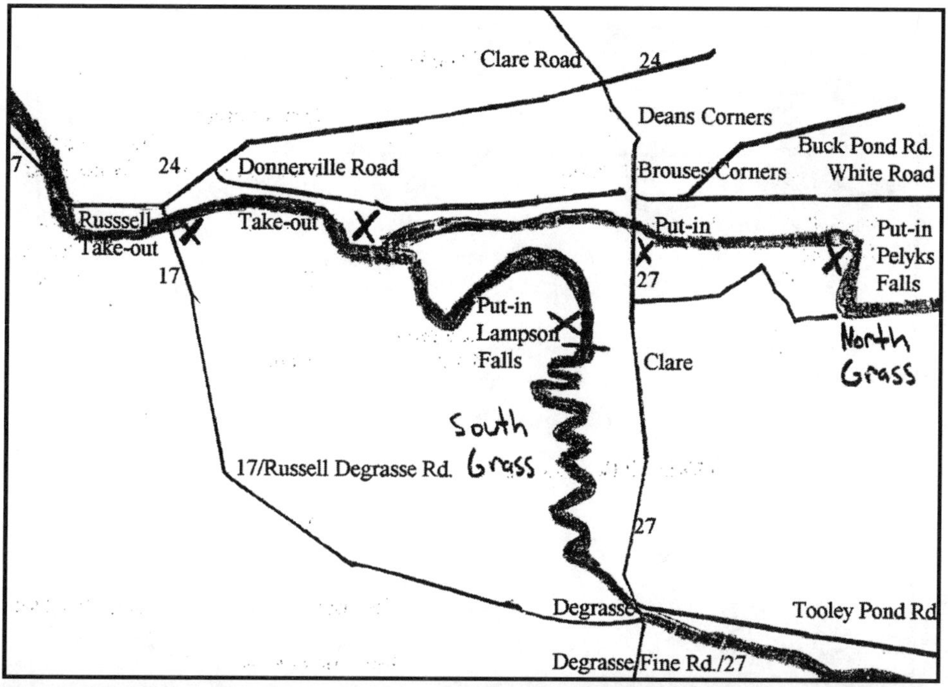

Tony Malokowski likes big rocks for breakfast. Photo by Julie Vickery.

River:	**Grass/Twin Falls*****(Degrasse)**
Scenery:	Very good (even though it's partly roadside)
Class:	IV-V+
Access:	.3-mile
Length:	6-10 miles
Average gradient:	60'/mile
Gauge:	Harrisville 750cfs and rising is enough / 1000-1200cfs is ideal
Water level:	Higher water (1600cfs or more) fills in the wide rocky parts of the river nicely, but it does make for some bad holes at the drops. It's important to know that this river holds water (it's swampy upstream) better than the gauge will indicate, which means if Harrisville is reading 850cfs and dropping you'd best be getting on the water that day -- there's still time!
Best betting time:	Early April-early May (it can run until June with decent rain)
Other local runs:	Upper Grass (I-III, V)** / Grass / Lampson Falls (III-IV+)*** (This seems to stay up longer than the rest of this river's sections) / East Oswegatchie (IV-VI)***
Boogie time:	70% -- scout the many big horizon lines
Time to do first run:	3+ hours for the 6-mile run and 5+ hours for the 11-mile run
First known descent:	Mike Duggan and the Kern brothers in the early 90's????
Raft:	Yes -- at 1100cfs or more (you'll walk a few and fall out a few)
Ducky:	Yes
Food and gas:	Degrasse -- or better options in Potsdam or Tupper Lake
Camping:	There's state land at Lampson Falls and just south of Degrasse
Page in the Gazetteer:	93/94
County:	St. Lawrence
Closest river store:	Wear on Earth in Potsdam

Directions: Take-out at the bridge in Degrasse or 2 miles upstream on the Tooley Pond Road at the new state access at Sinclair Falls. Drive about 6 miles upstream to the new put-in; or get in about .75 mile above the bridge at Newbridge (which is 2 miles further yet) and bushwhack down to the river. This lets you do the three-part (IV-V+) Copper Rock Falls and adds 3 miles to your day (and 1.5 hours). This will be a good 10 or 12-mile day with a lot of flat water in the first 4 miles.

Description/hazards: If you whacked your way into Copper Rock Falls, you'll be looking at 3 separate drops. First is a ledge falls that you can boof on the right, if it's not too high (and the new tree parked there moves out) -- next comes a heinous drop (which likes to flip you and snap your paddle into two pieces) which you may not want to run. If you go for it -- get right, and know that it's shallower next to the thing than it looks, and lastly you get a choice at the final part, you can go left and enjoy a nice **long** slide/ramp rapid or run another nasty looking thing on the far right-hand side of the river. After all that you'll get to enjoy easy water down to the first bridge and beyond. You'll run a few easy rapids and start getting bored just as you pass the new state put-in (which is hard to see from the river -- and where almost everybody now gets in) on the right -- you now have only a few minutes until you get to Rainbow Falls. This has been run several times -- which is O.K. if you like running class V+ drops. Portage on the left. Immediately below you'll find the left channel is more fun. Unless it's really high (my goodness -- what nasty holes) -- then you may want to take the right side.

At the huge horizon line you can go way right all the way down -- however, if that last hole is looking really big -- I wouldn't do it. When it's really high we go way left, all the way left. After a long stretch of class IV-ish stuff you'll notice the river getting very steep and tight ahead of you -- get out and LOOK. That last hole at high water is uglier than my old booties. If it's not too high, run it on the left and paddle hard (it likes to ender you and slam your boat and body against the left wall if you don't.)

Keep scouting all the horizon lines, especially the edge-of-the-earth drop (Twin Falls is its name), which is after that big ramp/falls (Adrenaline Falls). It's awesome. The experience is: skip, skip, and rocketing off the edge of the planet as you disappear into the foam. Don't try this at home. And lean forward all the way if you run this one.

There are two more drops down to the next bridge/take-out. Sinclair Falls starts under this bridge and is a fantastic drop to run and photograph. If it's high stay out of the hole at the bottom -- it's wild (experience speaking here). There's one more big boy to wrestle with -- run it kind of left-ish (there is a rock in the hole just left of center). Enjoy the **play spot** that's a little ways below and scout the last drop under the take-out bridge in Degrasse.

June of '96 was a very good month (it was raining a lot). I was lovin' my new RPM and running everything in it. Eric and Seth were just getting into creekin' and Peter was actually on the Grass in warm weather with few bugs around. Since we didn't have any virgins around to sacrifice (well maybe Eric), we had Peter along to appease the bug gods. I now assume that since the bugs didn't need appeasing Peter opted to provide the entertainment instead.

We had just enjoyed a great lunch at Twin Falls and were getting back in at the base of the falls. The last 20' or so is steep down to the water. I had just got in my boat when I heard rocks falling, a grunt and Seth yell out. And then there was a big splash right behind me. As I looked to my left I saw Peter's butt just above water level and his feet sticking straight in the air. His head was apparently planted in the river bottom. As Peter's face resurfaced and hit the air I noticed he looked a little red (in fact he looked even redder than he did that time in Maine when the college girls caught him skinny dipping in Baxter park). We proceeded to ask Peter a few questions to figure out if he was O.K. Apparently he was. This is one of infinite reasons why I paddle -- you just can't be that entertained by staying home and watching the Flintstones.

As a special comment I want to point out that it's very nice that the state (as of 2000) now owns this land. Several years before when I first paddled this it was posted and patrolled. My friend and shuttle bunny for the day, Joyce, informed me that trucks with <u>local armed hunters were looking for me.</u> Ah, the good ole days!

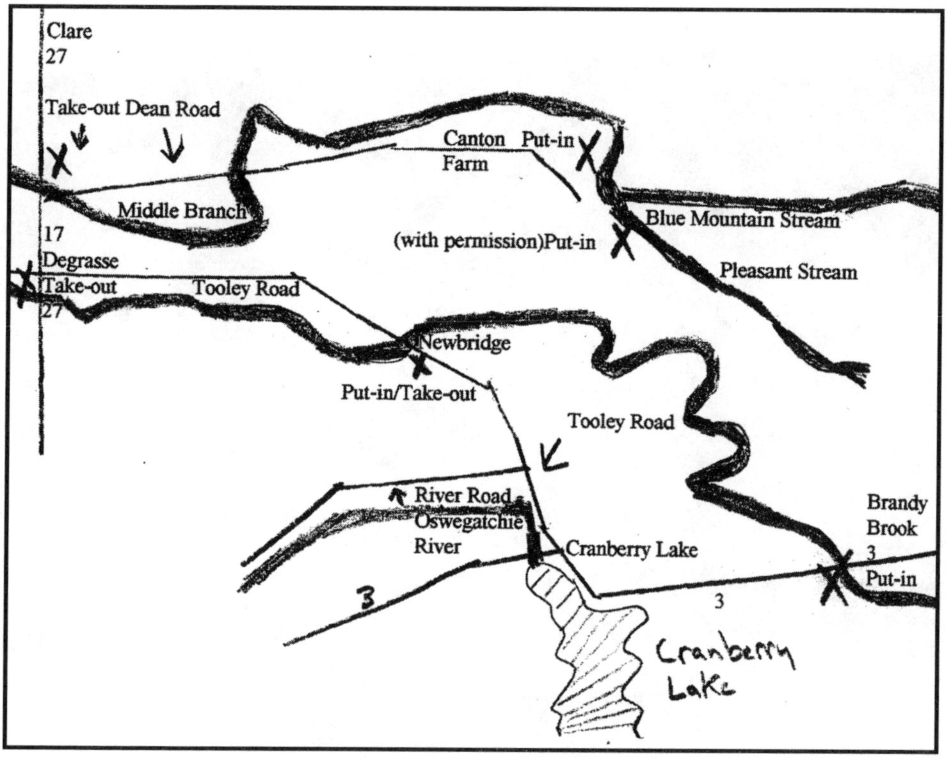

Notes

1
2
3
4
5

smell the roses

Dennis running Adrenaline Falls (high water). Photo by Sally Dewes.

River: **Grass/Upper***(Cranberry Lake)**
Scenery: Very good
Class: I-III, V
Access: Several miles -- with no houses close by
Length: 14 or 16 miles
Average gradient: 15'/mile
Gauge: Harrisville will be 750cfs or more
Water level: Due to the swampy watershed this stays a long time after rain
Best betting time: April-mid May
Other local runs: Grass/Twin Falls (IV-VI)*****/ Little (II-III)***
Boogie time: 90% -- make sure you scout Copper Rock Falls. It's about 10 miles into the trip.
Time to do first run: 5+ hours
First known descent: ?
Raft: Maybe -- there's a lot of flat water and the falls to deal with
Ducky: Yes
Food and gas: Degrasse or better options at Potsdam and Tupper Lake
Camping: State land at Lampson Falls and just south of Degrasse
Page in the Gazetteer: 94
County: St. Lawrence
Closest river store: Wear on Earth in Potsdam

Directions: Put-in at Route 3 where the river goes under the road. To get to the take-out go west through Cranberry Lake and turn up Tooley Road. After several miles you'll cross the river at Newbridge (easiest take-out). End your trip here or a few miles farther down at the new state pull off above Rainbow Falls.

Description/hazards: You can kayak or even canoe this piece. It's **remote** and woodsy. Mostly it's class I and moving water. The first mile is class I-III+ and has a hard drop about 1 mile down. If you are in a canoe expect a little portaging, especially if you're not a class III boater. The next several miles are flat water. As you get closer to Copper Rock Falls you'll find class II-III, be sure to scout the falls, they're a series of 3 drops with options -- rated class IV-V. You can get out at the next bridge or at the new pull off. If you use the lower take-out make sure you flag a tree (so you'll know when you get there) before starting down the run in the morning; you won't appreciate what comes next!

Notes

1
2
3
4
5

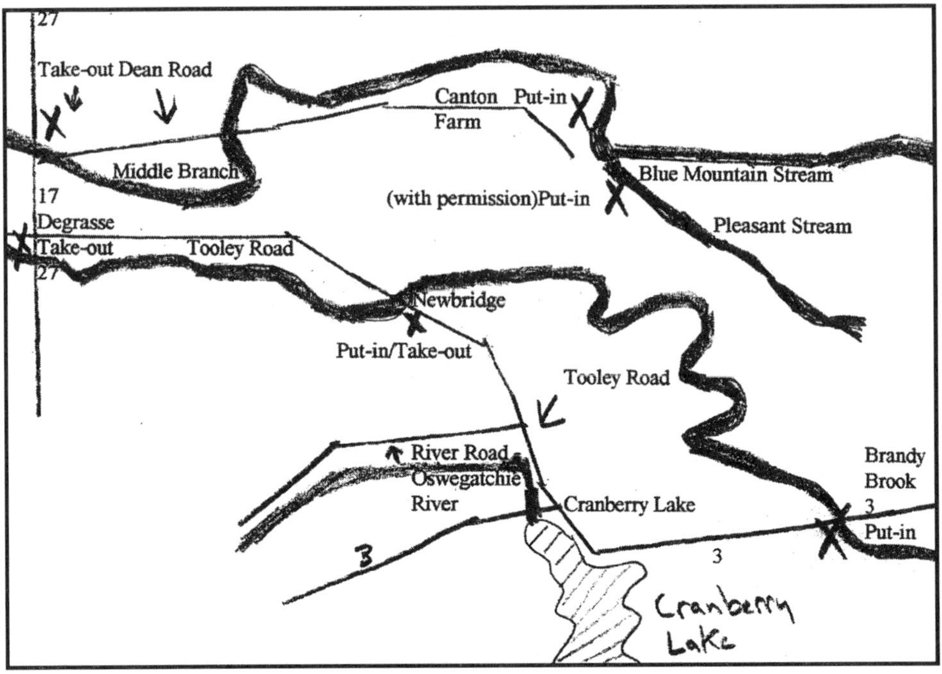

Jody Dixon isn't on the Grass, she's in the tree. Drive-by photographer.

River:	**Middle Grass***(Degrasse)**
Scenery:	Very good
Class:	III-IV+, and 2 drops at V/V+
Access:	1-mile
Length:	10.5 river miles if starting on state land at the stone dam (with permission from the Rainbow Club you could start even higher)
Average gradient:	35-40'/mile is the average for the described run and the several miles above that. This river has sections with big drops, broken up by long stretches of flat water.
Gauge:	Parishville has to be over 800cfs and Harrisville at least 1100
Water levels:	If the South Grass is high or you're looking to paddle something a bit easier -- do this. This branch doesn't run as often or stay up as long.
Best betting time:	Mid-April until early May
Other local runs:	Grass/Twin Falls (IV-V+)***** / North Grass (II-III+, V+)***
Boogie time:	90%
Time to do first run:	4 hours (not counting hiking time) if starting at the stone dam
First known descent:	Don Morris?
Raft:	Yes -- if it were fairly high this would be a great trip
Ducky:	Yes
Food and gas:	In Degrasse -- but don't get there very late
Camping:	State land in Degrasse and also south of town on Route 27
Page in the Gazetteer:	93/94
County:	Saint Lawrence
Closest river store:	Wear on Earth in Potsdam

Directions: The take-out is on Clare Road, 2 miles north of Degrasse; it's also possible to keep going, to paddle several miles of flat water down to Lampson Falls and do that section as well. It would make a nice overnighter. To get to the put-in drive up Dean Road (which is right there next to the bridge) and drive through the middle of a camp about 7 or 8 miles up Dean Road. A little ways above that you'll see a drop on your left, very close to the road. The spot that you're looking for is a couple of hundred yards beyond that drop. Find a small road on your left, right before a barrier/sign. You can park off the road and get in right there (quasi-legal) or better yet walk up to the state land/stone dam. The hike is 2.5 miles up a goat trail/old road. If it's late or you're not feeling oats-y you can walk just a mile and possibly paddle down the little brook that you'll cross. If you choose this option you'll find that the first mile (after getting to the Middle Branch) has lots of good class IV-ish stuff. This mile is my favorite part; it's well worth a measly 20-25 minute stroll with your boat.

Description/hazards: A local that knows (Denny is very, very wise) assures me that the put-in is state land (if you walk all the way up to the stone dam.) and therefore legal. Some of the local gun club members might disagree. They're wrong, but don't tell them that; they have guns. Be sweet and try to get permission from them. If that doesn't work,

I myself would probably sneak back 15 minutes later. I haven't the foggiest notion what you might do.

There are a couple of nice drops in the first mile, below where you parked, (because you were smart enough not to drive through that knee deep muddle puddle). Be sure to play a little. Endure some flat water. Enjoy the cool little drop under the bridge that you could have scouted on the way in, if you drove down the turn at that intersection you passed on your drive in. Scout the biggie. Run the long class III section next to the road. Flat water. And then you'll find more good drops. It's all runnable if you're not quite right in the head. If you're in the mood to paddle something that: is class II-IV, has breaks in between, is pretty and has a couple of big humongoes, (and a long, long class IV+ slide thing, which I've failed to mention), then you're in the right place (I know that there's no such word as humongoes -- don't care.)

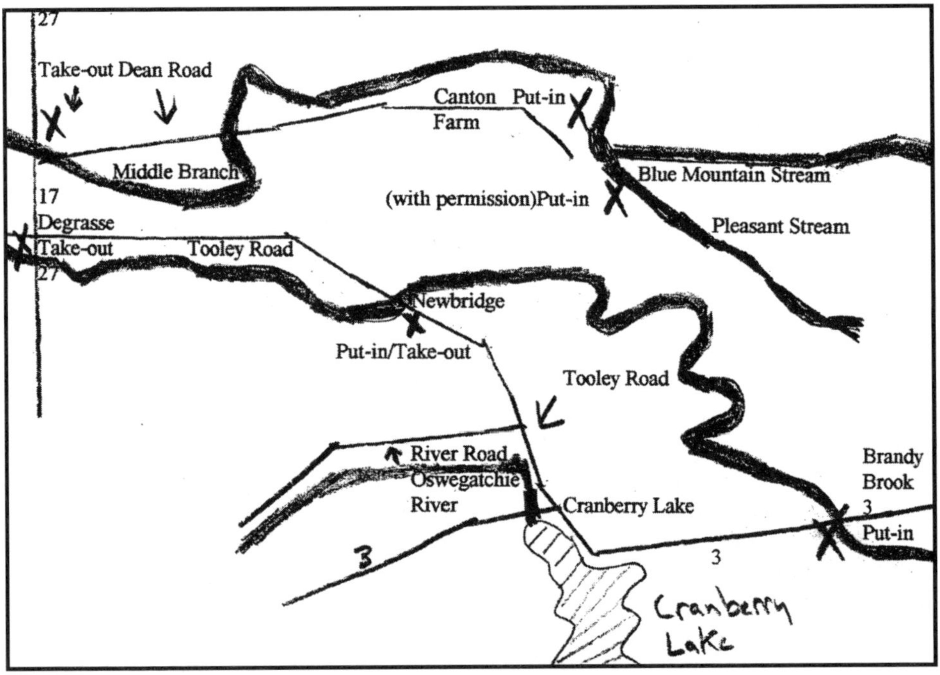

Notes
1
2
3
4
5

River:	**Grass/North Branch***(Degrasse)**
Scenery:	Good
Class:	II-III, V+
Access:	More than 1 mile
Length:	6.5 miles
Average gradient:	35'/mile, much of the drop in this run is at Harper's Falls
Gauge:	Harrisville should be 1100cfs or more
Water levels:	This run is better with lots of water -- and please, realize that if that's happening when you're in the area that there are a lot of other runs that are more shall we say, adventurous.
Best betting time:	April-early May
Other local runs:	Grass-Middle (III-V+)*** / Grasse/Twin Falls IV-V+)*****
Boogie time:	92% -- scout Harper's Falls
Time to do first run:	3 hours
First known descent:	?
Raft:	Yes -- if it's high and the raft isn't too big
Ducky:	Yes
Food and gas:	Degrasse or Russell
Camping:	State land along Route 27 just south of Degrasse
Page in the Gazetteer:	93
County:	Saint Lawrence
Closest river store:	Wear on Earth in Potsdam

Directions: Less than 8 miles north of Degrasse on Clare Road (Route 27) you'll drive over the put-in. Make sure that you're in the right place; it's easy to get on the wrong branch of the river. Not that there's a bad branch on the Grass, it's just nice to know where in the hell you are. If you do mess up, rest assured that all the branches run together and go through Russell (the other branches are pool-drop but may provide more excitement than you were counting on).

Description/hazards: Most of the whitewater in this run is class II-III-ish with lots of easy water in between. The big drop (which is really, big -- 40'-50') is called Harper's Falls and is almost 3 miles below the put-in on Clare Road. The scenery is pristine and you're in the North Country. What more could you want? The last leg into the main branch is flat and moving. On river right immediately after the confluence, is state land and a dirt road. This is the best take-out for the run (however it's hard to find). You could just paddle the 2-3 miles on the Main Branch, enjoying the class II-III stuff, all the way down into Russell.

I haven't done it, but it could be interesting to start 2.5 miles farther upstream by the camps above Pelky's Falls. The topo shows 60' of drop at the falls and 80' more, over the next 2 miles down to Clare Road.

Put-in Alert: If you put-in at the town building (on Clare Road, just north of the North Branch bridge) or right next to it on Buck Brook (which looks big enough), you'll save yourself 2 miles of meandering flat water at the start of the regular put-in.

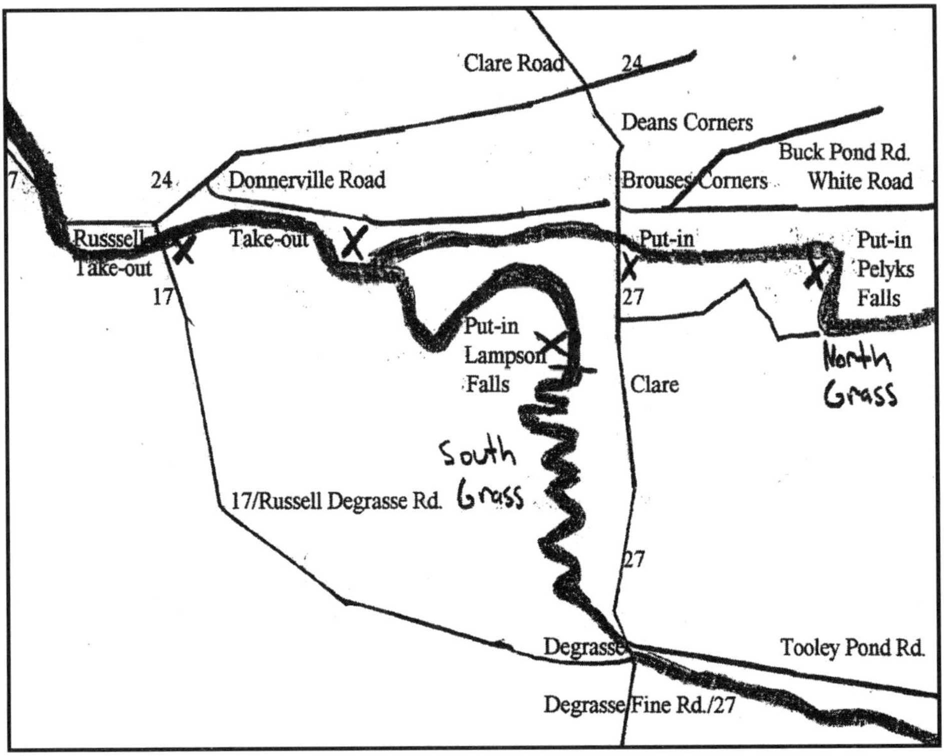

Notes

1

2

3

4

5

Buy Dennis breakfast

River:	**Independence****(Lowville)**
Scenery:	Very good
Class:	IV-V (last 3 miles) / above that is mostly I-III+
Access:	1-mile
Length:	3 miles or more
Average gradient:	120'/mile (last 3 miles) the last .25 mile drops 350'/mile
Gauge:	Donattsburg: 200cfs is minimum /400cfs is ideal /600-800cfs is awesome /above 1000cfs the last .25mile is orgasmic!
Water level:	This section takes 12-24 hours to peak after a rainstorm, so watch that gauge. In the summer the river often comes up to 100cfs -- this is still a fun level to paddle just the last .25-mile
Best betting time:	April and May.
Other local runs:	Otter Creek (III-IV+)***(do this before the Independence--it goes up faster and drops first)/Upper Independence (I-III+)***
Boogie time:	70% -- scout the last horizon…it's a dozzy.
Time to do first run:	3+ hours -- you'll be spending a lot of time scouting and re-running the bottom part.
First known descent:	Dennis and Peter Lippman in the early 90's
Raft:	Yes -- but I'd only do the bottom 3 miles
Ducky:	Yes -- even at 90cfs the last .25-mile is a blast
Food and gas:	Lowville or Boonville
Camping:	At the put-in on state land (the gauge is also here)
Page in the Gazetteer:	85
County:	Lewis
Closest river store:	White Water Challengers in Old Forge & Mountain Man in Inlet & Old Forge

Directions: Turn off Route 12 (south of Lowville) into the hamlet of Glenfield. Next you'll go over the Black River on Greig Road and take the first left onto Otter Creek Road. After a few miles you'll stop at Pine Grove Road; take a left. In about 1 mile you'll cross the Independence. Here you can drive up a closed road on either side of the river. The take-out is only .25 mile above Pine Grove Road at a closed bridge. To get to the put-in drive up (take a right) on Pine Grove and take the first right on Bradish. When you get to the T bear right and then right again at your next choice -- drive down to the river. This is the gauge bridge.

Description/hazards: Starting at the gauge bridge gives you about two minutes and forty-nine seconds to get ready for the games to begin (there is a fun little hole 200 yards above the put-in/gauge bridge).

After going around the second bend, you're in for it, especially if the river is high. The next mile is like the good part of the Boreas with more rocks and a few ledges thrown in. Two of these ledges have bad holes at high water (600cfs and above). If you run them take the first on the far right, and the second on either side -- don't get sucked in!

After doing a big drop with multiple choices you'll be faced with the last section **(The Fat Lady).** This section is almost as good as the river you've conjured up in your daydreams. There are multiple lines depending on the level. DO NOT run the far right side at the top at levels of 400cfs or more (and don't look at the hole over there for very long). The first time you do all of this last section your blood chemistry will be off the charts and only your best paddling pals will be able to stand being around you for a few days. To describe this section would be like using words to explain the sound of one hand clapping. Meditate on that one.

Extra! For a longer (or more moderate) run you can start up at Eric Canal Road or Bailey Road (which also has nice camping), this part is class I-III+. And for those that are curious, above that arc: miles of flat water, then a class IV-V gorge, miles of easy to moderate rapids and then a lot of gradient in the course of a few miles, and mostly flat and moving water above that. All of this would be a long two-three day trip with a lot of flat water.

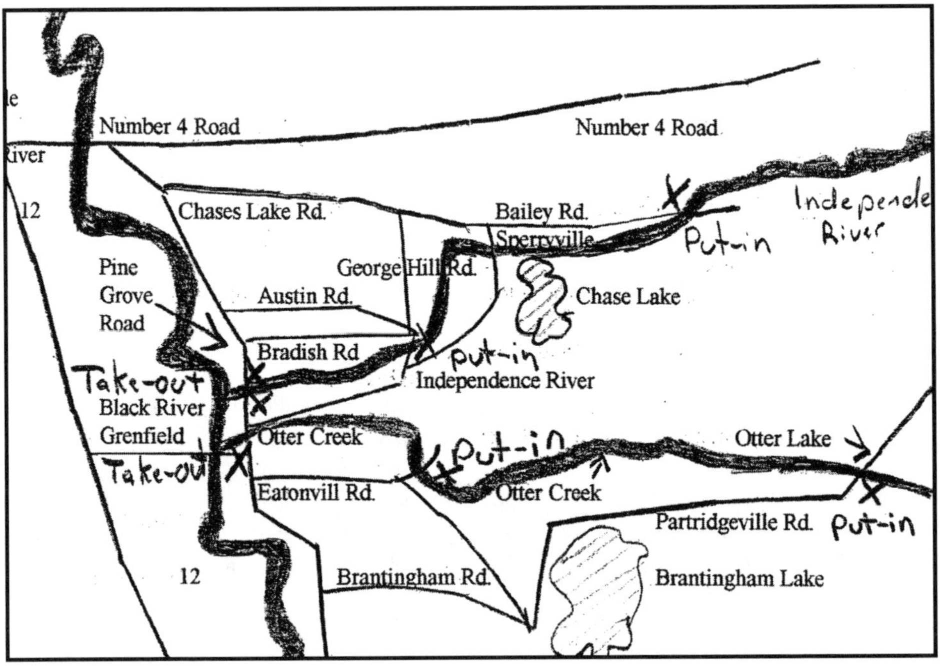

Notes

1

2

3

4

5

Dennis in the middle of The Fat Lady. Photo by Sally Dewes.

Dennis prefers dry red wine or a Corona (chilled) with a lime (very fresh)

River:	**Independence/Upper***(Lowville)**
Scenery:	Very good
Class:	These upper miles are I-III+
Access:	1-mile
Length:	7 miles or more
Average gradient:	60'/mile
Gauge:	Donattsburg: 200cfs is minimum/ 400cfs is ideal
Water level:	This section takes 18 hours to peak after a rain, so watch that gauge. In the summer the river often comes up to 100cfs -- a fun level to paddle the last .25-mile of the lower run (IV-V).
Best betting time:	April-mid May
Other local runs:	Otter Creek (III-IV+)***(do this before the Independence--it goes up faster and drops first) / Moose / Middle (I-III-IV-)***
Boogie time:	90% -- watch out for tree strainers
Time to do first run:	3 hours.
First known descent:	Dennis in the early 90's
Raft:	Yes -- above 500cfs
Ducky:	Yes
Food and gas:	Lowville or Boonville.
Camping:	At the take-out on state land (the gauge is also there)
Page in the Gazetteer:	85
County:	Lewis
Closest river store:	White Water Challengers in Old Forge & Mountain Man in Inlet & Old Forge

Directions: Turn off Route 12 (south of Lowville) into the hamlet of Glenfield. Next you'll go over the Black River on Greig Road and take the first left onto Otter Creek Road. After a few miles you'll stop at Pine Grove Road; take a left. In about 1 mile you'll cross the Independence. From here you can drive up either closed road on either side of the river. To get to the take-out drive up (take a right) on Pine Grove and take the first right on Bradish. When you get to the T bear right and right again -- drive down to the river. To get to the put-in drive back up this first hill and bear to your right. Stay on this road (don't cross the river) for roughly 7 miles. You can park (and camp) on state land just before the bridge.

Description/hazards: (Above this put-in are several miles of flat water. And then a spectacular class V gorge.... It's interesting up there -- hike up from the north side if you've got the extra time.)

Most of this run is moving water and class I and II water. There are 3 or 4 rapids that range up to class III+. This handful of drops is very rocky. They're a lot more fun with adequate water levels (300+cfs). There are a few low ledges that are fun (even though they might surprise you). A strainer mostly blocked one of the good rapids here the last time I ran this in the spring of 2000. There is a **fun little hole** 200 yards above the take-out/ gauge bridge).

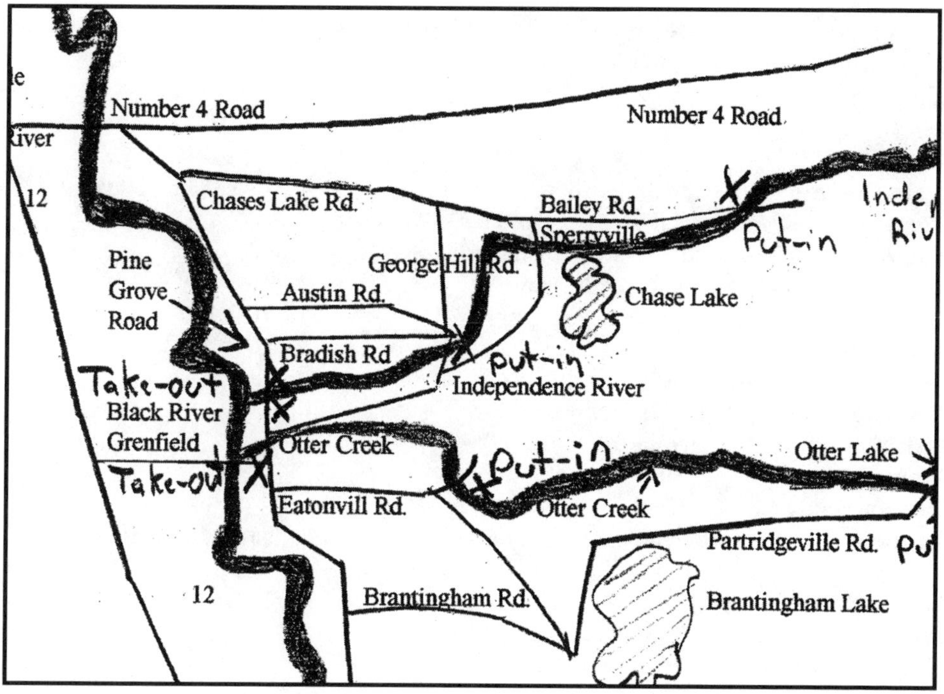

Notes

1

2

3

4

5

Have your pet frog neutered

River:	**Jenny Creek**(Harrisville)**
Scenery:	Good
Class:	IV-VI
Access:	.75-mile
Length:	5 mile
Average gradient:	80'/mile, some places drop at rates way exceeding 200'/mile
Gauge:	Harrisville should be 1000 cfs or more
Water level:	This stays up longer than you might think
Best betting time:	April-early May
Other local runs:	Oswegatchie / Fine (IV-VI)***/ Little (II-III)***
Boogie time:	60% -- there's lots of horizon lines to scout
Time to do first run:	3+ hours
First known descent:	**UNRUN**
Raft:	Nope
Ducky:	Yes
Food and Gas:	Harrisville
Camping:	State land on Fullerville or Jerden Falls Road or the motel in Star Lake
Page in the Gazetteer:	93
County:	St. Lawrence
Closest river store:	Wear on Earth in Potsdam

Directions: About 4 miles east of Harrisville (Route 3) you'll want to turn up Jayville Road. The take-out is actually right there on Route 3 in the hamlet of Pitcairn. As you drive up Jayville Road look to see if you spot the monster falls as you first get close to the river again. The second bridge that crosses the creek is a possible put-in.

Description/hazards: The topos suggests that you might be able to start a fair ways above this bridge. However -- from this bridge you'll have a good trip (no promises implied). There's a rocky IV-ish section to start. Then it flattens? It's small at the next bridge and there's a really big, nasty, unrunnable falls below that. Then it looks III-IV-ish down to a footbridge by the road (still III-IV-ish) -- and what's behind that house? Somewhere down there the contour flattens until it gets really juicy (IV-V?). Then you'll approach that really narrow falls (IV+/V) that you saw (almost in the road) on your drive up in. Below that it's easy next to the road and not much (?) happens until the monster falls. After you walk around the monster remember that the topo shows more drop-age before it flattens above Pitcairn.

Notes

1

2

3

4

5

Bob is such an idiot animal woman paddler!
Hi beautiful are you Jenny?

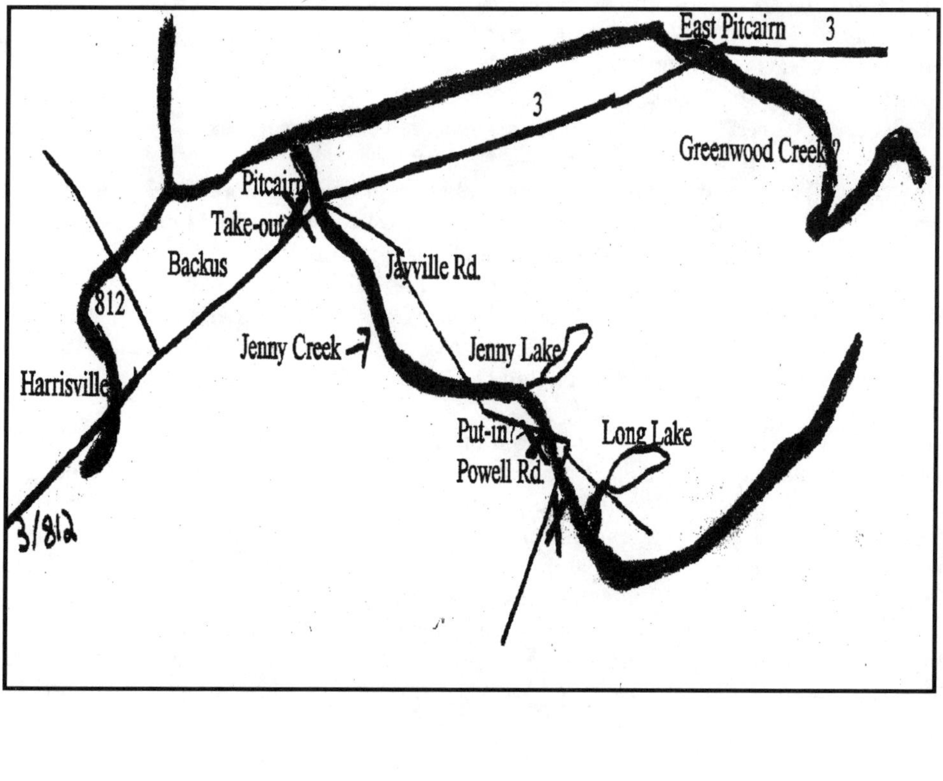
East Pitcairn
3
3
Greenwood Creek?
Pitcairn
Take-out?
Backus
Jayville Rd.
812
Jenny Creek
Jenny Lake
Harrisville
Put-in?
Powell Rd.
Long Lake
3/812

River:	**Johns Brook*****(Keene Valley)**
Scenery:	Great
Class:	V (2 drops are V+)
Access:	As much as 5 miles
Length:	6 miles (if you can carry your boat that far)
Average gradient:	300'/mile
Gauge:	East Ausable 4' or more -- the Hudson will be 7' or more
Water level:	If it's not raining while you walk in, make sure the level doesn't drop too low. Also if it is raining on the way in, be sure it's not rising too much. If it looks just high enough at the Route 73 take-out bridge -- you're golden.
Best betting time:	April (snowmelt with rain)
Other local runs:	North Fork Boquet (IV-V)*****/ The Branch at exit 29 (IV-V)****/ East Ausable (III-V)*** (this tends to run if Johns' Brook is too low)/ Lower / East Ausable (II-III)**
Boogie time:	65% -- if it's low enough to eddy-hop and boat scout
Time to do first run:	This depends on how far you walk in. Figure on 2 hours/mile (including the hike in). So get up early and start walking!
First known descent:	Spring of 1995 -- Dennis (yes I was alone).
Raft:	No
Ducky:	Yes -- this would be an awesome low water run
Food and Gas:	Keene or Keene Valley -- Noonmark Diner in Keene Valley
Camping:	Next to Split Rock Falls on the Boquet
Page in the Gazetteer:	96
County:	Essex
Closest river store:	Adirondack Lakes and Trails in Saranac Lake

Directions: The take-out is at the outdoor/climbing/mountain store (stick your head in the door) at the Route 73 Bridge in Keene Valley (check the level). For the put-in take your first right (after crossing the brook and heading south) in town and drive up the road. At the bridge you'll want to stop and take a quick look at what you're in for (if you're nervous that's good -- if you're really nervous, think again about doing this -- it's not any easier deep in the woods). When the road ends at the trailhead the hiking begins. If you just want to try a short run you'll only need to walk in about 15 minutes.

Description/hazards: If you want to do more than a short run (tough guy) get ready for combat: bring a water bottle, keep your dry suit tied at the waist, bring some food, have extra polypro. to change into and hopefully you'll have an ingenious carrying system (got your skirt?). The river is big enough to start way up at Bushnell Falls -- but nobody has been ambitious enough to start that high yet. From the falls down to Johns Brook Lodge the river is bouldery (IV-IV+) with plenty of wood to keep you company.

Starting at the lodge the riverbed transforms into a ledgey pool/drop challenge. The drops come fast and big for the next few miles -- you'll have to scout many of these and do safety on some. These few miles are very slow going -- the slowest of the trip. A few will have strainers and must be walked. The hardest drops are found in this section (V-V+). Without even noticing the river will again show its ability to change nature. There are boulders everywhere you want to be. Do the best you can -- and good luck! The river will be hard all the way down to the bridge above Route 73. If you and all your toys (and marbles) make it down to here, you'll find that things start calming down and your body's survival mode will start to relax. **You'll never fully recover.**

It was a cold rain mixing with a little snow as I climbed the trail. The top of my dry suit was tied around my waist to hopefully prevent overheating on this little hike -- it wasn't working. Between the sweat and the rain I was soaking wet. There were about 6-8 inches of snow on the ground, which made it easier to drag the boat but harder to walk. When I finally arrived at the gorge/bridge at Johns Brook Lodge I was: tired, pumped up, cold and hot all at once. It was disheartening to see the gorge was still frozen. So I crossed to the other side and started walking downstream. In about 10 minutes the river looked open enough.

What followed was a blur of reactionary paddling and boogie boating. The only other thing I'd done that was such a non-stop thrill/combat was the Boquet at near flood, with a fog from hell. I remember: walking the Energizer and getting stuck against rocks, getting out twice to pull my boat out of a pin and boofing and bashing for what seemed like forever. Was it a kayaker's heaven or hell? Well it doesn't get 5 stars for nothing!

At some point it was becoming apparent that it was going to be getting dark soon -- where was the take-out? It was pretty dark when I ran a particularly steep piece and felt totally out of control. O.K. -- I got the message. I'm out of there. Stumbling through the woods and almost running face first into an old sap house convinced me that maybe, just maybe I had pushed it once again. After about thirty or forty minutes of this I was exhausted, but there it was -- the bridge that's .5-mile below the garden parking area.

Why do people smile and shake their heads when I tell my river stories?

Extra! You can always carry the boat on you shoulder. You could even drag the boat with a piece of webbing around your waist. But the best deal may be a carrying system. You can build a yoke (that fits in the cockpit) out of wood and lined with foam. The ends of the yoke are shaped so that a bicycle tube can be attached to each end while running over the bottom of the boat. What ever you do, take a break, enjoy the scenery -- and **don't tell stories that will freak out your friends before starting down this river!**

Notes

1

2

3

4

5

No-No-No I am Not going to say it!!
this is my first time and I'm really excited!

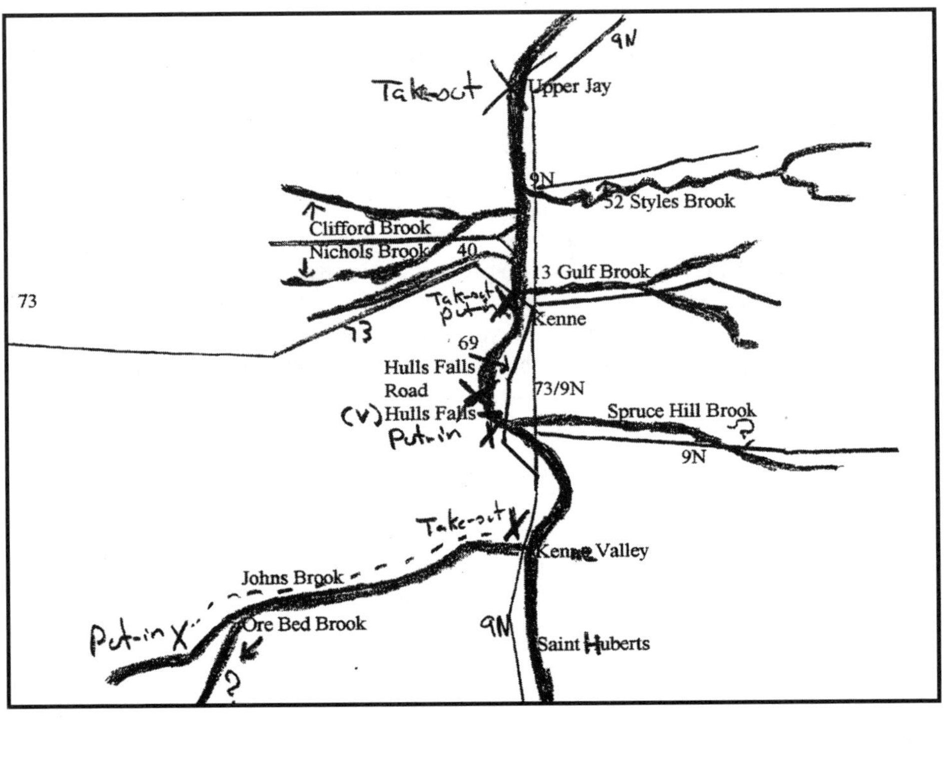
Take-out
Upper Jay
9N
9N
52 Styles Brook
Clifford Brook
Nichols Brook
40
13 Gulf Brook
73
73
Take-out put-in
Kenne
69
Hulls Falls Road
73/9N
(V) Hulls Falls
Put-in
Spruce Hill Brook
9N
Take-out
Kenne Valley
Johns Brook
Put-in
Ore Bed Brook
9N
Saint Huberts

Mike Duggan on the flat part of Johns Brook (low water). Photo by Ed Huber.

River:	Lake Ozonia Outlet***(St. Regis Falls)
Scenery:	Good
Class:	IV-V
Access:	.5-miles
Length:	3 to 9 miles
Average gradient:	60'/mile -- and 160'/mile the last mile
Gauge:	Parishville should be over 850cfs (this run peaks and starts to drop quicker than that gauge shows -- consider the lag time)
Water level:	Low water runs are rocky fun and high water is pushy and has some nasty holes (beware the wood moving down with you)
Best betting time:	April-mid May
Other local runs:	Deer (IV-V)**** / Deer / Lower (I-III)**
Boogie time:	65%
Time to do first run:	2 or 4+ hours
First known descent:	??
Raft:	No
Ducky:	Yes
Food and gas:	St. Regis Falls
Camping:	State land along the Deer River
Page in the Gazetteer:	100
County:	St. Lawrence/Franklin
Closest river store:	Wear on Earth in Potsdam

Directions: You could get in close to where Route 458 and Howe Road intersect (this will give you the shortest trip and the best stuff). As you drive farther up Howe Road there are other options -- like asking nice people if you can get in on their land (you'll have to walk downhill through the woods). There is also a place to start up where Lake Ozonia Road crosses the creek. Ask permission and don't start at the bridge by the lake. As it is -- most of the paddling in these top miles are flat and require whacking through the alder bushes (and I do mean whacking). The benefit is the occasional class IV drop.

Description/hazards: At the top most inny (what can I call it besides put-in?) the creek is small and slow -- it stays that way for about 4-4.5 miles with an occasional class IV drop. Starting farther down Howe Road you'll still have the passive-aggressive nature of the river to deal with. It's either flat or it's dropping in a big way. That last mile above Route 458, the aggressive girl really kicks in and kicks butt! It might be a wise thing to scout the section immediately below this bridge -- there's one really nasty drop in there. Pieces of wood and even a steel cable in the water have been foes in previous combats.

The guy standing next to my car didn't look very happy. Tony (who is infinitely wise) decided to stay in his truck while I got to go deal with the sourpuss. After a few minutes the unhappy landowner and myself were on good terms and Tony and I were driving back over to check out the level of the Deer River. When you're not

sure -- ask permission -- my experience is that people are accommodating if you ask.

For some reason Bonehead (at White Water Challengers in Old Forge) always lets me have a boat to abuse -- I mean-paddle-yeah-that's-what-I mean-paddle. The Micro 230 I was paddling had always been very predictable (even on Big Branch in Vermont). For some reason that day it decided to flip fast and hard for no good reason. The rock that I punched broke my knuckle making it hard to grip a paddle for several weeks. Must have been a paddle snake. It got me to thinking about armor-plated pogies again. SECRETE NOTE: I often wear pogies on warm days when paddling creeks; the bad thing about this is that you wind up with fewer scars on yours hands than other creek boaters, which makes it hard for boaters to identify you as a creek boater -- until you open your mouth anyway. And while I'm at it...another bad thing is when the leaves come out in the spring -- they suck up all the water -- bad trees -- bad.

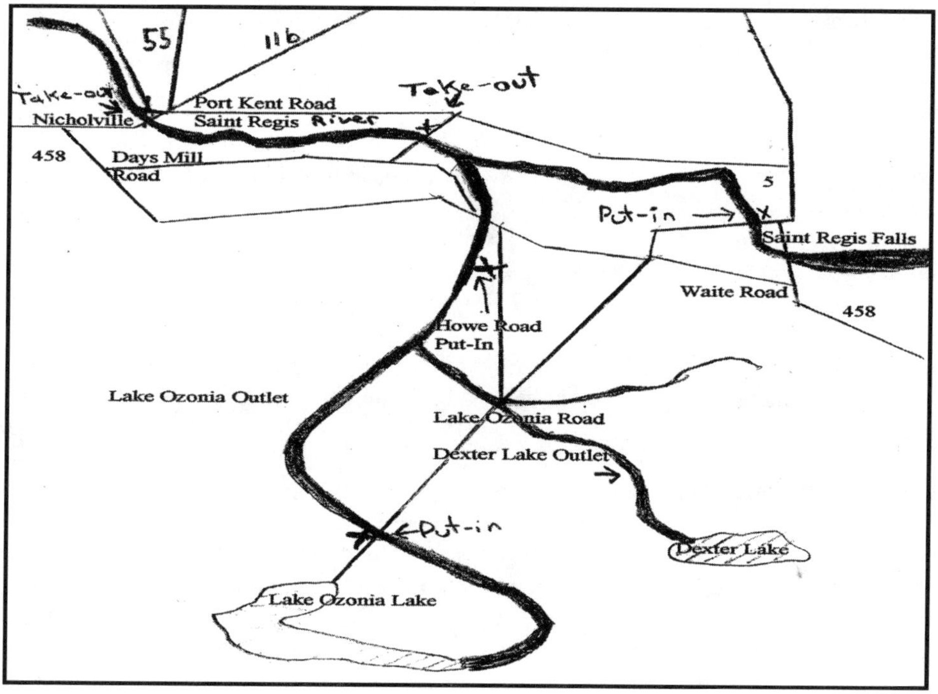

Notes

1
2
3
4
5

River:	**Little***(Star Lake)**
Scenery:	Good
Class:	I-III
Access:	1-mile
Length:	5 or 6.5 miles
Average gradient:	35'/mile
Gauge:	Guesstimate at the put-in; 200cfs is low / 400-600cfs is nice / 1000cfs is high
Water level:	Call Orion Power / Niagara Mohawk (Orion recently bought out much of Ni-Mo) and ask for the inflow of the Little River above Flat Rock power plant. (www.h2oline.com)
Best betting time:	April-early May
Other Local runs:	East Osweg. (IV-VI)*** / Grass/Upper (I-III, V)**
Boogie time:	95 -- 100% -- always watch out for tree strainers
Time to do first run:	2+ hours
First known descent:	?
Raft:	Yes -- at 400+cfs
Ducky:	Yes
Camping:	In Cranberry Lake or the cheap motel in Star Lake
Food and gas:	Star Lake
Page in the Gazetteer:	85
County:	St.Lawrence
Closest river store:	Wear on Earth in Potsdam

Directions: Put-in just above the bridge in Aldrich (just west of Star Lake and south of Route 3). For the take-out leave a car at Route 3 (5 miles) or on Brown's Falls Road (6.5 miles).

Description/hazards: This is a second hand report from Dan Sheer. To put it simply this is a little river. The gradient is moderate, but continuous. The river is full of small and medium size rocks. It's a rather remote run that is very enjoyable to just eddy hop down and practice skills on. You'll be out on your own -- away from it all for the first 4.5 miles -- enjoy. You could even paddle for a while with nothing on. Of course it will be cold and /or buggy -- you're in the Adirondacks after all. On a serious note, I can tell you that this becomes a big pushy class III run when it's over 1200cfs -- it would be a fast exciting trip at that level.

------I wasn't there, but Dan claims he was naked. For years he had been talking about naked canoeing and that day on the Little he finally did it. It was a warm day in early May -- perfect for a little exercise and a little sunbathing (while he was scaring the fish I was on my way down the Oswegatchie -- headed for the log jam and the swim with the dead pig/thing). After paddling the Little River, Dan was going to pick me up at my take-out in the hamlet of South Edwards.

-------Dan and I (fully clothed) had spent many days boating together. He loved doing ledge-y creeks in the Catskills just as much as I did. And we did have our share of mishaps, although now that I think about it, they almost always happened off the river. There was that day I locked my keys in my new (used) car and Dan was able to get his arm down to the button while I was prying open the door with his canoe paddle. And then there was the day he locked his keys in the car before we ran the Sawkill. After the run a cop showed up with a Slim Jim but wouldn't use it. It didn't matter; we still managed to get into the car.

-------It was probably one of life's most embarrassing moments. All I said was "Jeez, you think maybe they died?" The volunteer firemen that were by the river were not amused. They were standing by the side of the Sawkill River and looking at Dan's and my boats. We got the story from one of the firemen that another fireman lived up the river and had heard somebody in the river yelling for help. So he of course rang the alarm and called in the whole Zena fire department! I should mention that hours earlier Dan and I had stopped at the fire hall and asked if we could take-out there. While we had driven (after paddling) into Kingston for dinner (leaving our boats next to the firehouse) the alarm had apparently been sounded. All those firemen standing there had been looking for our bodies!

A few days later I told my friend Lenny about the debacle. He tells me he had heard all about it on the radio. So I naturally told a number of people about being on the radio and being semi-infamous. About a week later he 'fessed up and admitted he made it up, we hadn't really been mentioned on the radio. These are the kind of friends you can expect to wind up with when your life becomes twisted by a long-term exposure to the world of whitewater.

-------Dan, I hope you move back to N.Y. so I can pee (why do women say that men are dogs?) on your tires again; I miss that (as I was writing this he did...and I am!)

Notes

1

2

3

4

5

Buy a second book and give it to a friend

Hey that guy in the canoe is naked!
He has a nose like a turkey buzzard
Now I see why they call this the Little River
I hear he's that 'local expert' from New gersey
Hey you cutie come back - it's been a long winter
At least he's wearing his lifejacket

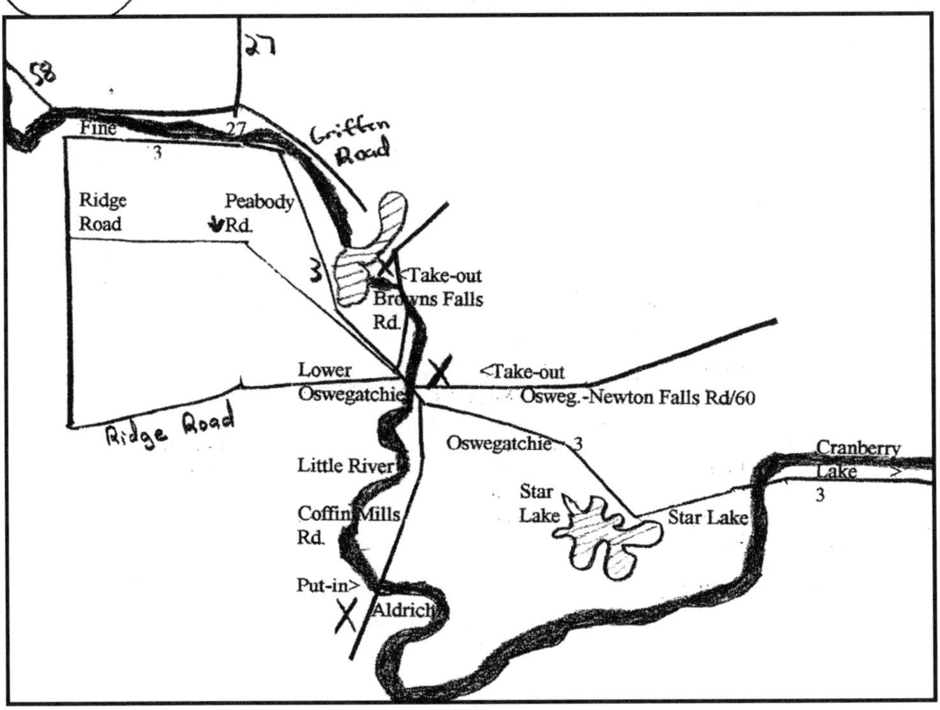
58
27
Fine
27
3
Griffin Road
Ridge Road
Peabody Rd.
3
<Take-out
Browns Falls Rd.
Lower Oswegatchie
<Take-out
Osweg.-Newton Falls Rd/60
Ridge Road
Oswegatchie 3
Little River
Coffin Mills Rd.
Star Lake
Star Lake
Cranberry Lake >
3
Put-in>
Aldrich

River:	**Little Black Creek*(Alder Creek)**
Scenery:	Good
Class:	II-V
Access:	1-mile
Length:	2.2 or more miles
Average gradient:	40'/mile -- the two rapids drop around 180'/mile
Gauge:	Boonville should be over 1000cfs to run this
Water level:	Beware the holes at the first rapid at high water
Best betting time:	April-middle May
Other local runs:	Moose / Bottom (IV+/V)*** / Moose / Middle (I-III, IV-)***
Boogie time:	90% -- scout the top and bottom rapids before getting in
Time to do first run:	1.5 hours
First known descent:	?
Raft:	No
Ducky:	Yes
Food and gas:	Alder Creek or Barnveld
Camping:	There's campground a few miles north on Lake Julia Road
Page in the Gazetteer:	77
County:	Oneida
Closest river store:	Mountain Man in Old Forge & Inlet & White Water Challengers in Old Forge

Directions: We put-in where Hughes Road crosses Little Black Creek (this is a dead end dirt road that you should drive up to from the south side). To find the take-out drive back out Hughes and go north at the T. Next take the first right onto Lake Julia and then the right onto Goldie Roberts. If you look to your right you'll find the take-out and a great looking rapid above that bridge. There is a nice class IV rapid at the Enos Bridge (on the Black River) a few miles away -- if you need something else to do.

Description/hazards: At the put-in is a great looking series of drops. They are in the class IV-IV+ range -- beware of wood and the last two ledge holes (particularly at high water). Then comes a long stretch of class II rapids. Then the rapids go away -- and there are trees blocking the river (only a couple). Paddle a ways and you'll see a great row of drops above a bridge. Enjoy them -- that bridge is your take-out. The gradient above this put-in suggests there may be some more drops (occasionally). There may be something below this take-out; the AWA inventory rates this as class II-V down to the Black River.

Notes

1

2

3

4

5

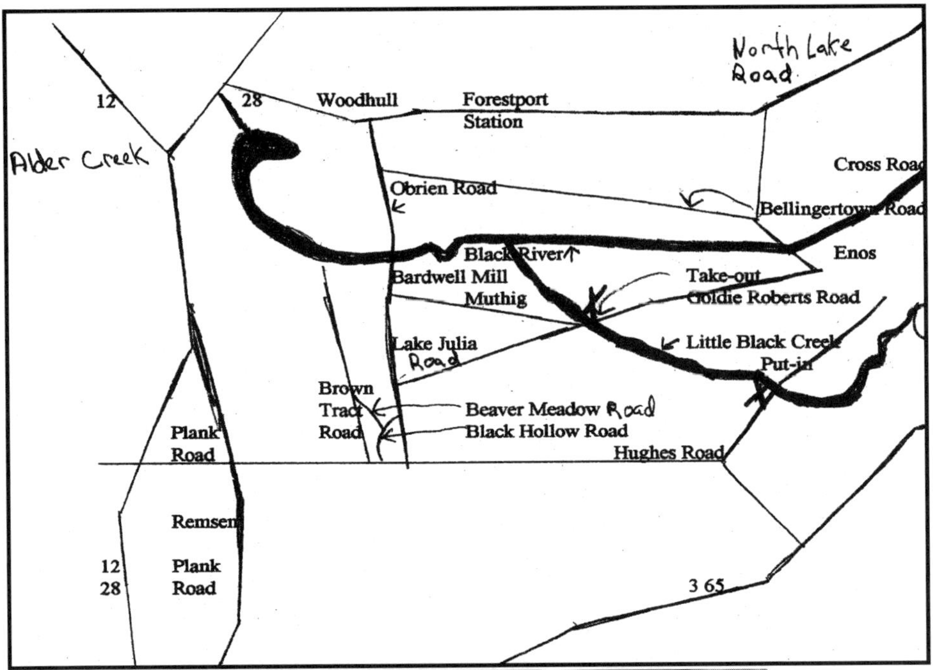

Chris Koll runs the Elbow Breaker on the Independence. Photo by Caron Koll.

River:	**Little Trout**(Malone)**
Scenery:	Good
Class:	II-III (IV)
Access:	.75-mile
Length:	2.5 miles
Average gradient:	115'/mile
Gauge:	Parishville isn't very close by but if it's over 750cfs you ought to be O.K.
Water levels:	I found this to be medium when the Deer (Dickinson Center) was high
Best betting time:	April-early May
Other local runs	Deer (IV-V)**** / Salmon / Malone (I-III, IV+)***
Boogie time:	96% -- scout the class 4 drop
Time to do first run:	2 hours
First known descent:	?
Raft:	No
Ducky:	Yes
Food and gas	Malone
Camping:	Campgrounds south of Chateaugay and state land on the Deer (go there)
Page in the Gazetteer:	101
County:	Franklin
Closest river store:	Wear on Earth in Potsdam

Directions: Put-in on the Montgomery Road / Route 36 Bridge just south of Burke. Find the take-out by driving north on Route 34. When you get to Route 11 take a left and park at the Route 11 Bridge.

Descriptions: Tony and I paddled this once several years ago. There was one obvious drop to be scouted and the rest was class II-II+/ish. We were disappointed. The run is pretty if you want a class II run. We were disappointed because we'd been told this section was class IV-V, it isn't. This river, as well as its neighbor the Trout, both have long (like 10 miles each) stretches of river that drop 100'-120'/mile. There must be something good in there (there's got to be) somewhere. If somebody knows where it is please tell me, so I'll know what I'm talking about (and paddling it would be nice). This got 2 **'s because it is a nice easy run, if that's what you're expecting -- it's good.

Notes

1

2

3

4

5

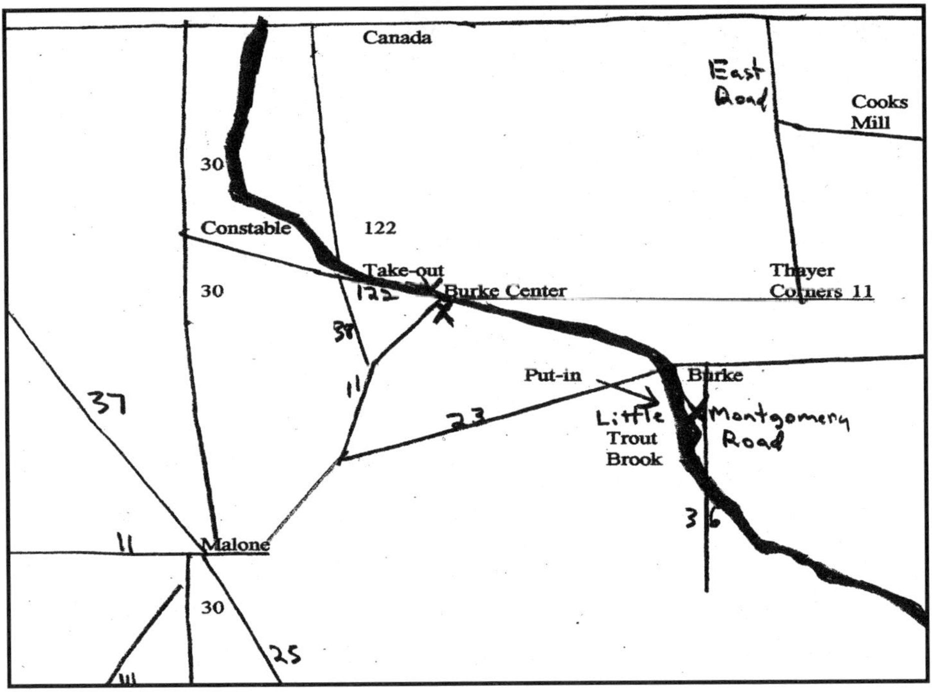
Canada
East Road
Cooks Mill
30
Constable
122
Take-out
Burke Center
30
122
38
Thayer Corners 11
37
11
Put-in
Burke
23
Little Trout Brook
Montgomery Road
36
11
Malone
30
25

River:	**Mad River**(Redfield)**
Scenery:	Good
Class:	III+/IV, VI
Access:	2-miles
Length:	4.5 miles
Average gradient:	42'/mile
Gauge:	The Fish should be 2.5' as a minimum
Water level:	At higher levels (4.0'+) beware the holes
Best betting time:	April-early May
Other local runs:	Fish (III-III+)***** / Salmon / Pulaski (II-III)***
Boogie time:	80% -- scout the top drops and walk the big falls
Time to do first run:	2-3 hours
First known descent:	?
Raft:	No -- a hard portage and annoying strainers towards the end
Ducky:	Yes
Food and gas:	Camden
Camping:	State land north of the put-in on Route 17
Page in the Gazetteer:	84
County:	Oswego
Closest river store:	Northern Outfitters is Syracuse and Utica

Directions: 20 miles north of Camden at the east end of the Salmon Reservoir is Route 17. You find a loop road off on the east side -- this is Harvesters Mill Road. The take-out is at a state fishing pullout on this road. To find the put-in head north back to Route 17 and stay on that until you see Otto Mill Road on the right side. If you drive down that a few miles you'll find a place to park just before the river, along with a suspension bridge. It might be possible to drive up the road that you just passed on the left -- but you'd better get permission. My understanding is that this put-in and the upper one are of a slightly/sort of questionable legal nature. This put-in is found by walking up the trail by the suspension bridge (a 12 minute walk).

There is a possibility of starting higher (it's easier up there I'm told). If you want to try that you shouldn't have turned off Route 17. You should have driven farther north on Route 17 and taken a right on Castor Hill Road. This is a slow narrow road that isn't usually passable until after the snow melts in mid-late April. A hunting club owns the land at the river and would probably appreciate being asked for permission. I've been told that at this point in time they tend to be agreeable if you are. From what I've heard -- there are a few things in these upper miles, just not enough to warrant the extra driving and paddling miles.

Description/hazards: From the lower put-in (the only one I've used) you'll find that the walk was worth the trouble. There are a handful of nice ledges to start off with (class IV-ish). There's a nice ledge right after you go and pass under the suspension bridge. At this point start thinking hard about getting to river right and do it fast. Below here is Mad River Falls. It's 30+ feet high and unrunnable. The portage is on the right side, right at the top of the falls. You'll get to run a short stretch of good stuff and then the river opens up and eases to class II and then I. The last .5-mile can be annoying because it splits into several channels and will probably have wood blocking it in one or two places.

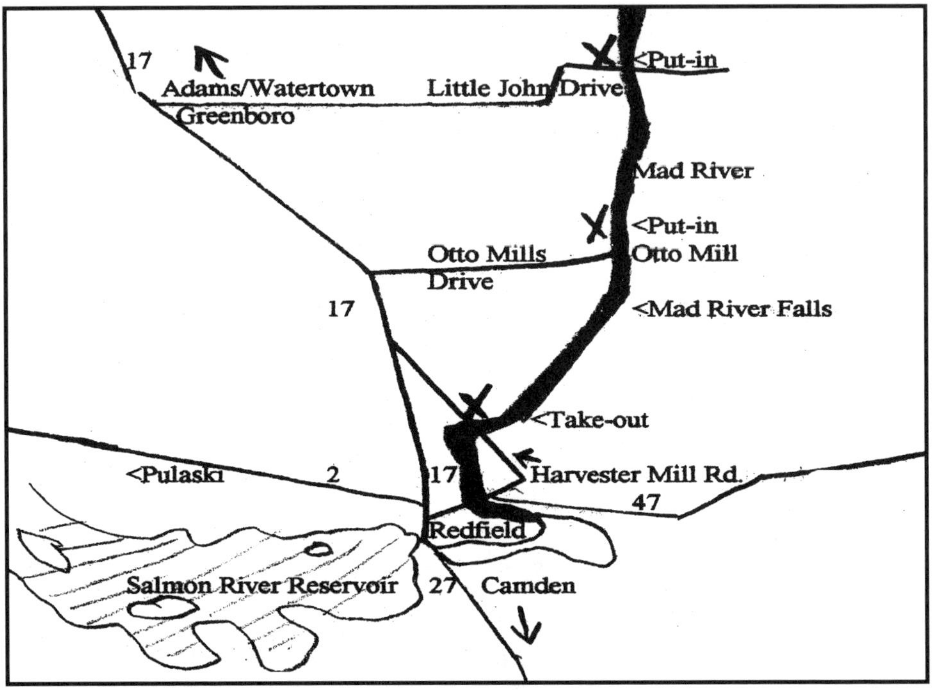

Notes

1

2

3

4

5

Lie -- tell Dennis he's brilliant

Give Peter a call for your basic flatwater and whitewater instruction

Surf us on the river and on the web
Ask for it in your local paddling shop
(Dennis likes it!)

River:	**Meacham Lake Outlet**(Malone)**
Scenery:	Good
Class:	III-V/V+
Access:	.5-mile
Length:	1.2mile
Average gradient:	90'/mile
Gauge:	Parishville will need to be 800cfs or more
Water levels:	If it's high enough for a good run the first series of holes right below the put-in will be incredibly nasty looking -- and acting
Best betting time:	April-early May
Other local runs:	Deer (IV-V)**** / Salmon (I-III, IV-)**
Boogie time:	75% -- scout the top holes before getting in your boat -- and then think twice about it
Time to do first run:	1-1.5 hours
First known descent:	?
Raft:	No
Ducky:	Yes
Food and gas:	Malone is your best bet
Camping:	Meacham Lake Campground
Page in the Gazetteer:	101
County:	Franklin
Closest river store:	Wear on Earth in Potsdam

Directions: Put-in at the Route 30 Bridge and take-out at Rice Brook on Route 458 (you'll probably see the huge parking area sign before you notice the brook).

Descriptions/hazards: The only line through the first holes at high water (V-V+) is a hero line, otherwise enjoy the short walk and notice the posted signs for the rest of the trip. You might find that you can sneak down this first drop on the left; the chances/consequences of messing up and becoming part of the log jam at the bottom are rather high however. After the top drop/heinous thing the river gives a breather before building to class III then IV. Not long after you'll want to look at a class IV+ section -- the total drop is around 20'. Your last rapids will be class III-III+ before fading to flat water and the take-out at Rice Brook. Simply paddle the short distance up Rice Brook to Route 458. If you're passing through this area stop and paddle this and watch out for all the wood parked in the river.

Notes

1

2

3

4

5

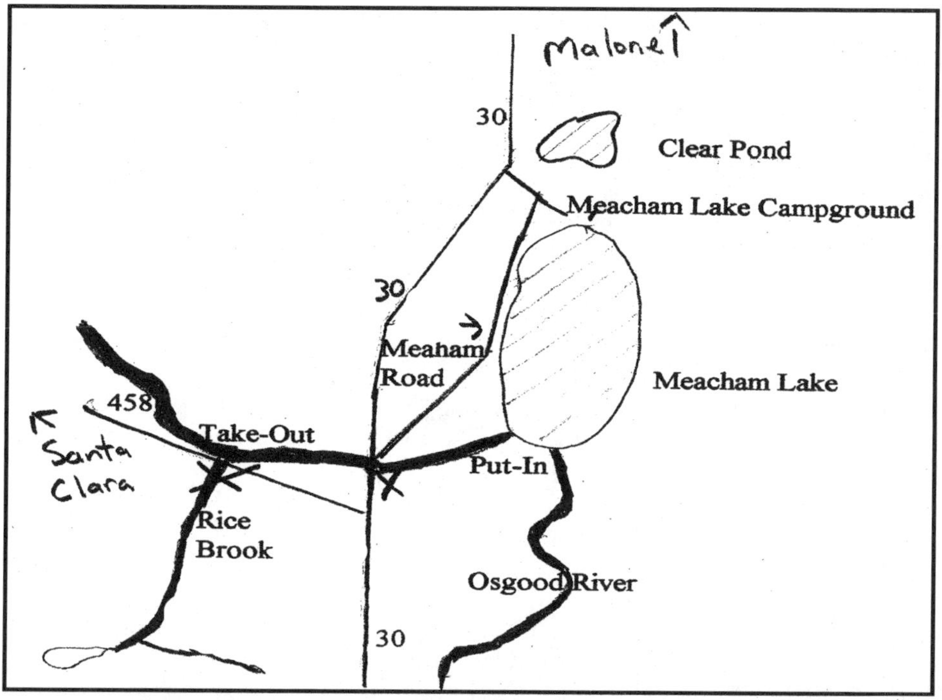

Dennis playing on the Oswegatchie. Photo by Sally Dewes.

River:	**Mettawee****(North Granville)**
Scenery:	Good
Class:	IV-V
Access:	.5-mile
Length:	4.5 miles
Average gradient:	50'/mile
Gauge:	Granville at 3.5' is very bony but doable /4.4'-4.8' is ideal
Water level:	This goes up easily and stays up a long time -- it **runs a lot!**
Best betting time:	Late March-late May
Other local runs:	Poultney**(III-IV) / Upper Poultney**(I-III+) See below*
Boogie time:	75% -- scout the horizon lines
Time to do first run:	3 hours
First known descent:	? This treasure has only recently become known
Raft:	Yes -- if it's 4.6' or more **(over 5' be careful)**
Ducky:	Yes
Food and gas:	Granville
Camping:	Campgrounds at Fort Ann or East Whitehall
Page in the Gazetteer:	81
County:	Washington
Closest river store:	Saratoga Outfitters in Saratoga Springs & Sacandaga Outdoor Center in Lake Luzerne

Directions: Turn north off Route 22, onto Truthville Road /Route 12. At the T take a left, the put-in is at the bridge. Or you can go right at the top of the next hill and get in at the fishing access a few hundred yards upstream (this is above the first hard drop you'll see at the bridge). For the take-out, get back on Route 22 and head west. In less than 2 miles you want to take the first right on Upper Turnpike and go about 2 miles on this. Then park at the big turn out on the right, at the falls.

Description/hazards: The first drop (IV+) at the bridge is a great spot for a photo opp. It's not as gnarly as it looks -- just stay right side up. The next goody (IV) is about .25 mile downstream. For the few miles that follow you'll find easy water and a handful of boat-scout-able drops. And just as you start thinking that the run is lame, a big horizon line (IV+/V) appears -- get out and scout/portage on either side. If you run this start down the right center and keep paddling all the way through -- things will happen quickly. As you get to the big ledge boof the left center and keep paddling (some nasty swims have taken place in the hole to your right). It you do get sucked back in, work your way out the right side. If you swim know that it can hold on to you until you swim deep or **go limp.** Enjoy the **play hole** immediately below.

The next drop is Z-turn (IV); watch out for the hole/undercut rock face at the bottom right (Sally's hole). This flows into the next steep (but easy down the middle) drop (III+). A few minutes more and you'll be at the falls and the take-out. The most exciting line here is way right -- with lots of air time -- right before lots of water (deep in your sinuses). Be aware that there's a small cave behind the right side of the falls. So far it's been more a source of humor than fear (so far anyway). If you don't mind a lot of scraping you can paddle this as low as 3.5' or 3.6'. That is if you really want to paddle badly -- the drops are still fun -- there's just not a lot of water in between them.

A large part of the reason that this gets 4****'s is that it runs so much -- be sure to save a day for the Mettawee!

Something(s) else! - Other than Button Falls (which is just above Granville -- and can be portaged on the right) you could do an easy (mostly flat-class I) paddle starting at Pawlet in Vermont (below the gorge -- please). We haven't paddled this but it looks mighty inviting over its dozen or so miles. That means there could be a surprise drop or two in there. Granville at 4.0' would probably be minimum for kayaking and 4.2' would be for canoeing. Be bold -- explore.

For another close by moderate run (II-III+) I'll mention the upper Poultney in western Vermont. The one time we did this we started about 4 miles east of East Poultney on Route 140 as it goes under a small bridge. There were a couple of small gorges (III+), easy water and a drop above East Poultney (VI) that we took out above. You can find this take-out by turning towards the river in town and crossing the bridge. Granville should be 4.2' or more to do this.

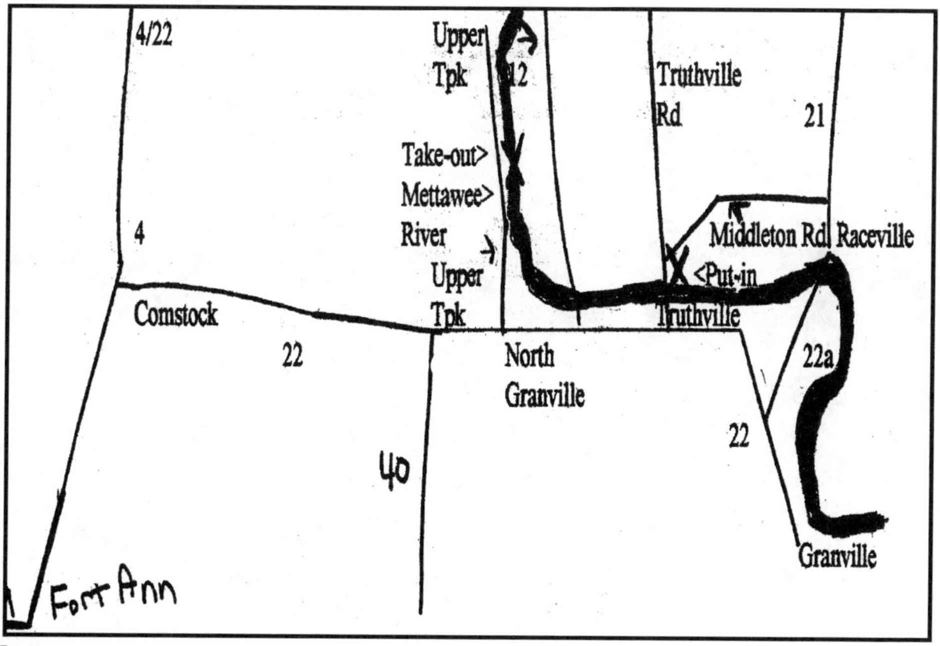

Notes

1

2

3

4

5

Tyler Maheu in the first drop of the Mettawee. Photo by Sally Dewes.

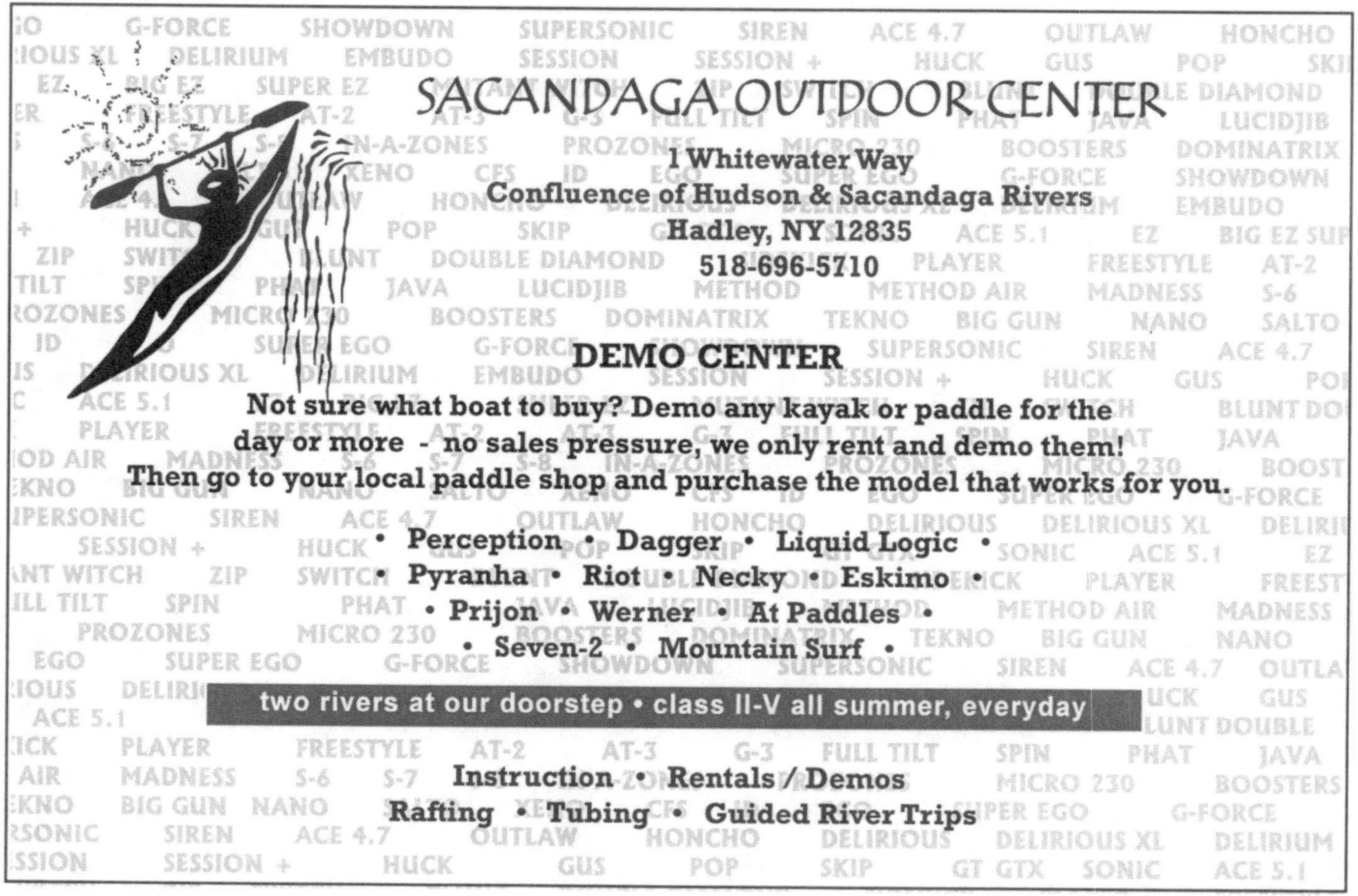
SACANDAGA OUTDOOR CENTER
1 Whitewater Way
Confluence of Hudson & Sacandaga Rivers
Hadley, NY 12835
518-696-5710
DEMO CENTER
Not sure what boat to buy? Demo any kayak or paddle for the
day or more - no sales pressure, we only rent and demo them!
Then go to your local paddle shop and purchase the model that works for you.
• Perception • Dagger • Liquid Logic •
• Pyranha • Riot • Necky • Eskimo •
• Prijon • Werner • At Paddles •
• Seven-2 • Mountain Surf •
two rivers at our doorstep • class II-V all summer, everyday
Instruction • Rentals / Demos
Rafting • Tubing • Guided River Trips

River:	**Mill Creek***(Lowville)**
Scenery:	Very good
Class:	IV-V
Access:	.1-mile and some of it is very steep to try to walk out
Length:	4 miles;
Average gradient:	100'/mile (in the upper half it's closer to 200'/mile)
Gauge:	Donnattsburg should be at least 400cfs
Water level:	High water is fast, pushy and presents some nasty holes
Best betting time:	April
Other local runs:	Independence (IV-V)**** / Deer / New Boston (III)**
Boogie time:	70%
Time to do first run:	3 hours
First known descent:	?
Raft:	Maybe -- if it's kind of high (and the first drop is tight…and then there's that ledge/hole under Route 12…maybe not)
Ducky:	Yes -- this is a great low water run
Food and gas:	Lowville
Camping:	On the Independence
Page in the Gazetteer:	84
County:	Lewis
Closest river store:	Mountain Man in Old Forge & Inlet & White Water Challengers in Old Forge

Directions: Put-in on Gordon Road (the second bridge, not the first). It might be worth getting in farther up one of the tributaries, but I won't swear to that. To find the take-out drive back into Lowville on Route 12. In the middle of town you'll cross the river and see a pizza place next to the bridge (it's pretty good -- had my first Greek Salad there). You should have turned right about .5-mile before this bridge. The 20' falls below the bridge is not runnable and there are no eddies the last 150 yards above it. A good take-out is at one of the last two bridges before the Route 12 Bridge.

Description/hazards: At Gordon Road Bridge you start off with the cows. The first drop is tight and has a surprise hole at the bottom. You'll find a lot of ledges -- they might be bigger than you first thought. The ledges are often long, but they don't go vertical, which is good since they all have shallow landings. The most exciting action starts when you can see the Route 12 Bridge high overhead. You'll be paddling down some very tight ledges with sheer rock on the sides; as you round this first corner (start on the outside) you're off to the races. As you approach the Route 12 Bridge you had better be on the right side of the river (the hole on the left will break you). This short section is twice as fast and drops twice as much as you thought it was going to when you looked at it from the Route 12 Bridge. Don't be surprised, I'm telling you so before you get there. In March of 2002 a solid boater had a horrible ride/swim in that hole on the left side; the results were: broken helmet, broken toe, torn muscles, sore knees, lost paddle and lost boat. **Stay away from that hole**. Any horizon line you don't like the looks of, get out and look. There is a big falls with a shallow landing just below the bridge in the middle of town -- get out before that (the hospital has enough business).

Notes
1
2
3
4
5

Drive shuttle for Dennis

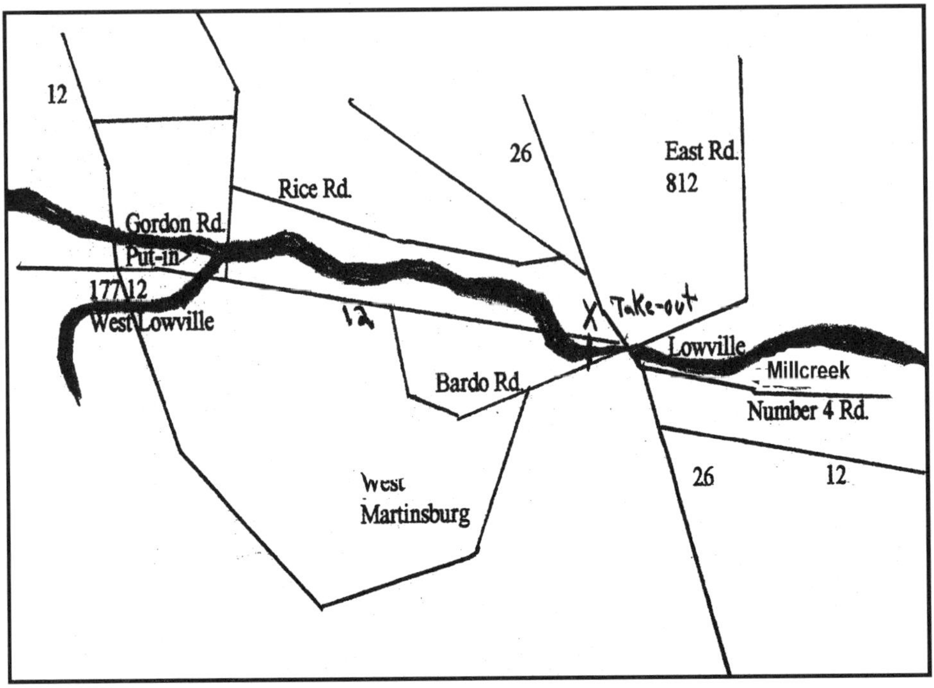
12
26
East Rd.
812
Rice Rd.
Gordon Rd.
Put-in>
177\12
West Lowville
12
X Take-out
Lowville
Millcreek
Bardo Rd.
Number 4 Rd.
West
Martinsburg
26
12

River:	**Mill Creek*(Port Henry)**
Scenery:	Fair-good
Class:	IV-VI
Access:	.6-mile
Length:	3-5 miles depending on put-in and take-out
Average gradient:	120'/mile below Moriah Center and 300'/mile in Port Henry
Gauge:	Putnam Creek should be at least 280cfs
Water level:	This drops very fast after the rain stops, so don't dally
Best betting time:	April
Other local runs:	Putnam Creek (IV-V)** / The Branch (IV-IV+, VI)***
Boogie time:	90% -- until just above Port Henry -- then get out!
Time to do first run:	2-4 hours depending on take-out
First known descent:	Dennis and Peter Lippman in 1995
Raft:	No
Ducky:	Yes
Food and gas:	Port Henry
Camping:	Split Rock Falls or Lincoln Pond
Page in the Gazetteer:	97
County:	Essex
Closest river store:	Adirondack Lakes and Trails in Saranac Lake

Directions: Take-out at the bridge just before getting into Port Henry and you won't have to experience falling off the earth. Drive back west on Route 4 to Moriah Center and get in at the bridge or just west of town.

Description/hazards: There's some nice class IV rocky creekin' in Moriah Center and it goes on for a while, just not long enough. Then the run eases up and doesn't do much until Port Henry. We didn't run the monster drop/thing or even take a good look at the two falls and gorge below. If it is doable, it's most likely class VI-ish.

As far as I know nobody else has run this thing. It is somewhat prone to wood and the last part is huge and huge. The day Peter and I got on it the rain had stopped for a while and the level was low-medium. On the steep part below Moriah Center Peter wanted to scout once again; I noticed the water was dropping and got impatient. I told him that his observations were nice but if he didn't get going there wouldn't be anything to paddle. Peter can be slow but he's great to paddle with and cooks his best food with a flashlight in his mouth!

Notes

1

2

3

4

5

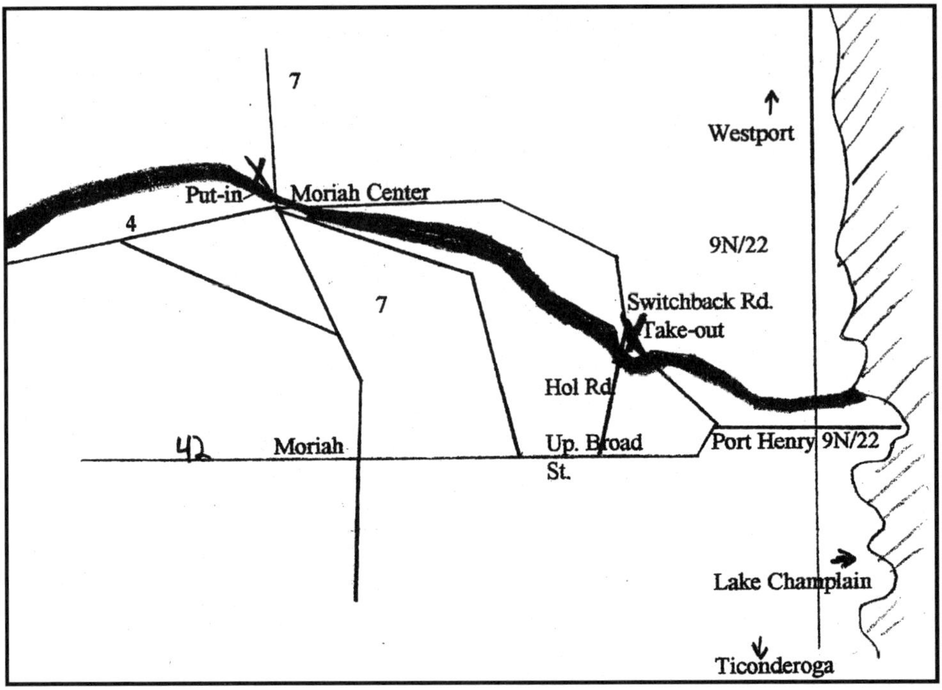
7
Westport
Put-in
Moriah Center
4
9N/22
7
Switchback Rd.
Take-out
Hol Rd.
42
Moriah
Up. Broad
St.
Port Henry
9N/22
Lake Champlain
Ticonderoga

Join AW

River:	**Moose/Bottom****(Port Leyden)**
Scenery:	Very good
Class:	IV+/V
Access:	l-mile
Length:	4.2 miles
Average gradient:	80'/mile
Gauge:	Mckeever at 2.5' is minimal / 2.7' to 4' is good / 5' and above is high / 6' is suicidal
Water level:	The weekend releases in the spring and again in the fall usually give you something in the 2.5'-4' range. The dam release only affects the last 4 drops. You are in reality only paddling on natural flow. The release means that they stop sucking water from the river.
Best betting time:	Spring and fall releases
Other local runs:	Independence (IV-V)**** / Otter (III-IV+)***
Boogie time:	50% -- there's lots of horizon lines to scout
Time to do first run:	3-4 hours
First known descent:	In the 70's?
Raft:	Yes -- a 12'er between 2.7' and 4' (maybe a little higher)
Food and gas:	Boonville
Camping:	Primitive camping at Lyonsdale Bridge and next to Fowlersville Falls on the right side
Page in the Gazetteer:	85
County:	Lewis
Closest river store:	Mountain Man in Old Forge & Inlet & White Water Challengers in Old Forge

Directions: The put-in is at Fowlersville Road Bridge. To get to the take-out drive south on Fowlersville Road and turn right on Hunkins Road, go through the next stop sign and drive by the big building (on your left) -- stay on this road. If you want to look at Lyonsdale Falls or find the camp spot, turn up this road and go over the bridge. For the take-out drive about 2.5 miles past the plant and turn right at the 4-way (Goulds Mill) intersection. Take the first right just as you get over the bridge and park by the powerhouse/falls.

Description/hazards: You can play at the drop above the bridge to get warmed up if you want. I mean, the next drop is a two stage 40'+ falls after all. Most people run left -- left. The hole below this is not good even at low levels. Stay left. The next one you can boat scout and run door #1 or door #2. The Funnel/Diamond Splitter is next and ought to be scouted the first time down (**inside info: the hole below the boof move way left at the bottom is worse than it looks**). The next two drops give you a choice of left or right, with the right being more exciting at both. Then you'll portage the dam and crawl up over the road. The lower half of this run has the exciting stuff you've heard about. At Agers you run a 10' sloping dam and then boof an 18' falls. You then get to run a big ledge that drops another 18'. The next big one is Shurform, you can do door #2 (IV-IV+) or door #1

(V-V-). Power line is around the corner (don't underestimate it), and then comes Crystal -- the rapid of the day. There are different lines to be had. Starting way, way right and moving to the center at the end is the least technical line. You can get out at the next dam or go for the gnarl, or the gnarlier. The gnarl starts with a run over the right side of the dam -- gets busy and ends in a 16' falls that you might see coming, or not. The gnarlier starts way left and is a thing called Morilla (a 20'+ falls/ thing). This is due to the fond resemblance to Gorilla on the famous/infamous Green River, down south.

I could've broken my neck. That thought was foremost in my mind as I finally rolled up below Magilla. The day before had been one of my first trips down this part of the Moose. I'd been paddling with Chris and Caron Koll and asked Chris what everybody was doing over there on the left side of the dam. As I recall he grunted something about a nasty drop. It sounded like something to check out. As I was scouting I noticed that Chuck and Willy Kern and a few others were running it. It did look nasty, but I saw the line and knew I'd make it. I did. It was so smooth that Willy himself paddled over at the bottom and congratulated me on the run of the day. Look at me -- big man on campus!

The next day all was not going well in the top half of the rapid. Instead of coming off the top of the big approach rock like the day before -- I'd some how slid off the left side (my sense of urgency factor obviously wasn't high enough). Next thing you know the boat was against the left-side wall and doing a sliding splat. Survival mode kicked in. The move is to be way right and setting up for an angled boof at the lip of the falls. Well now with the adrenaline booster the boat somehow got too far right (urgency factor was too high). The front of the boat caught dry rock and stopped dead. The current pushed the backend over the falls. Still upright (front pointing to the moon) the boat fell several feet -- the backend hit rock and stopped while the water now pushed the front end forward. All was not going smoothly. In fact the front kept going over and twisting to the left. Landing more upside down than not, this pilot noticed his face and neck were very exposed and close to the wall on the left.

Slaps on the back really don't mean much. You'll probably remember it a lot longer if you break your neck.

Notes

1

2

3

4

5

Buy ADK books

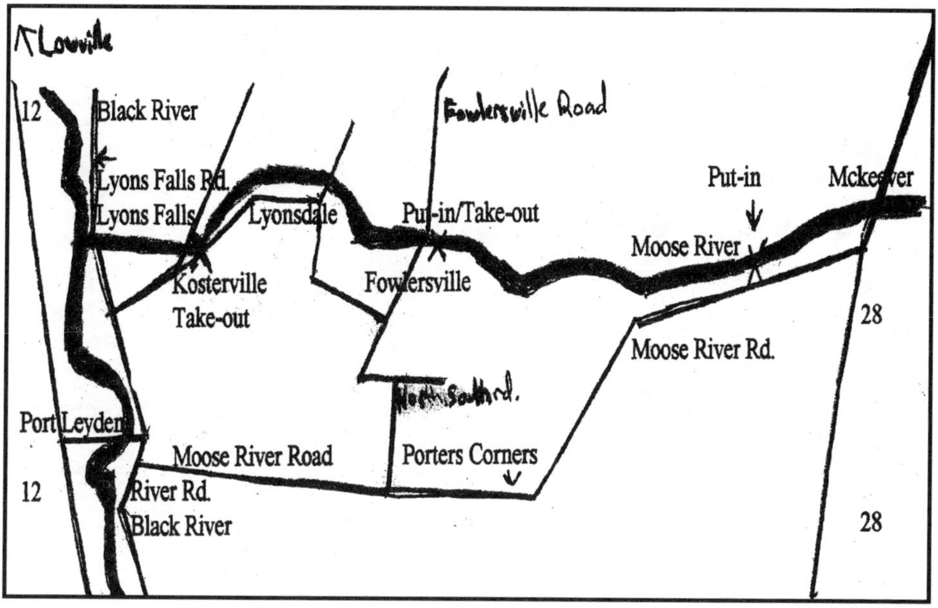

Sally Dewes on the right side of Shurform. Photo by Dennis.

River:	**Moose/Lower**(Old Forge)**
Scenery:	Good
Class:	III-IV+ (3.5'-4') / IV-IV+ (4-6') / IV-V (over 6')............and it keeps going up.
Access:	1-2 miles
Length:	10 miles
Average gradient:	40'/mile
Gauge:	Mckeever
Water levels:	4' is low / above 8' is class V in places / this drops quicker than you'd think for something with this big of a watershed / 5.5'-6" is a **great surf level** and a great raft level
Best betting time:	April
Other local runs:	The Bottom Moose (IV+/V) is the place to be if this is too low / if it's 5' or above go check out a creek (i.e.-Independence (IV-V)**** and / or the Otter (III-IV+))*** / Middle Moose (II-III, IV-)**
Boogie time:	80% -- at the very least -- scout Mixmaster
Time to do first run:	3-4 hours
First known descent:	??
Raft:	Yes -- over 3.9' (3.6' is doable but very bony)
Ducky:	Yes
Food and gas:	Old Forge or Boonville
Camping:	Singing Waters Campground just west of Old Forge
Page in the gazetteer:	85
County:	Lewis
Closest river store:	White Water Challengers in Old Forge & Mountain Man in Old Forge & Inlet

Directions: Fowlersville Bridge on Fowlersville Road is the take-out. For the put-in go south on Fowlersville Road then left at the T on Penny Settlement. Immediately turn right on North South Road and then left at the next T. Now drive several miles east on Moose River Road until a big obvious pull off about 3 miles west of Route 28 -- this is.... yes! You guessed it.

Description/hazards: 5'-6' is a fun level for this run. It's ideal for an April raft trip too. At this level there's a lot of fun stuff to surf. Not many people paddle this in April because it's a long cold day with the wind in your face. If you do brave the elements you'll find some big rapids with a lot of easy water separating them. First comes Iron Bridge -- this is a fun rapid at most levels -- at levels above 7.0' it changes into pure hell -- especially if you don't make the dogleg -- moving hard to the left (and watch out for holes all the way down). Don't even think about getting pushed to the outside (right) -- the hole at the top of the island over there is death at high water. The next biggie comes up quickly -- Tannery -- you can go right center all the way down and then move right at the bottom (or stay way left all the way if it's high). WHATEVER you do **stay out of the**

Whaleback hole at the bottom center -- it is big enough to hold a whale...........and has! Following closely is -- Rooster Tail; go with the waves and stay out of all those big holes--at really high water you may want to start (and stay) way right, to miss those monsters. The next morsel is Froth Hole -- run it right center -- but not too far right or you'll land on a piton rock. Mixmaster is now up to bat and you'd better scout. Elevator Shaft is next to last and tends to hit you hardest on the right -- go straight down the middle. Even though the last drop at the take-out bridge looks innocent it can be hungry -- beware the last hole in the center.

The very first weekend my girlfriend and I spent together we went to the Moose (romantic huh?). The river was low but we didn't care -- we were getting to know each other (smooching along the river). Because we had started late (it's complicated) we decided to start a ways above the usual put-in spot and were just enjoying the day and each other's company (more smooching). This all meant that by the time we got to the bottom of Rooster Tail it was getting dark (no time for smooching). I had hiked out here on a previous trip but this time found it hard going in the waning light (was she still behind me?) I got to the road and found the bike we'd stashed earlier just in case we were to run out of light (smooch too long).

I'd done the shuttle quickly and came back in the dark looking for my Sweetie (I wanted to smooch some more). Actually being chivalrous was the real reason -- where was she? The concern was starting to grow. Turning back and making a slow pass I saw her -- she was on the other side of the road -- with a glass of wine in her hand! It seems she met some nice people that invited her over to their camp for food and drink. Since that day I've often run/biked/hitched and suffered greatly to get back to her as quickly as possible -- so she wouldn't get cold, lonely, bored or worse -- only to find her in dry clothes -- eating and drinking. As I write this I think about all the time we used to smooch on the river -- whatever happened to that?

Notes

1

2

3

4

5

Give out more unsolicited hugs

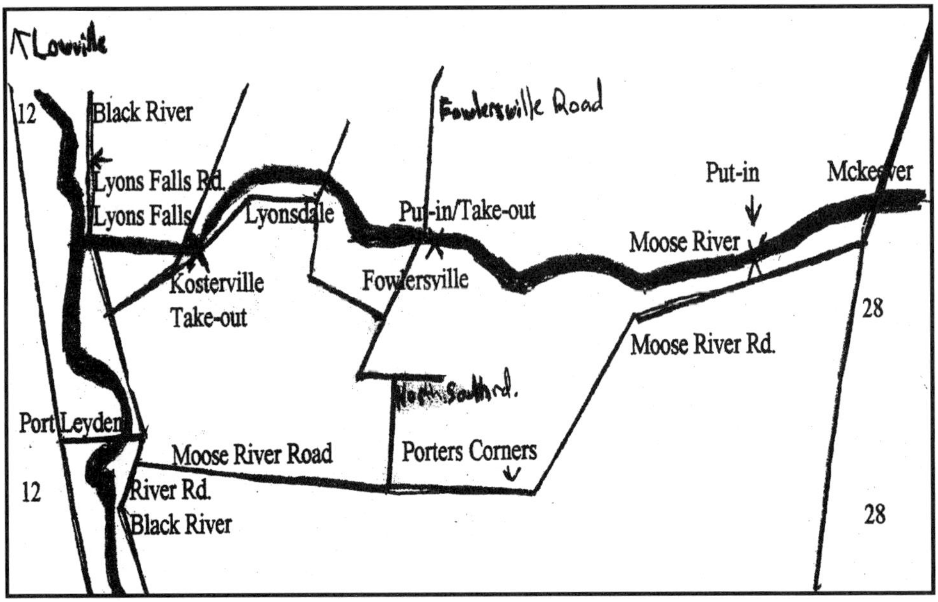

Lower Moose. Photo by Ceci Mendez.

River:	**Moose/Middle***(Old Forge)**
Scenery:	Good
Class:	II-III, IV-
Access:	1-mile
Length:	6-9 miles
Average gradient:	30'/mile
Gauge:	McKeever
Water levels:	2.5' is min. /3-4' is nice /above 5' is high (and class III, IV)
Best betting time:	April (high)-May -- most of the summer and again in the fall
Other local runs:	Moose / Lower (III-V)** / Moose / South Branch (II-IV)****
Boogie time:	95% -- you may want to look at Gordon Falls
Time to do first run:	3-4 hours
First known descent:	?
Raft:	Yes -- in fact a 16'er is fine if it's over 3.5'
Ducky:	Yes
Food and gas:	Old Forge
Camping:	Singing Water Campground
Page in the gazetteer:	85
County:	Herkimer / Oneida / Lewis
Closest river store:	White Water Challengers in Old Forge & Mountain Man in Inlet & Old Forge

Directions: You can put-in at the campground or just below -- where the river comes next to the road. For the take-out you can use the Route 28 Bridge (5.5 miles) or further down the Moose River Road. The first 2 pull-offs on the right side of Moose River Road are good spots (this will extend your trip by 2-3.5 miles).

Description/hazards: The river is moving and nice at the put-in. You'll encounter occasional rapids -- and somewhere in the middle of the first 4 miles you'll want to scout the falls. This is a rocky rapid with a nasty ending -- if the water is kind of high be very careful here. As you pass under Route 28 the river will be looking calm -- don't be fooled -- there are some good rapids if you keep going. The remaining rapids will be class II-III or more if the river has a good amount of water. You can probably guess which take-out I'd recommend. This section gets rafted and duckied during the summer months -- it doesn't take much water to enjoy. And at the other extreme the last drops are big water class III-IV at 8.0' or more.

Notes

1

2

3

4

5

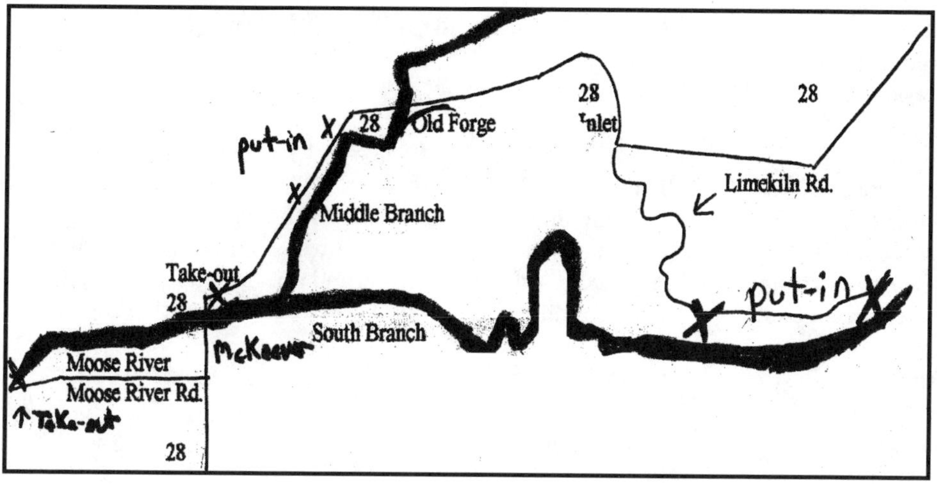

28
Old Forge
28
Inlet
28
put-in
Limekiln Rd.
Middle Branch
Take-out
28
South Branch
McKeever
put-in
Moose River
Moose River Rd.
Take-out
28

River:	**Moose/South Branch****(Old Forge)**
Scenery:	Great
Class:	II-IV
Access:	Several miles
Length:	22 or 27 miles (shuttle is 30-35 miles and not a fast one)
Average gradient:	30'/mile
Gauge:	3.0' is minimum / 3.5' is nice / 4' is better
Water levels:	You can run this above 5' -- just watch out for the big drops
Best betting time:	May 1 (ALC-agreement)-June and usually again in the fall
Other local runs:	Moose/ Middle (I-III, IV)*** / Moose/Lower (III-V)**
Boogie time:	99%
Time to do first run:	At least 10 hours from lower put-in and 12 from the upper
First known descent:	?
Raft:	Yes -- over 4'
Ducky:	Yes
Food and gas:	Old Forge
Camping:	State land below the ALC land
Page in the Gazetteer:	85/86
County:	Hamilton/Herkimer
Closest river store:	Mountain Man in Inlet & Old Forge & White Water Challengers in Old Forge

Directions: The take-out is at the Route 28 Bridge, on the right side, south of Old Forge. To get to the put-in drive east on Route 28 until you get a little east of Inlet. When you see Limekiln Road on your right, turn there and head out into the boonies. In about 12 miles you'll get to the trail (on your right) -- which takes you into the Rock Dam, the lower put-in. To get to the upper put-in, drive up the road another 4.5 miles or so until you get to the bridge.

Description/hazards: If you start at the bridge/upper put-in you add 5 miles to the trip and don't have to carry in. The first 5 miles move along quickly, are pretty and give you 1 mile of shallows to deal with if it's less than 3.4'. If you start at the Rock Dam you have to walk in almost a mile. Around a mile below this point you'll run into a class IV ledge. From there it's less than a mile to the ALC land (you'll see a sign). This club requires that the gauge must read at least 2.65' the day you start the trip and that you only paddle this between May 1 and October 15. This is the agreement -- several people went to jail in 1991 to get you this route, respect it. No picnics or camping for the next 12 miles; only scouting.

For the next 6 miles it's class I-II+. Three feet is minimal for a decent run on this section in a canoe -- especially down to Otter Brook Bridge. From there it's 1 mile to Grindstone Rapids (III-III+). Below it's easy for a ways until Limekiln Falls (class IV) -- then flat and easy. You'll start getting class II's for a ways as you approach Remsen Falls (class IV); after the falls it's long class II's down to the take-out at Route 28, on the right side. There are lean-to's by Remsen Falls that can be accessed from a trail off of Route 28.

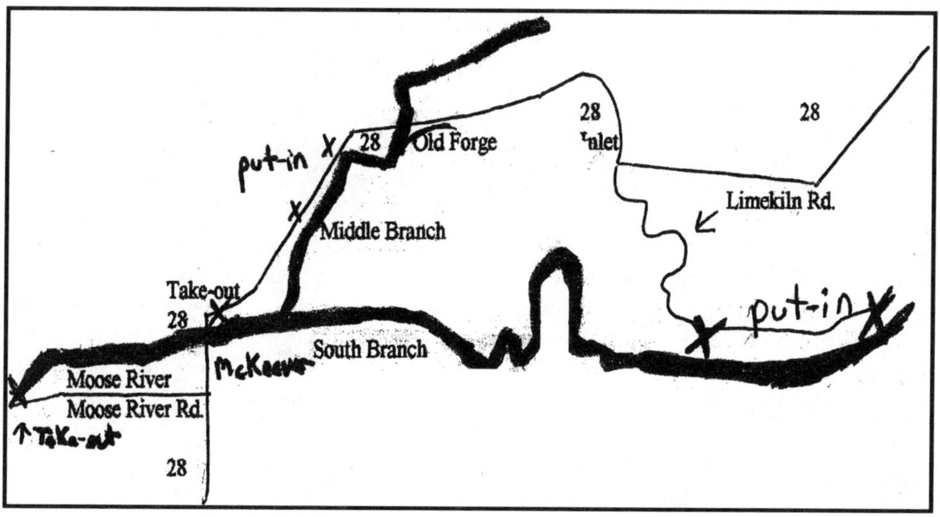

Notes
1
2
3
4
5

River:	**Negro (N0) Brook**(Lowville)**
Scenery:	Good
Class:	IV+/V?
Access:	.5-mile
Length:	1 or more miles
Average gradient:	150'/mile
Gauge:	Donattsburg will be over 600cfs
Water levels:	There's usually a lot of snow on the Tug Hill Plateau, it's melting for you. Why aren't you there?
Best betting time:	Late March-early May
Other local runs:	Mill Creek (IV-V)*** / Deer / New Boston (III)***
Boogie time:	75%
Time to do first run:	3 hours
First known descent:	**UNRUN**
Raft:	No
Ducky:	Yes
Food and gas:	Lowville
Camping:	Sleepy Hollow Campground off Route 26
Page in the Gazetteer:	84
County:	Lewis
Closest river store:	T. I. Adventures in Clayton

Directions: The take-out is at East Road -- a few hundred yards south of the real Negro Brook. To get back to the put-in, head south on East Road and take your first right (Sharp Road). Then drive up Sharp Road and head straight across Route 26 -- you'll find it is now called Boshart Road. Just as you hit Patten Road you'll cross the put-in. If you are up to running the drop above the bridge -- great -- if not, start lower.

Description/hazards: Starting just above the intersection of Boshart and Patten is a very short but exciting looking section. The drop above the bridge is a series of several drops -- all within one biggie. This is a short gorge and the water zips going under the bridge. The one thing you really need to know is that there is barbed wire below the bridge. Barbed wire across the water is bad. Personal experience has taught me that. You'll have to cut the wire and the tree behind it if you want to run this drop. The next 1.5 miles looks to be pretty flat (and may have more wire). What we'll probably do when we finally get on this run is start at the bridge above Route 26. It looks like there is some gradient worth checking out. From Route 26 down to East Road is just over a mile -- it drops 170' -- this section appears to be more bouldery. Get out at East Road, if you go beyond that you'll find yourself in a big swamp.

Several years ago my friend Lenny and I where suppose to go paddle. Plans had been made several days ahead of time (which isn't like us usually) to paddle a particular river on that day. Well, I checked and found out it was running a really good level that day. So I called Lenny in the morning, really excited. He starts to moan about having a lot of work to do (he and his wife own a hotel/resort). Lenny

always has special events going on to attract extra business. He was moaning about having to set up for a wedding or something. Anyway, things needed doing -- he said something about setting up a bunch of chairs. My interest in this line of conversation was waning fast. Then he said he wanted me to come down to help him! Was he nuts? He lived an hour away. Yours truly is stoked to paddle and he wants me to blow off paddling, drive an hour, and set up chairs for some whoop-dee-doo at his place? What in the hell was he thinking? Feeling annoyed and properly indignant (after all, the water was up damn it), I said "I shouldn't even be talking to you now!' Meaning I had better things to do -- like paddle! That phrase -- "I shouldn't even be talking to you now!" became an often-repeated joke for years after that.

You have to let people know when they get their priorities messed up. Set up chairs indeed!

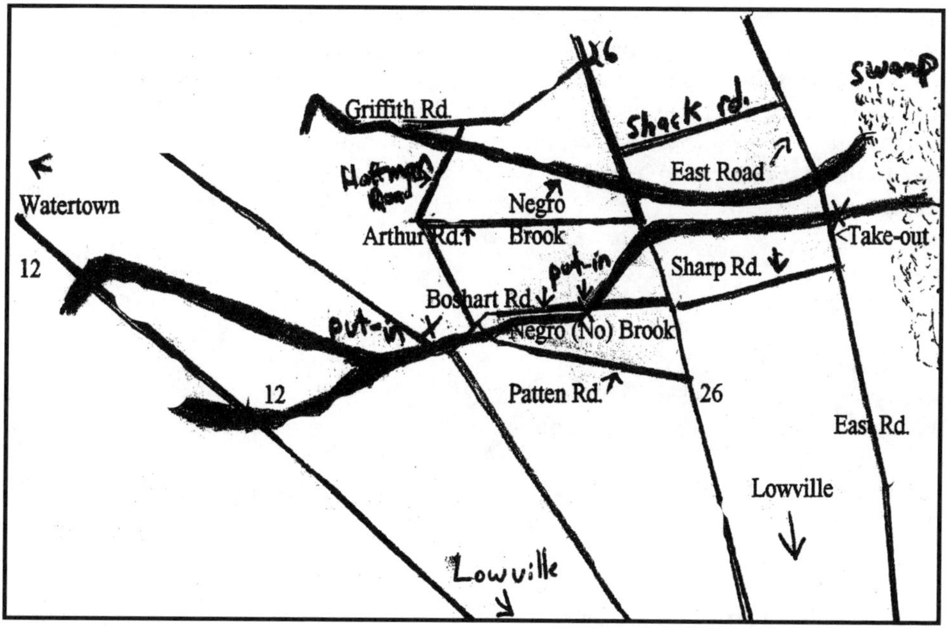

Notes

1
2
3
4
5

River:	**East Branch of the Oswegatchie***(Fine)**
Scenery:	Good-very good
Class:	IV-VI
Access:	3-miles
Length:	7 miles
Average gradient:	60'/mile
Gauge:	We're working on getting a contact person with Orion Power.
Water level:	450cfs is bare minimum / 800-1100cfs is ideal. Much more and somc of the drops will take a courageous soul. Up till now we've always struggled to get a real person that would give us real info at Orion/Niagara Mohawk. So check this out when you're in the area (the Middle Branch Osw.) and the Grass arc very close by). This tends to have a long season because it drains Cranberry Lake (which is huge). If the wide part of the river in Fine looks high enough to just get down -- you're set.
Best betting time:	April-early June
Other local runs:	Little River (II-III)*** / Grasse / Twin Falls (IV-VI)*****
Boogie time:	50% -- there are many horizon lines to look at
Time to do first run:	4-5 hours -- keep 'em moving
First known descent:	??
Raft:	Yes -- over 750cfs
Ducky:	Yes
Food and gas:	Harrisville or Gouverneur
Camping:	State land just south of Degrasse
Page in the Gazetteer:	93
County:	Saint Lawrence
Closest river store:	Wear on Earth in Potsdam

Directions: The take-out is at the bridge in the hamlet of South Edwards. The put-in is .25-mile above the upper bridge in Fine on Route 27 -- where the parking is only 30' from the river.

Description/hazards: (What follows is a sampling of the drops -- some of the most exciting have not been mentioned -- bon voyage!) Enjoy the easy warm up rapids; it's going to be a long day. Coming under the first bridge you'll be enjoying some big waves -- **catch a surf** if you can. Next comes a choice -- we usually take the far right door. As you're bouncing down shallow rocks right above the second bridge (if you're not scraping you'll have your hands full at the constricted drops) realize that this is the widest and lowest spot on the river. Go right at the island. Let's make a deal comes next (3 separate doors to choose from). Peter Pan follows and is a must scout on the left. You probably won't believe me but the hole isn't as bad as it looks. If the water is high the **surfing at the next drop is great**. You'll find one more good drop before you paddle across the reservoir. If there's water below the dam it's a lot of fun to paddle the gorge (getting in is very tricky). There's another dam and then a nasty class V drop (stay out of those big holes). Next comes an easy drop and then you'll see the last bridge. The drop below this bridge is great fun; you can run it on the right or left side (the right is more fun). As a finale there are some **fun holes to play in.** Just get out and walk through the brush and trees to your car.

Extra! If you are lucky enough to be in the area when everything is high (or was the day before) you should go check out the Browns Bridge section of this river. Just drive several miles east of the Fine put-in on Route 3 and take a left on Browns Bridge Road. In a few minutes you'll cross this section **(class V).** You'll know right away if it's up -- just hike upstream with you boat and have a blast! You'll find falls and slides on this 1.6 miles section.

It had only been about a month since the short cast came off my leg (see the Katterskill story in volume #2) and I didn't want to swim and bang my leg. It was mid-spring and this was my first time down this. I had left Dan's jeep at the take-out for the Little River for him and he was going to pick me up after paddling solo down that. The water was at a good level on the Oswegatchie and all was going smoothly. I even ran Peter Pan (it didn't look as bad as the portage). At Black hole Falls the smart thing seemed to be to run the optional left route, which looked class IV-ish. Yes, I did scout and yes, I saw the logjam in the middle. It looked to be easy to miss. Being wrong when you paddle alone can be very dangerous to your health.

Starting down the left side: I bumped a rock-it pushes me towards the logjam-no biggie-I hit something else-now I'm close to the logjam-still no biggie. When I bump again and slide up against the tree it's starting to get big. Leaning towards the tree I'm figuring the current is moving in the direction that will actually push me off. There must be a limb just below the surface. I stop cold. Even though I'm leaning hard downstream the front of the boat is driven underwater. The bear hug that I have around the top tree keeps my head above water. The boat is leaning so far over that the cockpit is blocked. There's no way to get out! It's been a minute or so and the current is pushing the bow even deeper. The bottom of the boat collapses against the back of my legs. "I'm dead -- I'm dead!" The thought tears through my brain. Something happens next that shouldn't be possible.

You hear about miracles, about what you can do if you put your mind to it. Especially when the adrenaline kicks in. Only a second before I'd thought I was gasping my last breath and then I'm standing on top of the logjam. How did I get there? I still tell people that it wasn't physically possible for that to have happened. My next move was to reach into the kayak and grab my throw bag. I clipped into the back loop on the boat and tossed the bag across the current and on to shore. The paddle was right behind that. Then came the exciting part. I was still in the middle of a log-strewn class IV rapid with a barely healed leg. I scouted out a swim line and hopped in. The plan had been to backstroke behind some holes and get to shore quickly. The little trashing I took in the first hole changed my mind. I decided to swim the rest of the rapid and then head for shore. I took some hard butt shots because I was holding my gimpy leg (it was still recovering from that little situation on the Katterskill in January) really high to protect it. When the rapid ended the stroking for land started. The eddy was more powerful than I had figured so I had to try a second time for solid ground. "What in the hell is that?" I heard myself yell out loud. Just as the sickening smell overwhelmed me I bounced off the thing. "Oh my

God" -- it was a...a...bloated carcass of a dead pig/animal/thing. It takes a lot to induce an overpowering urge to puke in a raft guide. I didn't lose my cookies -- but I did gain the shore -- and dam quick too.

My attempts to do a vector pull to get my boat out of the logjam had failed so I started to hike down the side of the river in search of the unknown take-out and my buddy Dan. The walk took awhile. As I came out of the woods the first earthlings that saw me were the two kids on a riding lawnmower. They had that look you only see the first time the locals see you in your brightly-colored-other- worldly-paddling-gear. As I walked down the road towards Dan the first two kids were joined by every kid in town -- all riding their bicycles around me. I sent two of them ahead of me in the falling darkness and told them to let the guy with the canoe on his car know that I was coming. Afterwards Dan laughed and said I looked like the Pied Piper coming out of the dark leading all the kids in town.

The kids didn't know about Rule #1 – Never follow Dennis

Notes

1
2
3
4
5

Buy Dennis dinner

What stinks? Hey this isn't a piece of wood!
WHAT the Fu..!!

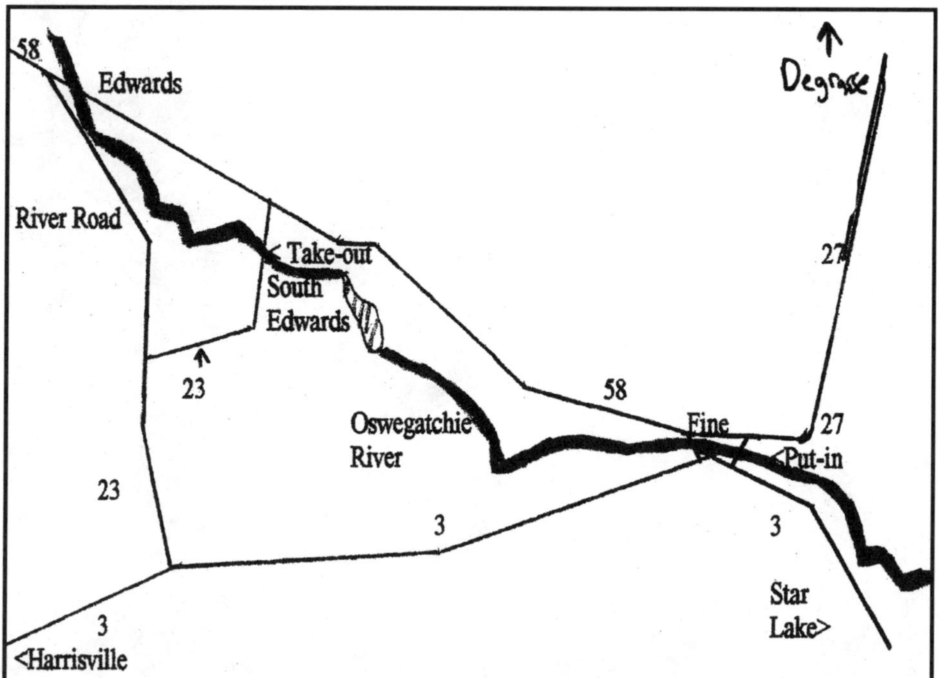
58
Edwards
River Road
< Take-out
South Edwards
23
23
Oswegatchie River
58
Fine
27
<Put-in
27
Degrasse
3
3
Star Lake>
3
<Harrisville

Tim Kelley at Humpy Falls (that hole is a nightmare). Photo by Chris Koll.

River:	**Mid. Branch of the Oswegatchie****(Harrisville)**
Scenery:	Great
Class:	IV-V, VI-
Access:	Many miles
Length:	4.5 miles-26.5 miles (the shuttle for the longer runs are much longer than the river miles)
Average gradient:	80'/ mile. Runs #3 and #4 have much steeper sections
Gauge:	Harrisville at 900cfs and rising or 1100cfs and dropping is minimum. If it's been really high (above 1800), and seems to be dropping very slowly, you may need 1200cfs to meet this acceptable minimum. The reason being that the gauge shows the combined flow of both branches, and the West Branch holds water longer.
Water level:	1200cfs and rising or 1800cfs and just starting to drop should be about right for starting at the top (longest) runs. You can run just the bottom 4 miles at 800cfs and fly off huge class V-VI drops or walk around some great photo opp's.
Best betting time:	Late April to mid May -- after the gates are opened. The top section is gated by the D.E.C. and opens late April, after mud season. Call them in Watertown, N.Y. to find out when it's open. The gate at Bryants Bridge opens late April, when Lassiter gets to it.
Other local runs:	West Oswegatchie (IV-V+)** / Little (I-III)***
Boogie time:	90% (make that 50% in run #4)
Time to do first run:	Varies greatly -- just keep moving (don't stare too long)
First known descent:	?
Raft:	Yes -- if it's fairly high, you're really good and can manage the really, really nasty portage at Rainbow Falls. Skip run # 4.
Ducky:	Yes
Food and gas:	Harrisville
Camping:	For the shorter runs you can camp on state land along Jerden Falls Road. For the longer runs you can camp along the upper river.
Page in the Gazetteer:	93
County:	Herkimer / Lewis
Closest river store:	Wear on Earth in Potsdam

Directions: Listen closely; this may be a little tricky. This river has 4 different sections. The take-out for any section becomes the put-in for the next section. The #1 put-in is found by driving east out of Belfort (on the Beaver River) and driving up the Long Pond Road. At the end is a gate that is opened after mud season (mid or late April). This next 10 miles is in good shape as of the end of 2001. The put-in is next to the road about 10 miles past the gate. You've probably noticed this is a very long shuttle. This river section ends about .5-mile above Mullins Pond (still in Herkimer County). There is a primitive camp road on your left (just before a series of class IV ledges). This is too much driving to do as a single run -- combine it with #2 and #3.

To reach the put-in for # 2 you'll have to drive up Bryant's Bridge Road (if the gate's open). Go 3.5 miles, bear right and drive to the T and take a left and then bear right when it looks like the road is disappearing. This ends in .3 mile at an old camp. This is the start of section 2. This is all normally doable in a car. But the big rains in the fall of 2001 changed that. There is a huge wash out preventing you from driving the last mile into the old camp (you could walk).

The put-in for # 3 is down the hill, about 3.5 miles upstream of Bryant's Bridge Road Bridge. That sounds righter than bridge bridge don't it? The bridge bridge (Bryant's Road) is the take-out for #3 and the put-in for #4.

Take-out #4 is on Jerden Falls Road in Middle Branch Corners. The big rains in the fall of 2001 also made the shuttle for #3 a lot nastier. Now you need a 4-wheel drive with fairly high clearance to get to put-in #2 and #3. There aren't many camps up there, so who knows when they'll get around to fixing up the road.

Description/hazards: Section one has a lot of flat water. Which is what you'll have for a ways at the beginning of the trip. This **(16 mile long)** section has some incredible vistas. Appreciate how far out in virgin country that you truly are. In the middle of this is a long (2-3 mile) stretch of white water. It's mostly class II-III, but there's a fair amount of class IV and a spot or two that approaches V-ish. Most of the easy water on this section is at least moving along.

The ledges at the start of #2 **(this section is 2 miles long)** are a lot of fun. You could just boat scout them -- they're class IV. But it's narrow and wood would be a bad thing. You get to do these ledges and a class III gorge if you paddle this part of the river. The small wooden bridge you'll see is the put-in for #3 **(4 miles long).**

A dynamic entry off the bridge is the usual put-in method here. This section of the river is everybody's favorite. This part is about 4 miles long, takes about 3-4 hours and has 2 portages. The first hard rapid is about .7 mile below the bridge. Scout along the right side. Walking is easier and much quicker if you stay as close to the river as possible. The hole at the end of this section gets very hungry at high water. The next hard drop is portaged on the left side (it's been run at low water). For the next few miles you can boat scout the class IV ledges and short gorges. Always stay alert for strainers and all the big bad holes if the water's high. The huge horizon about 3 miles into the run is just the foreplay to Rainbow Falls. Scout and walk on the left side (get out 100 yards above the first drop or you'll be swearing while you crawl under all the downed trees in the woods). People have run the top falls and the big ledge on the left, below the falls. Nobody has run the really big falls below that yet; somebody will. After you get tired of staring at all of this you have to start roping your boat down into the gorge below the big falls. It's an easy climb down to the water about 50-60' below the top. If you have friends that are afraid of heights you might do what I've done -- don't tell them about this part ahead of time. It worked for me, what you do depends on how thoughtful (or sadistic) you are. That's most of the run. If you made it this far you can figure out the rest yourself.

The put-in for #4 **(4.5 miles long)** is at the bridge (this is the Sluice Falls section). Plan on walking almost everything in the next 4.5 miles. That is unless it's 800-900 cfs and you're here with the big dogs -- ready to run huge class V-V+ drops. This is worth paddling if you have the time, even if it's higher and you're not feeling like a big dog. This is some of the biggest, could be runnable-ist stuff you'll ever see. Bring your camera and your gonads / brass ovaries (that wasn't as much work as I thought).

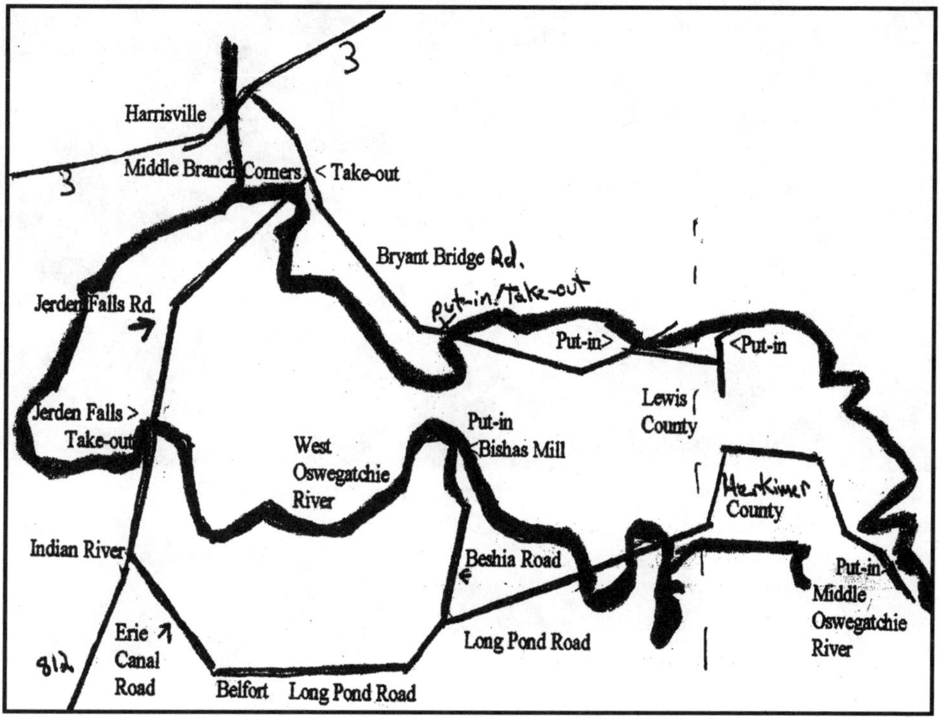

Notes

1

2

3

4

5

You'll want to buy every book that Dennis ever writes

Sally Dewes in Section #3. Photo by Dennis.

River:	**West Branch of the Oswegatchie***(Belfort)**
Scenery:	Good-very good
Class:	IV-V+
Access:	3-4 miles
Length:	10 miles (the shuttle is twice as long)
Average gradient:	35'/mile (the drops are often 20'or more)
Gauge:	Harrisville at 1000cfs and rising or 1100cfs and falling slowly is minimum; we are going on the working theory that the West Branch takes longer to go up but stays up longer than the Middle Branch. These are low levels. 1600cfs is high.
Water level:	The reading at Harrisville is the combined flow of this run and the Middle Branch run.
Best betting time:	From ice out until early May or big rain events -- this often comes up in the fall, after the leaves have changed over.
Other local runs:	Mid. Branch of the Oswegatchie (IV-VI)**** / Little**(I-III)
Boogie time:	65% -- stop and scout all the horizon lines
Time to do first run:	4+ hours (with slow friends 5+ hours)
First known descent:	?
Raft:	Maybe -- if it's high and you're really good…exciting!!!
Ducky:	Yes
Food and gas:	Crogan or Harrisville
Camping:	State land along Jerden Falls Road
Page in the Gazetteer:	85 and 93
County:	Lewis
Closest river store:	Wear on Earth in Potsdam

Directions: Take-out: from Lowville take Route 812 north and in Indian River take a right onto Jerden Falls Road and drive to the take-out bridge at Jerden Falls. Put-in: drive back to Route 812, head south and take the first left. This is Erie Canal Road. Drive six miles and bear left onto Long Pond Road. Go about five miles and take a left onto Besha Road and go about 7 miles. Shortly after you first see the river on your right you'll come to a fishing access parking area. This is the end of the road and the put-in.

If you want some adventure -- start .5-mile above Round Pond. Drive to the end of Long Pond Road and stop by the gate. You'll be parking in the big parking area next to the large camp/club on the right side. Now carry your boat for .3 miles on the trail and get in by the footbridge. There is: class IV and then a big falls, lots of flat water, a long stretch of class I, a small lake, some class IV-V thing, flat water, a class IV-V big ledge thing, and then a few miles of flatness down to the normal put-in. To do all this and the normal run in one day would be long and contain about 9.5-10 miles of flat water. This section brings the total run to 18-20 miles.

Description/hazards: The run starts off with a little flat water, a washed out dam and the river narrowing down. About 1-mile into the run you come to a great section of ledges, which we boat-scouted down. Shortly comes a big horizon line. This is a 25' falls, which has been successfully done on the left. It is shallow though. What follows are miles of class IV and V. You'll quickly notice that these are big drops and most of them seem to have at least one nasty rock exactly where you won't appreciate it (which is the only reason why this river doesn't get 4 ****'s). About half way down flat water will make an appearance, enjoy the breather. This calm stretch lasts about 4 miles. And believe me you'll want to scout the next 2 drops (a IV+ and a V). Get out at the bridge.

After hearing that our friends Tom and Tony loved this run, we were amazed how many times we'd driven over the take-out bridge and didn't know what we were missing!
The shuttle seemed long and the river flat but, we were kind of, sort of, sure that the end of the road was the put-in so Sally, Derek and I started down the river. At this point we were laughing that it was August and spring creeking season was never going to end. The gleeful mood continued, as I was thoroughly enjoying my new Eskimo Diablo and we were getting better acquainted with each other. We really savored the first stretch of class IV ledges. And we opted to walk the 25' falls that showed up a few minutes later. Tom and Tony had run this drop a few weeks before, but they are bolder and cuter (Dennis speaks only for himself). Actually though, the falls looked fairly shallow and I respect my ankles and didn't want to bang up my new boat. Yeah! That's it, that's why I didn't run the big nasty rapid!
In the next several miles we found many class IV and V rapids. At a small footbridge the river narrowed down to 10' and disappeared down and left. So we scouted, and then...? The next footbridge proved to be even more exciting.
This was a 2-part class V drop/falls (we later found out that the first part is normally not run) -- now they tell me! But I'll let Sally tell the story...I lied, nobody is telling it -- I'm only saying that after boating together for 4 years Sally finally got the chance to bag my sorry as.... and keep me from swimming over a big nasty class V falls. O.K. I lied again -- Sally also threw me a rope in Idaho once.

<u>YOU MUST READ THIS –</u> The first big falls you come to has broken the backs of two people in the last several months; the people that have run it on the left side have been fine, the 2 guys that got hurt ran it more in the center- DO NOT RUN THIS 25' FALLS IN THE CENTER. For some reason (so I've heard) the first party that got hurt decided to keep it a big secrete -- if that is true I can't print what I think of that decision.

Notes

1

2

3

4

5

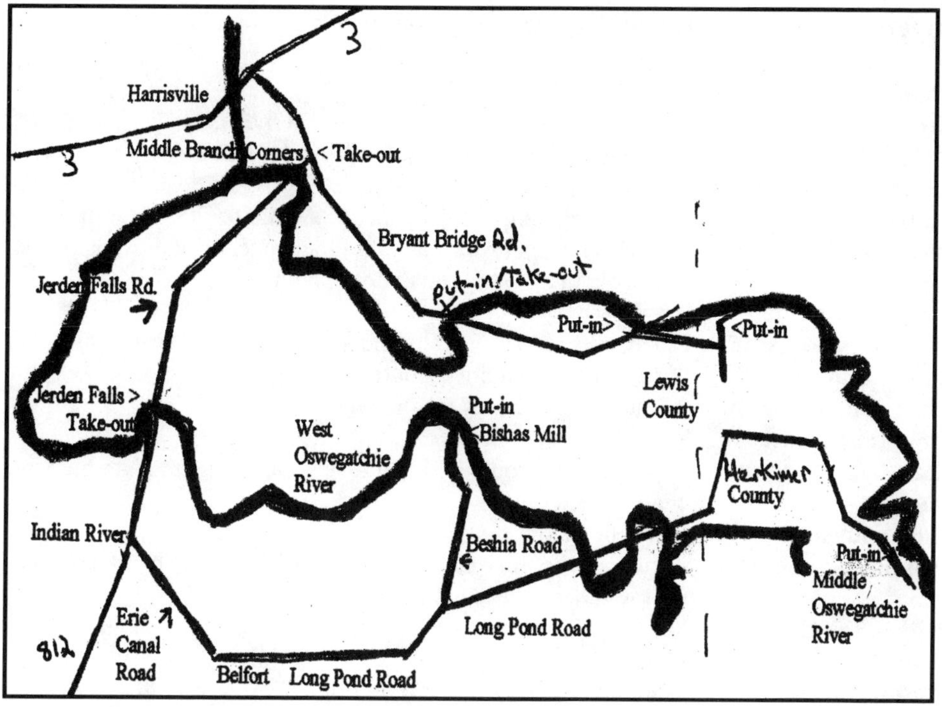
3
Harrisville
Middle Branch Corners
< Take-out
3
Bryant Bridge Rd.
Jerden Falls Rd.
put-in/Take-out
Put-in>
<Put-in
Jerden Falls >
Take-out
Lewis
County
Put-in
<Bishas Mill
West
Oswegatchie
River
Herkimer
County
Indian River
Beshia Road
Put-in
Middle
Oswegatchie
River
Erie
Canal
Road
812
Long Pond Road
Belfort
Long Pond Road

River:	**Otter Creek***(Lowville)**
Scenery:	Very good
Class:	III-IV+
Access:	.25-miles (or over 1 mile if starting at the lake)
Length:	2.5 miles (15 miles if starting below the lake)
Average gradient:	80'/mile
Gauge:	Donattsburg on the Independence should be 300cfs or more
Water level:	This creek rises faster than the Independence and drops quicker, so paddle this first if you're doing both.
Best betting time:	April-early May
Other local runs:	Independence (IV-V)****/Independence / Upper (II-IV)**
Boogie time:	90% -- if you're a boat scouter.
Time to do first run:	2 hours / or 4+ hours for the long run
First known descent:	??
Raft:	Yes -- a 12'er would be fun above 600cfs (bigger if it's higher)
Ducky:	Yes
Food and gas:	Lowville or Boonville
Camping:	At the put-in for the Otter (permit required), or at the put-in for the Independence (state land).
Page in the Gazetteer:	85
County:	Lewis
Closest river store:	Mountain Man in Inlet & Old Forge & White Water Challengers in Old Forge

Directions: The take-out is where the creek crosses under (hopefully) Pine Grove Road. If it looks low (here) but doable -- there's surely enough water upstream. Park about 200' below the bridge at the pull out. For the lower put-in drive south on Pine Grove and turn left on Eatonville Road. In something like 1.6 miles you want to turn left at the Y in the road. You'll cross the river in a minute and ooh and ah at the sight of the first drops. For the upper put-in don't drive up Eatonville Road (it's usually all dirt and mud for miles). You want to stay on Pine Grove (heading south) for a few more minutes and turn left on Brantingham Road. In around 4.5 miles you want to turn left on Partridgeville Road. Take this all the way to the end. Park by that last bridge and walk upstream a couple of minutes so you can do that shallow class IV-ish ledge.

Description/hazards: If you're feeling feisty you can start way up at the end of the road just below Otter Lake. You'll find **easy class II-III and three or four drops in the class IV-IV+ range**. Then you'll come to several miles of flat, but moving, water. The suggested put-in (the lower one) is at the power lines because the 3 or 4 miles (in the long easy stretch) above are blocked by a fair number of logjams as of Nov. 2001.

Starting at the power lines (lower put-in) is just plain fun! The run starts off with multiple drops that are class IV-ish and sure to please. Most of the following drops are fair game for boat scouting. When you arrive at the dam, take-out on the left and check out the tiny, ugly channel on that side (yup, it's been run). After bumping down the shallows watch out for wood. It won't be long until you come up on the hardest drop (IV+) on the lower run. Do safety and watch out for old rebar at the top.

The river's up and I'm stuck in the damn mud in the middle of nowhere. Don't you hate when that happens? Peter and I had just run the Independence for the first time and were stoked to do the Otter. Peter's car was at the bottom and we were driving my car up trying to figure out the put-in (you don't know how much I've suffered for your benefit). The going had been dicey up to that Y intersection on Eatonville Road so I decided to stop and turn around -- guess I should've had more speed. Half of the front tires were soon out of sight -- buried in the mud. I pulled out the shovel and starting flinging mud away at a fast clip. There was a new creek to paddle -- it was still light out and we were going to be out of here in no time! The attempts at driving and shoveling weren't helping -- a certain type of panic over came me. We're going to be out of here in few minutes -- damn it! Wrong. Being far wiser than I, Peter opted to stay out of the way during the height of my frenzy. As true discouragement was setting in two local guys on ATV's show-ed up -- and then ran home and got a come-a-long to pull out the car. The amount of tension on the cable right before the mud suction was dispelled was scary as hell. We didn't have time to paddle.

School of Hard Knocks for the day (pay attention): 1. Don't drive on dirt roads when the frost is going out (mud season) 2. Since you'll probably ignore rule #1 -- bring a shovel and a come-a-long 3. If you've got a rope or a cable under a lot of tension, wear your helmet and lifejacket, stand back and stand at an angle to the battle (a smaller target presents less flesh to be pierced).

Notes

1

2

3

4

5

Buy Dennis a beer

The damn mud is deeper than that creek we just paddled!
The guidebook said not to drive on dirt roads during mud season!

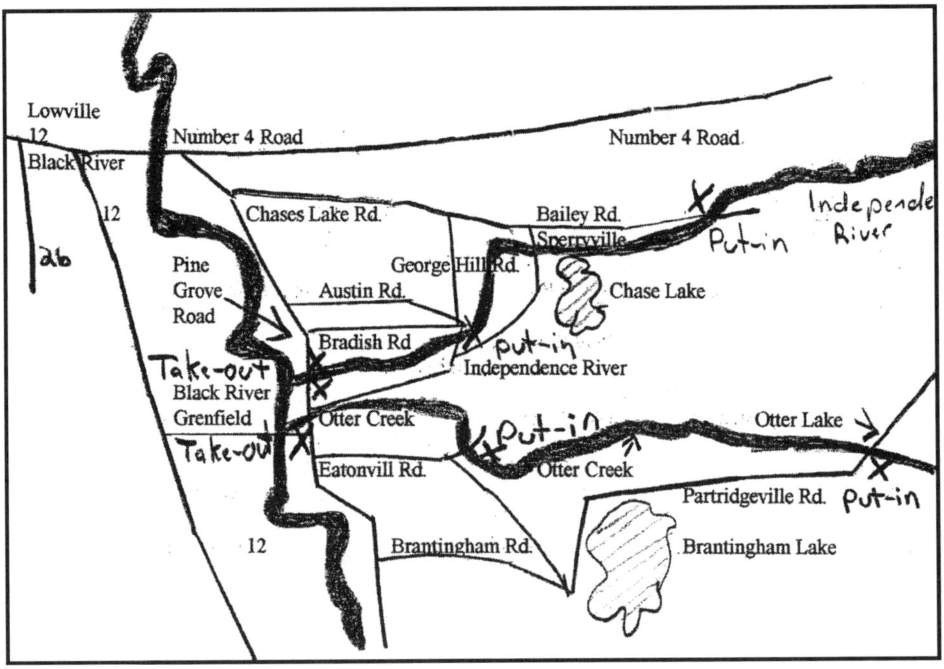
Lowville
12
Black River
Number 4 Road
Number 4 Road
12
26
Chases Lake Rd.
Bailey Rd.
Sperryville
Put-in
Independe
River
Pine Grove Road
George Hill Rd.
Austin Rd.
Chase Lake
Bradish Rd
put-in
Take-out
Independence River
Black River
Grenfield
Otter Creek
Put-in
Otter Lake
Take-out
Eatonvill Rd.
Otter Creek
Partridgeville Rd.
Put-in
12
Brantingham Rd.
Brantingham Lake

River:	**Poultney*(Fair Haven)**
Scenery:	Fair-good
Class:	III-IV
Access:	.4-mile
Length:	4.5 miles
Average gradient:	35'/mile
Gauge:	Granville should be at least 4.0' / When you figure out the Fair Haven gauge on the Poultney let me know.
Water level:	This doesn't run as much as the nearby Mettawee -- but it does run quite a bit
Best betting time:	April-mid May
Other local runs:	Mettawee (IV-V)*** / Poultney/Upper (II-III+)**
Boogie time:	90% -- at least get out and look at the first 2 drops
Time to do first run:	3 hours
First known descent:	?
Raft:	Yes -- Fair Haven should be 500cfs or more
Ducky:	Yes
Food and gas:	Fair Haven or Whitehall
Camping:	East Whitehall Campground
Page in the Gazetteer:	97
County:	Washington
Closest river store:	Sacandaga Outdoor Center & Saratoga Outfitters in Saratoga

Directions: The put-in is at the Route 4 Visitor's Station, right on the N.Y. and Vermont border. To find the take-out, drive back toward N.Y. and take the first right. At the T go right and take the first left on Manchester. Bear right in 1.5 and then turn right again. This takes you up the dead end (Carters Falls) road to the powerhouse and your take-out.

Description/hazards: There is a fun class III+/IV drop right below Route 4. Around the next corner is a big long drop that is way fun to run. It's class IV-ish and something worth running more than once. This is the big drop of the day. There is flat water and occasional class III-III+ ledges. Some of these will have unpleasant holes at high water. Towards the end is a long stretch of flat water. This is a fun, intermediate run.

Extra! For another close by moderate run (II-III+) I'll mention the Upper Poultney in western Vermont. The one time we did this we started about 4 miles east of East Poultney on Route 140 as it goes under a small bridge. There were a couple of small gorges (III+), easy water and a drop above East Poultney (VI) that we took out above. You can find this take-out by turning towards the river in town and crossing the bridge. Granville should be 4.2' or more to do this.

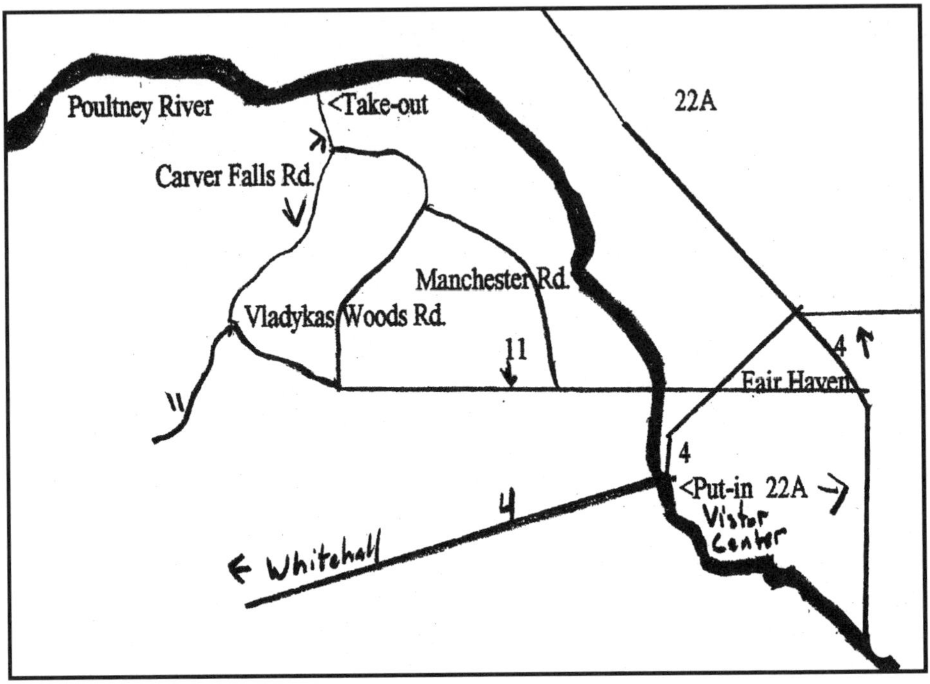

Notes

1

2

3

4

5

Buy wine for Dennis

River:	**Putnam Creek**(Crown Point)**
Scenery:	Good-very good
Class:	IV-V+
Access:	.1-mile
Length:	5.5 miles
Average gradient:	120'/mile
Gauge:	Crown Point -- 240cfs is minimal for the next to the last mile 280cfs is low for the run and 400cfs is high
Water level:	Beware of the next to the last mile (the place where the river is on the north side of the road). This is class V above 350cfs.
Best betting time:	April
Other local runs:	Mill Creek (IV-VI)**in Port Henry / The Branch (IV-V)**** at exit 29
Boogie time:	50% -- scout the many drops from shore first
Time to do first run:	4-5 hours.
First known descent:	Dennis in the early 90's
Raft:	No
Ducky:	Yes
Food and gas:	Ticonderoga and Port Henry
Camping:	Spilt Rock Falls and even closer (but not free) are Putnam Pond and Lincoln Pond.
Page in the Gazetteer:	89
County:	Essex
Closest river store:	Sacandaga Outdoor Center & Saratoga Outfitter in Saratoga

Directions: Put-in at the Penfield Pond in Ironville, just ask the people at the house at the historic site. They're accommodating, if uninterested. For the take-out drive down the road about 2 miles and bare left, this follows the river. Notice the posted signs. I have been given a hard time (by a grumpy landowner) at the third bridge. Stop and look at this section where the road starts to go down steeply. Look for the wood (it will come up on you fast at river level). As the road T's at Factoryville take a right and cross the bridge; this pull-off is the take-out. Remember this bridge. You can drive up this road (on the other side of the river), back to the top. After going only about 150 yards look to your right -- this is the falls where I blew my ankles.

Description/hazards: Running the little dam at the beginning is a great way to start off the day. Then look out for the drops above the next bridge, which come up fast. These drops are class IV-V and are woody. The falls below the first bridge has been run at low water, and yes -- it is nasty. The next couple of miles down to the next bridge are mostly class II-III. This next bridge rapid is class IV-V and full of wood. Get used to it. Scout when in doubt -- there is a lot of wood in the last few miles. You'll know when you hit the hard part because it builds up quickly and then gets even harder and steeper. I hope you scouted this out on the drive. This section is sheer terror or joy depending on the level, wood placement and your perverted senses.

Below the next bridge we often walk the double ledge on the left (it's shallow). Dodge the wood and holes. Scout the next steep ledge. The left is a walk. The right is runnable if the trees ever move out of there. The next biggie is a 20' falls. If you run this, go over the right half and don't pencil straight down in. Enjoy the last .2-mile, and get out before the 30' falls at the next bridge (it is only about 4'deep).

Extra! If you want to see something awesome go look at the water screaming down the La Chute -- it's right in Ticonderoga.

Tony and I drove by Putnam Creek on the way to the Vermont creeks. There wasn't any water in Vermont, so we came back for a closer look at Putnam. We found a low but reasonable level. Running the first several rapids and dodging sticks was fun. And even more fun when we got to be the first to run the Black Hole Falls (which is 400 yards below the put-in). With much water it could prove to be more than one may want to chew on.

The run had gone smoothly and the kids (we) were having a great time. The last falls had seemed easy enough when I ran it the year before. This time there was this little nub that pushed me left -- stole my speed and allowed the boat to pencil down. Three feet of water isn't nearly enough to slow a boat falling 20', before it slams into the basement floor. Upside down in the hydraulic at the bottom of the falls my brain screams, "You're hurt -- maybe broken -- where's Tony? Is he gonna' land on my sorry head?" Fortunately he knows enough to wait 30 seconds and hits the line, not the nub. I pull my boat up on shore and do a <u>body survey</u>. Both ankles are sprained, perhaps worse. I get in the boat and paddle to the take-out, which is thankfully near at hand. After getting home, both ankles swell and stop working totally for a few days. I had to drive (my standard) with a stick (again) for a while.

Lesson: Kayaker (in lbs.) + boat (in lbs.) x distance (in feet) x water (depth in inches) cubed and then subtract those (impossible to quantify) nubs ='s the total damage done to lower body extremities (multiple this number by two if you don't have a foam bulkhead).

<u>Secret of the day:</u>

I have found that with extra foam in front of the foam bulkhead (against your feet) gives more strength to the deck and absorbs even more shock (just in case you might ever impact a rock from any significant height). I do realize how foolish this statement is -- because that could never happen to you. Yeah right!

Notes

1

2

3

4

5

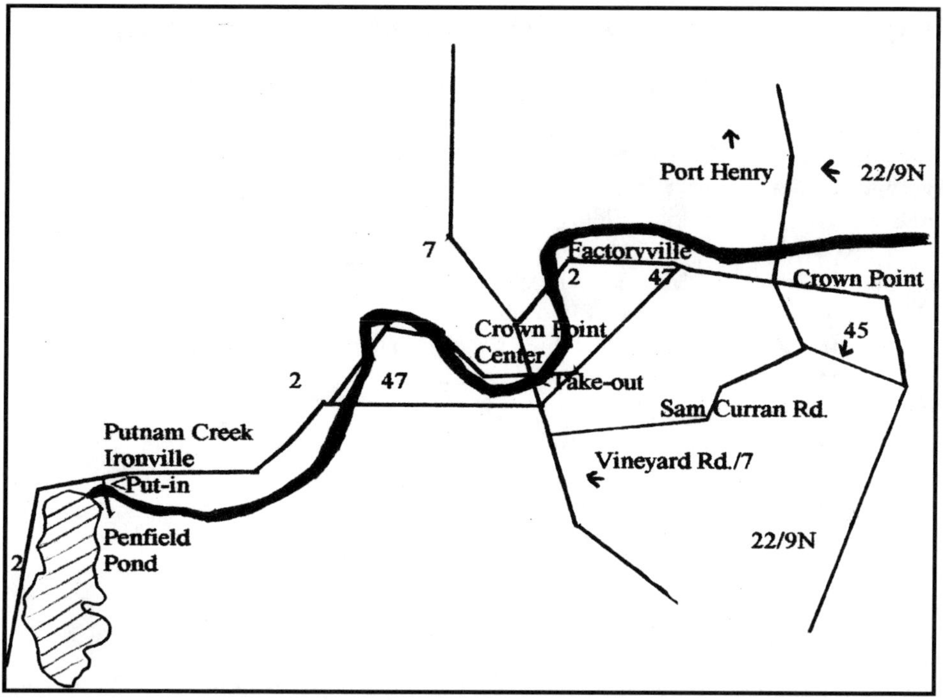

Is it a: bird, plane, fish or…no it's Tom Vickery. Photo by Julie Vickery.

River:	**Raquette**(Piercefield)**
Scenery:	Very good
Class:	Flat-V+
Access:	3-miles
Length:	16 miles
Average gradient:	18'/mile
Gauge:	Piercefield
Water levels:	6.0’ is low and above 8.5’ is high
Best betting time:	May-early June
Other local runs:	Bog (II-V)* / Grass/ Upper (I-III, V)**
Boogie time:	95% -- the three big drops all come towards the end
Time to do first run:	One very long day or a nice overnighter
First known descent:	?
Raft:	You betcha’ (yep) -- above 6.0’
Ducky:	Yes
Food and gas:	Tupper Lake
Camping:	On state land by the take-out
Page in the gazetteer:	94 / 95
County:	Franklin / St. Lawrence
Closest river store:	Wear on Earth in Potsdam

Directions: The put-in is right below the Piercefield Dam on Route 3. The take-out is about 13 miles downstream at the state site for Jamestown Falls. The sign is small (yellow-on-brown) -- look closely. If you turn off and see concrete road and campers you went downstream too far -- go back upstream and find the dirt road.

Description/hazards: This is a great late spring -- early summer run. This is just the ticket for a raft (over 7') trip / overnighter with friends. You'll find a remote and beautiful run (some of my friends pick on me for saying the word beautiful). Starting below the dam at Piercefield you'll have a long stretch of easy rapids that are fun and bouncy. Then some flat water until the island -- you want to go left. And scouting would be good -- since this is a class IV drop. Lots of flat water follows. Then a nice long stretch of waves (II-III) -- this is Moosehead Rapids. The next drop is the biggest so far--Moody Falls (IV-V) -- the line depends on the level. When you get to Upper Jamestown (IV+/V) you'll be impressed -- the hole is a nightmare at most levels. Lower Jamestown follows quickly (V-V+) and will likely be a walk -- or the beginning of a good story. The take-out is about 250 yards down on the left side.

Notes

1

2

3

4

5

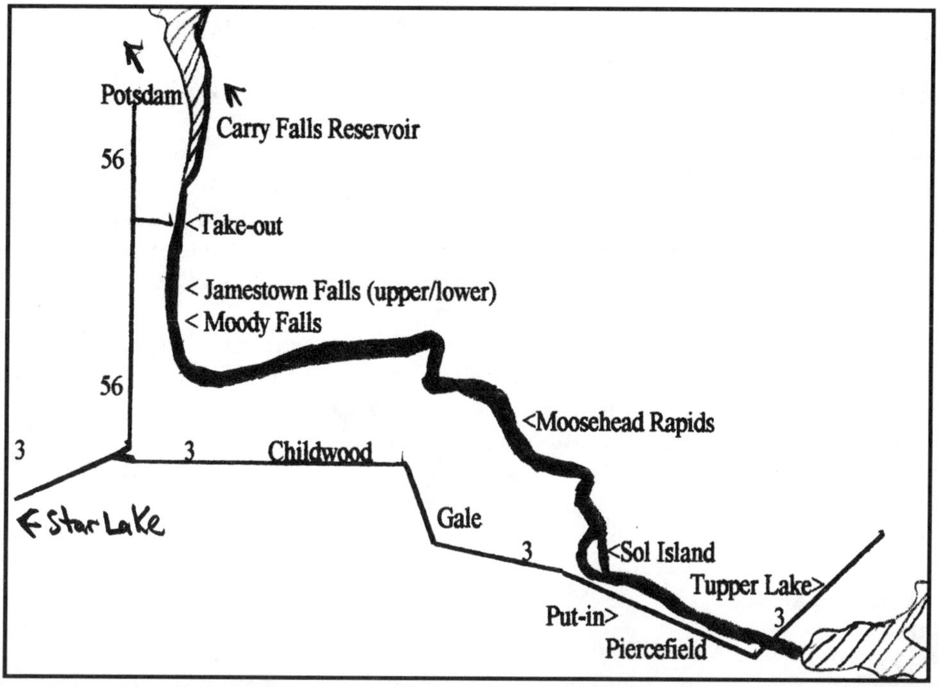

Upper Jamestown Falls. Photo by Sally Dewes.

River:	**Raquette River/Stone Valley****(Colton)**
Scenery:	Good-very good
Class:	IV+/V+ (IV-IV+ if you're doing a low water run)
Access:	1-mile
Length:	1 or 4.5 miles
Average gradient:	First mile is 200'/mile -- the next 3.5 miles drop another 40'
Gauge:	If Parisville is running 400 cfs this should be up. Unfortunately, the Colton gauge is below the good stuff so it doesn't tell you much (since the power company takes out so much water). Check out **www.h2oline.com**
Water level:	Fortunately this can be run at a wide range. It runs all spring since we get to paddle the leftovers and the huge watershed upstream takes a long time to drain down.
Best betting time:	May-June (too high in April)
Other local runs:	W. St.Regis/ Parishville (III-IV)***/ St Regis/ act II (II-II+)**
Boogie time:	40% -- you'll be scouting a lot the first time
Time to do first run:	2+ hours for the first mile (with a walk back up a trail on either side) and 3+ hours for the whole run
First known descent:	??
Raft:	No
Ducky:	Yes
Food and gas:	Colton or Potsdam
Camping:	Stowe Bay Park in Colton
Page in the Gazetteer:	100
County:	St. Lawrence
Closest river store:	Wear on Earth in Potsdam

Directions: The Put-in is right in Colton, on river right. Just drive across the bridge above the dam and park in the little parking area and walk 200'. If the sight of this first long rapid terrifies you, turn around and get in your car and leave -- it doesn't get much better (or worse -- depending on your perspective and what you're looking for). If you're doing the short run (which is what I'd suggest if you're doing a low water bone run), just walk back up the trail (on either side of the river) after the last juicy drop and take-out here. If you've got at least 300-400cfs just take-out at Brown's Bridge. To get there drive north on Route 56 about 4 miles and hang a right on Route 24; you'll cross the river in a minute and find the take-out.

Description/hazards: This seems to have a fish level flow, which is just barely enough water to run this **all summer long.** It might be 75 cfs -- maybe. But it's fun if you're in the neighborhood. The rapid at the put-in may be the longest, hardest rapid you've ever started off the day with -- enjoy! At medium (and above) levels the hole that's located on river left, 500' downstream of the put-in, is just plan horrible. If you've got water, scout everything on this run. If you are doing a bone run enjoy the chutes and explore the options. A few hundred yards below the end of the first beast is a river wide ledge, beware the piton-angle left. Go left at the island drop. Beware of the undercut most of the way down the left channel. Just scout everything. If you're boating this without somebody who knows it and it's high you should really take your time. When you get to the second island, which is like big drop #6 (not much more than 1 mile down the river), go right if it's low. And go left if there's much water. Scout this well. At low water the approach is long and rocky and gets tight and nasty. The locals call this 50-50. That's because those are your odds of not getting slammed off the left wall at the bottom. This is the last hard drop. You can walk back up the trail or boat the 3 miles or so of easy stuff down to the next bridge.

Notes

1

2

3

4

5

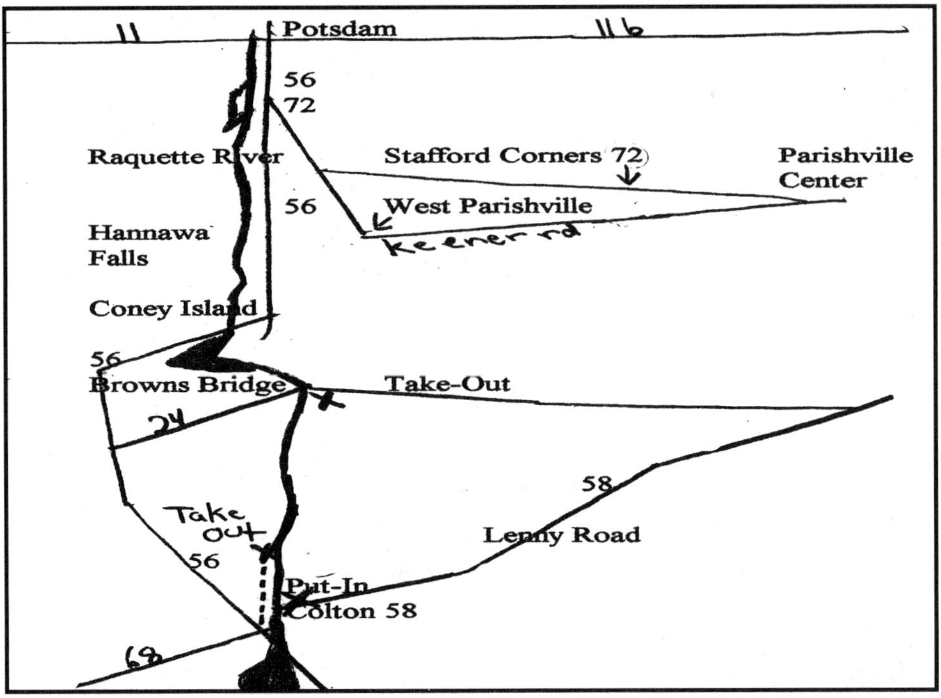
Potsdam
56
72
Raquette River
Stafford Corners 72
Parishville Center
56
West Parishville
Keener rd
Hannawa Falls
Coney Island
56
Browns Bridge
Take-Out
58
Take out
Lenny Road
56
Put-In
Colton 58

River:	**Roaring Branch*(Lowville)**
Scenery:	Good-very good
Class:	IV+/VI
Access:	The falls in the state park have sheer walls
Length:	2-6 miles
Average gradient:	The last mile drops 300'
Gauge:	Donnatsburg will probably be 500cfs or more if this is running
Water level:	You want enough water to pad the shallow ledges but not so much that the holes get bad.
Best betting time:	Late March-early May (when that 300+ inches of snow is melting off of the Tug Hill Plateau).
Other local runs:	Independence (IV-V)*****/ Otter (III-IV+)***/ Moose / Middle (II-III-IV-)***
Boogie time:	50% -- you have to scout every horizon line!
Time to do first run:	3+ hours
Raft:	Never
Ducky:	Yes -- especially since the drops all have shallow landings
First known descent:	Dennis in the early 90's
Food and gas:	Lowville or Boonville
Camping:	At the put-in, of either Otter Creek or the Independence
Page in the Gazetteer:	84/85
County:	Lewis
Closest river store:	White Water Challengers in Old Forge & Mountain Man in Old Forge & Inlet.

Directions: The put-in I used was in Martinsburg, and the take-out was below the last drops at the Route 12 Bridge.

Description/hazards: There is a beautiful and very tight mini-gorge in Martinsburg that could be run at the right water level. Below the gorge it's rather easy going until the 80'+ falls in the park. How can you tell it's coming? I only have got a clue, there is a steep drop and you go under a bridge just as you enter the park (so the falls are drawing near). All I can say is don't go over it. The portage is on the right side (yes I know it's steep isn't it?) Rumor has it that someone did run the beast. The next few drops (30'+ and 20'+) may well be runnable; I was too dizzy (chasing my boat) to notice. The last stretch has multiple drops which all land shallow but are runnable.

The map had shown Wittaker Falls, where was it? I had started right below an incredibly tight mini-gorge. Then the going was pretty easy for miles. As I paddled on there was something noticeable happening. There were no real rocks in the river -- but it was moving quickly. Nervousness isn't usually a factor, but that day -- it was growing. The river bottom and the banks were all solid rock -- the same piece of rock. I ran a big ledge drop (just before a bridge) without scouting that got me really

cranked up. After that the little voice that sometimes speaks to me was screaming louder than it ever had, "Get out -- NOW!" It was tough crawling up the rock/bank. Around the corner was a sight never to be forgotten. The falls are 80' high. I had caught the very last eddy (well, sort of an eddy).

It took awhile to portage on the right side. But then caution now seemed to be wise. After all, this was a first -- who knew what other surprises lay below? As soon as I got back in the water the next surprise was apparent. Ferrying over to the other side, I climbed out to look at a 30' falls. I thought it was too big to run alone. And only sheer walls on the sides. I guessed I could climb down there after dropping my boat into the big eddy (after all it's practically totally cut off from the downstream flow -- what could happen?). The boat splashes down and seemingly possessed flings itself through the small channel and into the river. The current pulls it out of my sight.

My boat has disappeared around the corner and gone over another big horizon line. It's an hour and a half before dark. What should I do? Save my boat and paddle the rest of the river -- that's what.

It took awhile but I managed to climb down the 30' drop and the 25' one that followed. The river bottom was deep within sheer walls that were darkening as the day was ending. Not surprisingly the boat was going around in circles in the eddy -- on the other side of the river. So I jumped in and swam across. After wrestling the boat to shore, it was obvious that it had landed hard on its stern. Even though it was an impressive dent, it hadn't cracked.

As it started to get dark I came staggering up the bank at the take-out. I had run some of the last drops and walked some. The last stretch had held some good multiple drops -- all landing on shallow rock. I'd suggest using somebody else's boat for this run -- and a parachute.

Notes
1
2
3
4
5

Smell the roses

What's that noise?
Damn the suction from that hole almost sucked me out of the sky

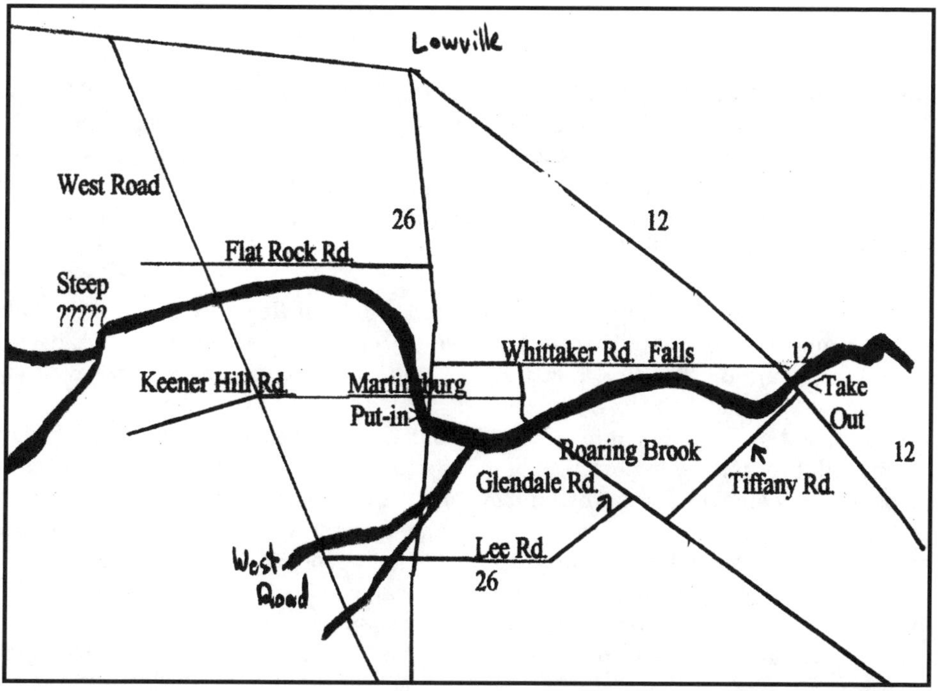
Lowville
West Road
26
12
Flat Rock Rd.
Steep
?????
Whittaker Rd. Falls
12
Keener Hill Rd.
Martinsburg
Put-in>
<Take
Out
Roaring Brook
12
Glendale Rd.
Tiffany Rd.
Lee Rd.
26
West
Road

River:	**Round Lake Outlet***(Tupper Lake)**
Scenery:	Very good
Class:	Flat or IV-V
Access:	1 -2 miles
Length:	8.5 miles
Average gradient:	40'/mile (some sections are 150'/mile)
Gauge:	If the Hudson is 4.5' or more this will probably be running
Water level:	This run has two very large lakes that it's draining. So realize that it takes a while to peak -- but then it stays up for several days. Paddle this right after other stuff has dropped.
Best betting time:	April-late May
Other local runs:	Bog (I-V)**/Grasse / Twin Falls (IV-V+)*****
Boogie time:	80% -- there's several things to get out and ponder
Time to do first run:	3+ hours
First known descent:	?
Raft:	Maybe at high levels, but there's the flat water and wind…..
Ducky:	Yes -- fun at low water
Food and gas:	Tupper Lake
Camping:	State Land by the Bog/Round Lake take-out
Page in the Gazetteer:	94/95
County:	Hamilton/St. Lawrence
Closest river store:	Adirondack Lakes and Trails in Saranac Lake

Directions: Drive up Circle Road towards Whitney Headquarters. As you drive over a small bridge that divides two bodies of water you're crossing the put-in. As of 2002 there's no legal place to park here -- so drive up the road a little ways and park at Whitney Headquarters. To get to the out-take (I'm tired of typing it the right way) drive north on Circle Road until you hit Route 30 -- go north on Route 30 until you see Route 421 on your left. After you turn up this you'll quickly be crossing over the Bog -- park right there by the bridge. There are picnic spots just around the next corner (I know -- it's where the black flies picnicked on me in mid-May).

Description/hazards: The only real way to check the level (if you're afraid it might be too low) is to park about .3-mile south (on Route 30) of the Horseshoe Lake turn off and run in over a mile on the very faint trail and eyeball the level. Do you see why that Gazetteer comes in handy?

The first 4 miles of this little treat is all flat water (the last few miles across the lake the wind will probably be in your face or a crosswind). At the end of the lake things start to happen pretty quickly. It's narrow in there and there are several shallow ledge drops in the class IV range. Just when it looks like things are getting easy you'll run into some more drops. Keep in mind that some of this needs to be scouted. The biggest drop is class IV+ even at low levels. At high levels it's hard class V. This rapid is awesome and way cool (you'll see). All too soon the rapids go away completely and you're wondering if that's it. It's not. There's more goodness and then it eases as you paddle into the Bog River. Nothing much happens for a bit, but then you'll see a horizon line and the approach to Bog River Falls. The falls is class IV-IV+ and makes a spectacular sight as it drops 25' into the big (Tupper) lake (framed nicely under the bridge on Route 421).

As of the spring of 2002 the Nature Conservancy has bought a lot of land around this run. The state is supposedly going to buy it from them. The camp owners in the area aren't happy, they have to move out. Like many of the recent land acquisitions by the state, the previous landowners had long-term leases with hunting clubs and camp owners that will be staying there until their leases are up. Some of them aren't happy with having to go. Always be patient and pleasant with the locals (remember most of them have guns).

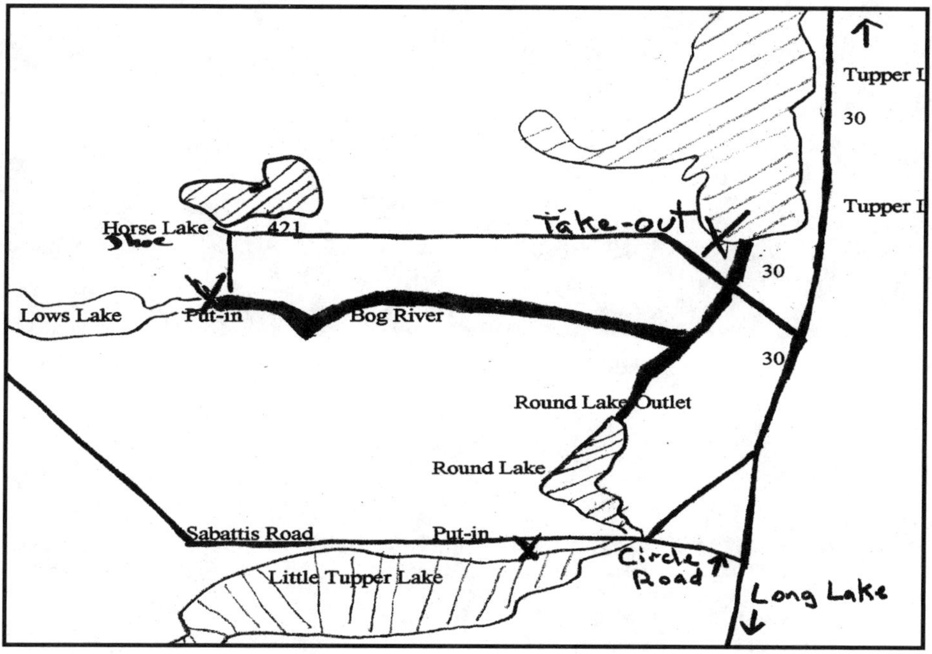

Notes

1
2
3
4
5

Sally Dewes shows off her paddle on Round Lake Outlet (low water). Photo by Dennis.

River:	**Saint Regis/Parishville***(Parishville)**
Class:	III-IV, VI
Access:	.7-mile
Length:	6.7 miles
Average gradient:	40'/mile
Gauge:	Parishville at 600cfs is a fine level & 1000-1200cfs has some good play
Water Level:	This is often runnable at a low level (400cfs)
Best betting time:	April-May
Other local runs:	Deer (IV-V)**** / Deer/Lower (I-III)**
Boogie time:	90-100% -- after Sylvan Falls that is
Time to do first run:	3 hours
First known descent:	?
Raft:	Yes -- if it's 800cfs or more
Ducky:	Yes
Food and gas:	Parishville
Camping:	Higley Flow State Campground in South Colton
Page in the Gazetteer:	100
County:	St. Lawrence
Closest river store:	Wear on Earth in Potsdam

Directions: If you are heading east on Rt. 72 you'll cross a bridge in the middle of Parishville. The next right turn is Slyvan Falls Road -- take it. Immediately on your right side is the parking for the take-out (see the water). Park out of the way -- nothing pisses off the locals like parking in front of the firehouse door. If you drive up Slyvan Fall Road around 8 miles you'll find a big ugly sign. Turn around and go back to your second house on your (now) left side. Go find the nice people. And if you've ever thought about going to New Zealand ask them about their winter there; you'll then know that you have got to go there yourself!

Description/hazards: Slyvan Falls is a Twin Falls and both are awesome. As of this writing a caretaker won't let you start there. Just stop at the last permanent house on your right before the big bad sign scares you away. These people have been gracious the two times I've stopped by and wanted to get in behind their house. They own goats and a natural soap factory and..... oh yeah...you want the description to the river...that's right...O.K. If you walk down the hill behind their house you'll find a wide path takes you straight to the water in seven or eight minutes. The first rapid is long and easy. In fact there isn't anything more than class III until you see a horizon line. This is IV-ish and would have some ugly hole action at high water. Both times I was here I scouted from the bridge downstream before the run. It's not that close to the drop, but then someone you don't want to encounter owns this land, and after all, you're walking around in, HER woods. Can you tell there's been trouble here before? As you come down under the bridge you'll be in the thick of the best part of the river. There are **waves and holes all over the place -- hope you brought your play boat**. The next drop is class IV and deserves a scout. After that I remember the scenery and some class III-III+ stuff. At the end is 15 minutes of flat water. The take-out is at the sandy public beach (a great picnic spot, just off the Slyvan Falls Road) on the right or 5 minutes farther downstream, in town, behind the firehouse.

Extra: I haven't looked at it myself, but my buddy Tom scoped out Allan Falls. This section is just below Parishville. Below the impoundment and dam in town is another impoundment and then the Allan Falls section. It hasn't been run yet; it's very short and very nasty. The way I hear it -- it takes less than 100cfs to make this look runnable. I'll warn you though, the way Tom described it -- it sounded pretty…dicey.

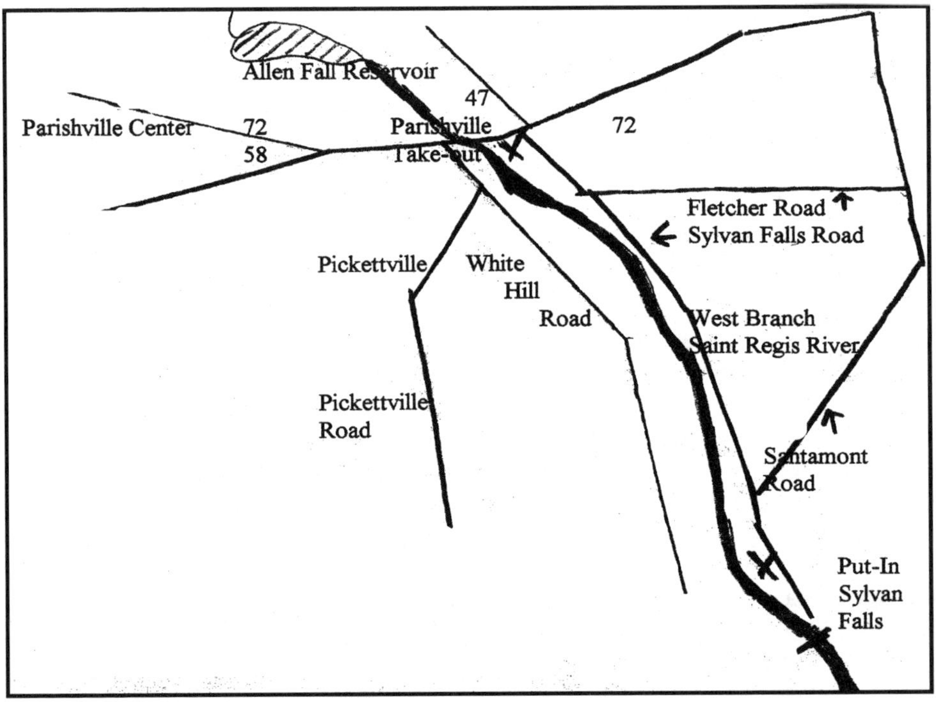

Notes

1

2

3

4

5

River:	**Saint Regis/Silver Staircase**(St. Regis Falls)**
Scenery:	Good
Class:	III-IV
Access:	.9-mile
Length:	6 or 10 miles
Average gradient:	45'/mile
Gauge:	Parishville at 450 cfs is minimal / 800-1200cfs is ideal
Water level:	Waves in the run just keep getting bigger as the level goes up
Best betting time:	Late March-early May
Other local runs:	Deer /Lower (I-III)** / Lake Ozonia (IV-V)***
Boogie time:	100% (yes -- that's right 100%)
Time to do first run:	3-4 hours
First known descent:	?
Raft:	Yes -- above 800cfs
Ducky:	Yes
Food and gas:	St Regis Falls
Camping:	At the put-in there's a campground
Page in the Gazetteer:	100/101
County:	Franklin/St.Lawrence
Closest river store:	Wear on Earth in Potsdam

Directions: The put-in is right below St. Regis Falls. Just as you drive east into the town of St. Regis Falls (on Route 458) you'll cross the river and take the first left. This takes you down to the campground and the put-in. There is a nice covered pavilion to eat under if the weather is great for boating, but not so great for enjoying your supper. The falls themselves (class V) have been run. Yes -- the holes are nasty if the water's up. To get to the take-out drive west on Route 458. Be sure to gawk at the rapid above the bridge as you cross over Lake Ozonia Outlet (as if you could help it!). That run is short and fun -- if you are up to it. A little over a mile after you cross into St. Lawrence County is a right hand turn, take it. The first take-out bridge is just a minute away. For the lower take-out -- stay on Route 458 until it T's with Route 11B and turn right. The take-out bridge will be right there.

Description/hazards: The falls (class V) at the put-in have been run. You'll probably want to start at the base of them. This is a big wide river -- the rapids are pretty constant for the first half of the trip. Just below the put-in there's a ledge with a hole behind it that bears watching. Then you get to enjoy miles (class III-IV) of rapids (they'll be big if the gauge is over 1000cfs). The one time I ran this it reminded me of running the Hudson Gorge at a good level (6 feet), just without the drops thrown in. As you get down this section the intensity gradually diminishes. Notice Lake Ozonia Outlet coming in on your left. If you want to tackle something harder try that -- or the Deer River. The first bridge you get to, which is about 6 miles down, is a good place to hop out if you just want to do the harder rapids on this river (or you're in a hurry to get on Lake Ozonia). The rapids here will ease up to class II by the lower take-out.

Act ll

From the lower take-out in Nicholville all the way down to Buckton, which is about 12 miles, the river averages 40'/mile. From what I've seen this should be class I-II. It ought to make a nice canoe trip.

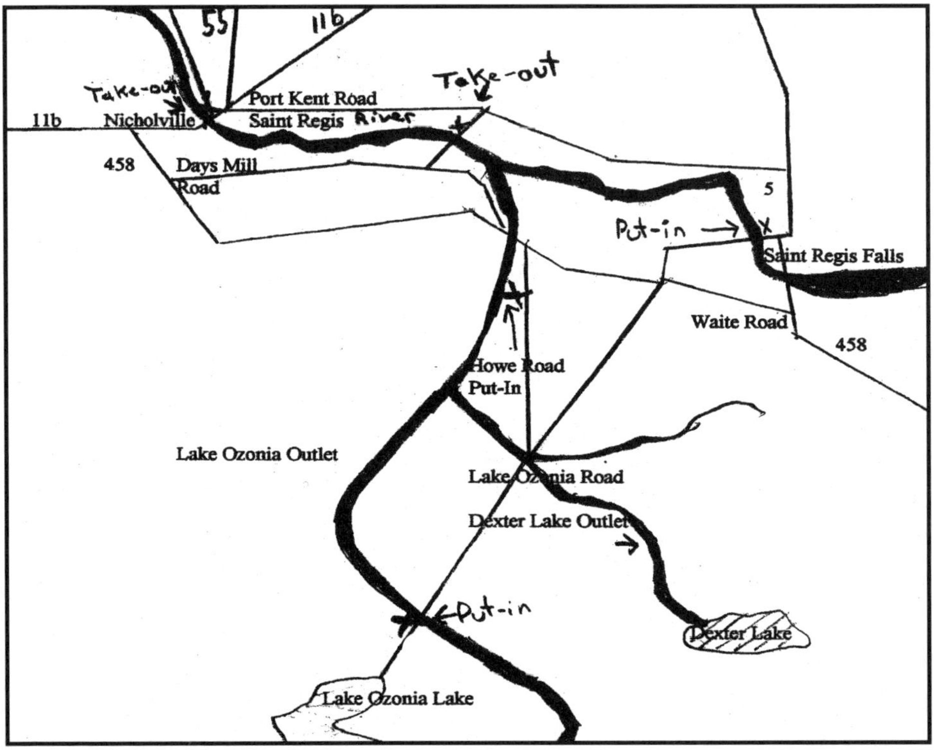

Notes

1

2

3

4

5

Join AW

River:	**Salmon***(Malone)**
Scenery:	Good
Class:	I-III, IV
Access:	.25-mile
Length:	5 or 7 miles
Average gradient:	45'/mile
Gauge:	Parishville should be at least 400cfs
Water levels:	This river has a big drainage which includes a lot of marshy areas and several good sized ponds and lakes -- like the St. Regis it takes a day to come up and then it stays up.
Best betting time:	April-late May
Other local runs:	Little Trout (II, IV)** / Deer (IV-V)****
Boogie time:	97%
Time to do first run:	3 hours
First known descent:	?
Raft:	Yes -- over 600cfs
Ducky:	Yes
Food and gas:	Malone
Camping:	There is state land to the south off of Route 27/Pond Road
Page in the Gazetteer:	101
County:	Franklin
Closest river store:	Wear on Earth in Potsdam

Directions: You can get in at the picnic site, which is on Route 25, at the end of the awesome Chasm Falls rapids. To get to the take-out, drive north on Route 25 and take a right at the 4-way in Whippleville. The take-out is at the bridge. To get to the lower take-out, keep driving north after you cross the bridge. You can take-out along the road where it looks easiest.

Description: You'll start off paddling class II for a bit, (just make sure you get in below the powerhouse.) It will calm down and then go back to class II as you see the second bridge. For a mile the river is wide and straightforward. When you spot some big boulders on the left get out and look at the next drop. It's big. As I recall it drops 30-40', I don't remember if it's runnable (V?). Portage on the left side. The next 400' is made up of class II+/III ledges and boulders. Lots of class II is next on the menu, down to the next bridge. From that bridge to the next is class I. Shortly below that one the river goes back to class II and then jumps to class III- as you come into Whippleville. If you keep going towards Malone you'll have class II rapids to enjoy. Get out before town so you don't have to deal with the dams in town.

Big Extra! Chasm Falls hasn't been run -- it's class V+/VI and has the most continuous series of non-stop drops you could possibly imagine. Here Willy! Here Willy!

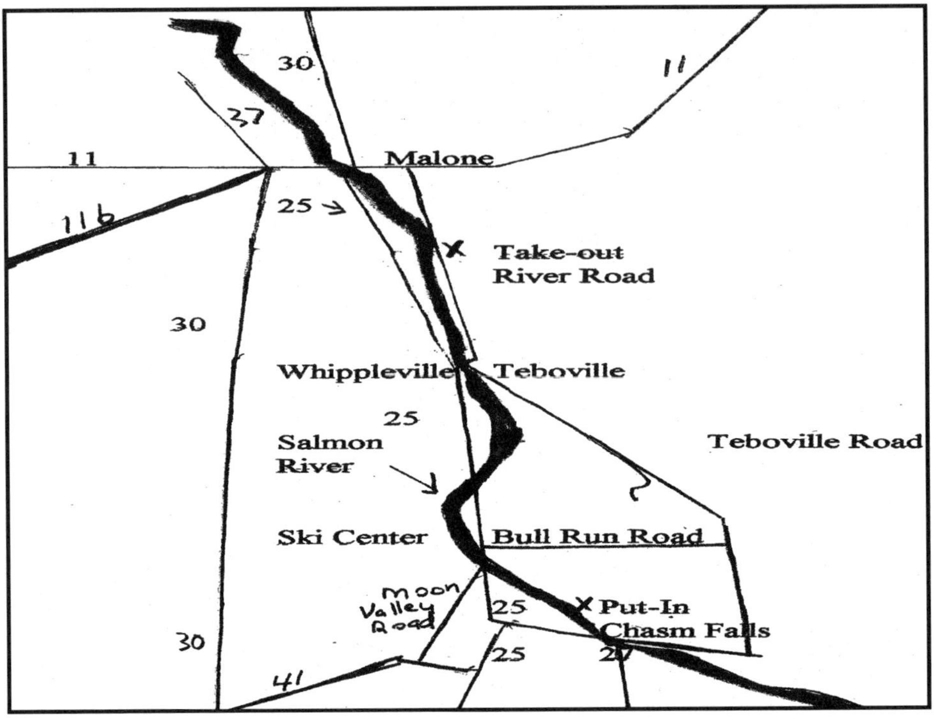
30
11
37
11
Malone
116
25
Take-out
River Road
30
Whippleville
Teboville
25
Salmon
River
Teboville Road
Ski Center
Bull Run Road
Moon
Valley
Road
25
Put-In
Chasm Falls
30
25
27
41

Notes

1

2

3

4

5

River:	**Salmon***(Pulaski)**
Scenery:	Good
Class:	I-III
Access:	.5-mile
Length:	10 miles
Average gradient:	25'/mile
Gauge:	Call Ni-Mo for release levels (315-298-6531)
Water levels:	You want to have at least 600cfs releasing
Best betting time:	March-April and releases -- check with the AW journal
Other local runs:	Fish (III-III+)***** / South Sandy (III-V)***
Boogie time:	100%
Time to do first run:	2 + hours
First known descent:	?
Raft:	If it's at least 900cfs
Ducky:	Yes
Food and gas:	Pulaski
Camping:	Campground in Pineview or the Redwood Motel
Page in the Gazetteer:	83
County:	Oswego
Closest river store:	Northern Outfitters in Syracuse & Utica

Directions: The upper put-in is by the bridge in Altmar -- this section is class I. If you drive west on Route 13 for about 2.6 miles you'll come to Pineveiw; this is the lower put-in. If you keep driving west on 13 you'll pass the 2A Bridge. This is also a possible put-in if you want a short trip and the best of the rapids. From here drive down 13 and take a right (north) on route 11, into Pulaski. In town you want to head west on Lake St., and just a little ways down you'll find a parking area on the left. Close by is the treatment plant take-out. For the lowest take-out and the longest trip drive west on Lake St. or Route 13 (on the other side of the river) and take a left on Route 3. You'll quickly see a sign for Selkirk Shores Park on your right -- head that a way. There is a pull-off a little ways down this road--take it, it's the take-out.

Description: There is some nice playing just before the bridge in Pulaski and again shortly after that at **a great play hole called Titanic**. O.K. -- those are the highlights!

Actually what you'll find is class I and II for a few miles if you start up at the upper put-in. From the lower put-in you start off with class II. The first corner above Pulaski is where the river changes to class III and **good play spots appear**. The holes are fun and bouncy. As you come around the corner and see the bridge you'll find some good playing. As I recall (it's been about 10 years) this stuff needs to be played on the way down. There are only a few eddies. If you learn how to do sharp ferries and catch eddies you get to play more! Below town is a really fun hole called Titanic. Hang out for a while. The take-out is down on the right side. If you paddle down to the lower take-out all I remember is easy water and a surprise drop that was much easier than it first looked from upstream.

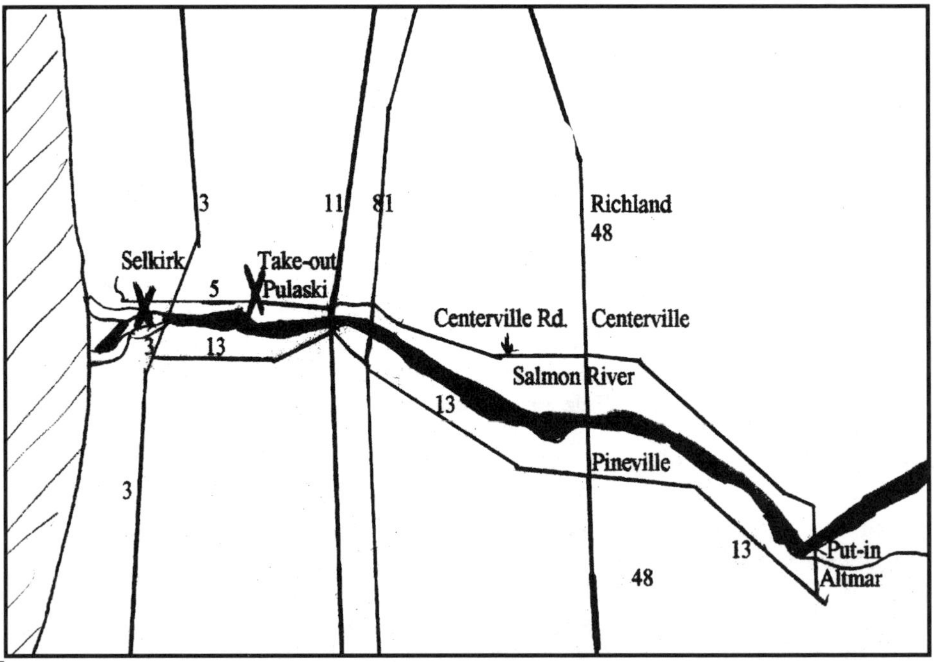
3
11
81
Richland
48
Selkirk
Take-out
Pulaski
5
Centerville Rd.
Centerville
3
13
Salmon River
13
Pineville
3
13
Put-in
Altmar
48

Notes
1
2
3
4
5

Hug your kitty

River:	**Salmon*(Schuyler Falls)**
Scenery:	Good
Class:	III-V?
Access:	.4-mile (over 1 mile if you run all the way through to I-87)
Length:	2 miles or more
Average gradient:	The steepest 2 miles drop 125'/mile (and 160'/mile at I-87)
Gauge:	You're going to need 1800cfs or more on the Ausable gauge
Water levels:	There are big ledges -- watch out for holes at high water
Best betting time:	April
Other local runs:	Ausable Chasm (IV-V)**** / Saranac (II-IV)**
Boogie time:	Who knows?
Time to do first run:	3-4 hours
First known descent:	**UNRUN?**
Raft:	No
Ducky:	Yes
Food and gas:	Plattsburg
Camping:	Campgrounds north of Keesville
Page in the Gazetteer:	103
County:	Clinton
Closest river store:	Adirondack Lakes and Trails in Saranac Lake

Directions: Put-in along Norrisville Road a few miles above Schuyler Falls. To do the steepest and shortest section, drive into town and take a right (head east) on 22B. Turn left at your first chance and use the bridge you'll cross as the take-out. The river drops 50' down to the next bridge and very little in the next 3 miles. There's a short section just off the River Road down by I-87 that drops 80' in .5 mile; you might want to give it a look.

Description/hazards: This run has a lot of wood in it! There are some ledges on this stretch. It looks to be class III if you start at the Conners Bridge. You could start up at the dam at the little park if you want to start real easy. As you approach the bridge in town (you probably just walked around some wood -- and you better get/stay ready to do it again) you'll find yourself on **a 300 yards long (IV) ledge** (yahoo!). There is a lot of flat water until you get down by I-87, where you'll find another huge ledge. That's all I can really tell you. There's got to be some more drops than I've seen and lord knows about the strainer situation. If you are a solid class IV boater and feel adventurous -- check this out, carefully.

I'd been driving over this river for years when I was way up north boating. It seemed like I was always zooming south when I noticed the water cranking down this big steep ledge just to the west of I-87. I had wanted to check it out for a long time. Inspired by the upcoming printing date of this book I just had to check this out for myself in March of 2002.

What I found was a creek with a fair amount of wood in it, especially above town. The 300 yard long ledge under the bridge in town looks to be big fun. The drop down by I-87 also looks to be a good one. I won't be able to tell you more until I paddle it.

Scouting can be almost as much fun as paddling -- if you like exploring. During the summer when there is no water in the creeks is a great time to get some exercise and look at a run for the first time. Just hike upstream while jumping from rock to rock. This also gives you a good river level look at the gradient and the hazards you'll find. Its how I scouted out Johns Brook the summer before running it.

Notes
1
2
3
4
5

Give Dennis gas money

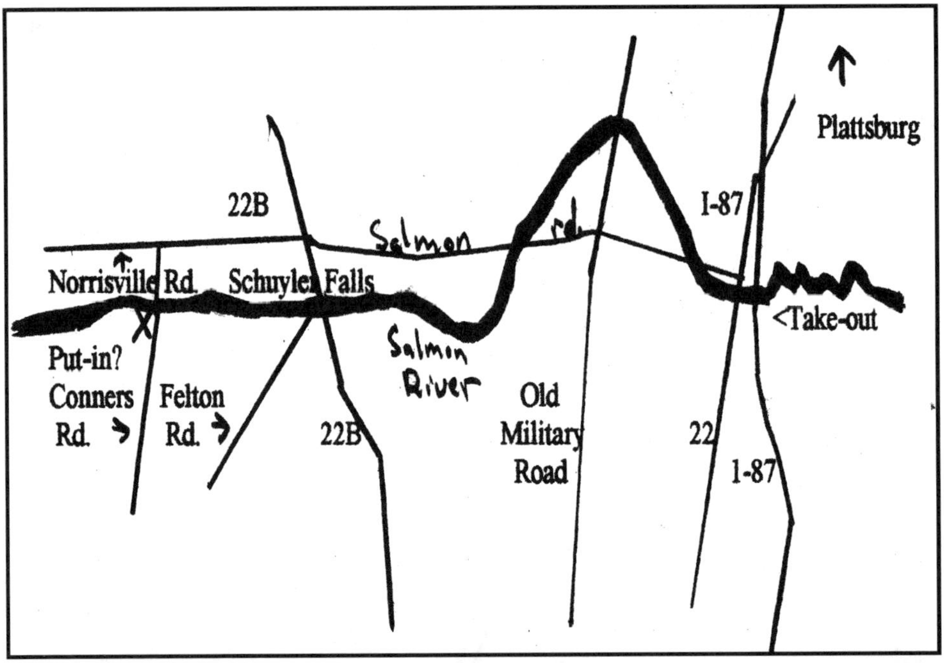

Al Baker on Black Hole Falls (East Oswegatchie). Photo by Chris Koll.

River:	**Sandy**(Adams)**
Scenery:	Good
Class:	I-V
Access:	.4-mile
Length:	8 or 10 miles
Average gradient:	50'/mile
Gauge:	The Fish needs to be at least 2.5'(?) / 3' would be better, call Northern Outfitters at (800-249-4112).
Water levels:	Be careful of the holes, especially those down by Woodville
Best betting time:	Late March-early May
Other local runs:	South Sandy (III-V)**/Lorraine Gulf (III or IV if it's high)***
Boogie time:	75% -- scout the falls
Time to do first run:	3-4 hours
First known descent:	?
Raft:	Yes
Ducky:	Yes
Food and gas:	Adams
Camping:	Campgrounds in Pulaski or Sandy Creek
Page in the Gazetteer:	83
County:	Jefferson
Closest river store:	T.I. Adventures in Clayton

Directions: The put-in is in Adams at Route 11. From there head west on Route 77/Smithville Road for 2 miles and turn left on Route 178 (you'll pass by the alternate put-in). Take a left on Route 75 and go through Belleville and keep going west. You'll notice that the map shows the road names changing; just stay on the same road until Route 3. At this intersection turn left and take-out at the bridge as it passes over the river. You can also do a drive-by to check out the river at the bridge in Woodville.

Description/hazards: If starting at Adams expect the first few miles to be easy ledges and flat water. Starting at Route 178 will shorten the trip by about 2 miles. Much of this section is flat water with an occasional class IV-ish drop. When you get closer to Woodville the excitement picks up as the ledgey bottom tilts down hill. This section goes on for a ways and is the climax for a nice run. If the water is high, scout from shore before running this, so you'll know where the holes are that will eat you alive (the ones on the right side won't even spit out your bones).

Notes

1

2

3

4

5

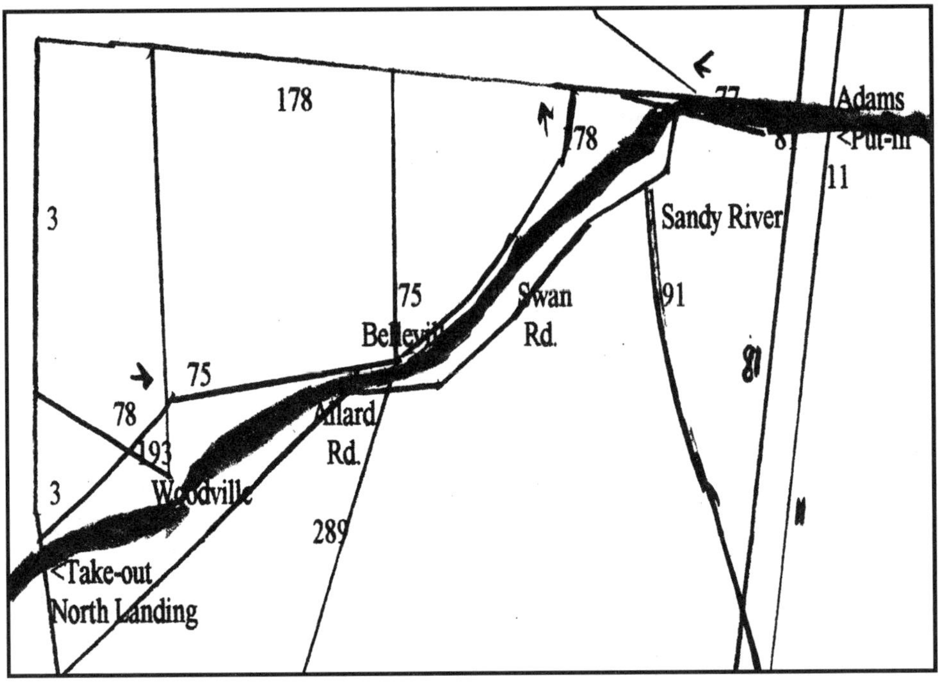
178
178
Adams
<Put-in
11
3
Sandy River
75
Swan
Rd.
91
75
78
193
Woodville
3
289
<Take-out
North Landing

River:	**South Sandy***(Ellisburg)**
Scenery:	Good
Class:	III -V
Access:	.75-mile
Length:	7 miles
Average gradient:	50'/mile
Gauge:	Fish Creek has to be at least 2.75' (?) / 3' is nicer, call (800 - 249 - 4112) and be sure to thank the nice people at Northern Outfitters in Utica/Syracuse (or spend money there) -- ask for Brad and tell him you like his style -- he likes that.
Water levels:	Watch out for BIG holes below ledges / falls at high water
Best betting time:	Late March-early May
Other local runs:	Sandy (III-V)** / Lorraine Gulf (III-at high water it's IV)***
Boogie time:	85%
Time to do first run:	2-3 hours
First known descent:	? I know it was rafted at high water in the early 1990's by the A.R.O. raft guides (I heard they had a great time).
Raft:	Yes
Ducky	Yes
Food and gas:	Ellisburg or Adams
Camping:	Campgrounds at Sandy Creek or Pulaski
Page in the Gazetteer:	83
County:	Jefferson
Closest river store:	T. I. Adventures in Clayton

Directions: The take-out is at the bridge in Ellisburg. To get to the put-in drive east on Route 193 until you hit Route 11. Then head north to Giddingsville and hop in at the Route 11 Bridge.

Description/hazards: Like the other runs in this area, you'll be amazed at the ledgey river bottom of this river. For long stretches the riverbed is solid rock. This run can be very fast and continuously pushy (with a few drops/falls thrown in to up the ante); high water will be exciting and is not to be underestimated. The bridge a few miles above Ellisburg has a big drop under it -- it's even more exciting because it has a small dam at the top of it. If you're in a hard boat that surfs you'll have a really fun day. The river is much more manageable when it's not so high. It can still be fun -- mellow fun that is -- not, scary fun. Thanks for the input on this run, Cameron. Personally I'm going to make sure I get on this in 2002; I've heard from a number of people that the **surfing is really good on this run.**

As of March 2002 one of the big drops has a hard to see/bad tree strainer in it.

Free Love Free beer
playboy bunnies on the prowl
Drops and surfing— how could it get any better??

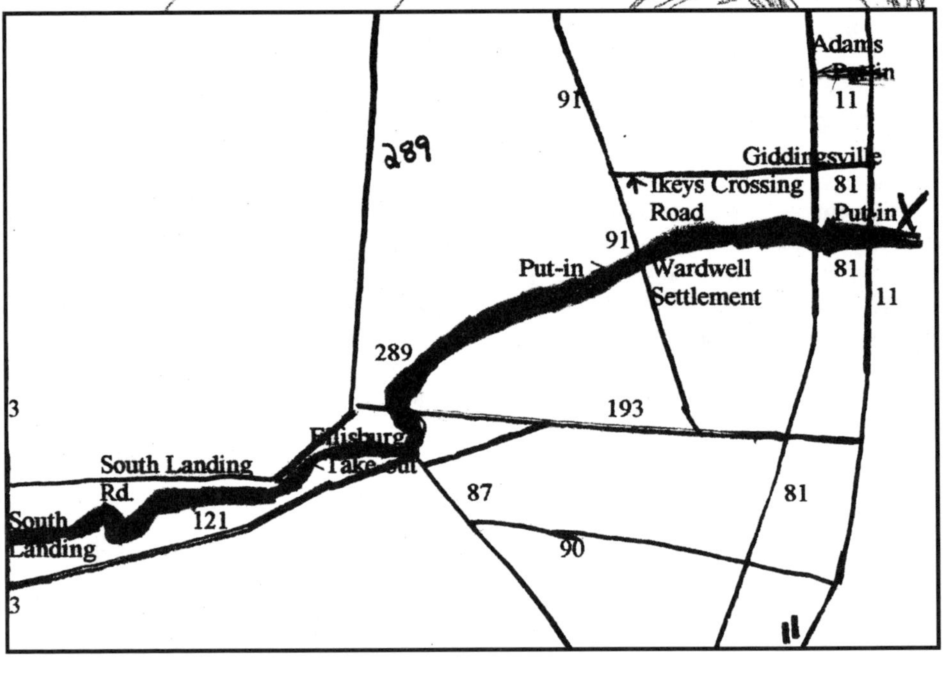
Adams
Put-in
11
91
289
Giddingsville
Ikeys Crossing Road
81
Put-in
91
Put-in >
Wardwell Settlement
81
11
289
3
193
Ellisburg
Take-out
South Landing Rd.
121
87
81
South Landing
90
3
11

Tom Vickery likes to play. Amen. Photo by Julie Vickery.

River:	**South Sandy/Lorraine Gulf***(Adams)**
Scenery:	Very good-sheer walled for miles
Class:	(III) or (III-IV) at high water
Access:	Sometimes it's only 30' away -- but, it's straight up
Length:	11 miles
Average gradient:	45'/mile -- the last 2 miles are 60'/mile
Gauge:	The Fish needs to be at least 2.5'. Call Northern Outfitters at (800 - 249 - 4112)
Water levels:	High water may be hard to find, but it would make things brutal if somebody has a problem.
Best betting time:	Late March-April
Other local runs:	South Sandy (III-V)*** / Sandy (III-V)**
Boogie time:	99.3% (You'll at least want to stop to pee, won't you?)
Time to do first run:	3-4 hours
First known descent:	?
Raft:	Yes -- if it's high
Ducky:	Yes
Food and gas:	Adams
Camping:	Camping at Pulaski or Sandy Creek
Page in the Gazetteer:	83
County:	Jefferson
Closest river store:	T. I. Adventures in Clayton

Directions: Put-in at Bullock Corners at County Road 95. Then head south and take your first right, going until it T's. Head west on Route 189 for several miles. You'll cross the river and turn left/west on Route 97. At Route 11 turn left and find a place to take-out at the bridge in Giddingsville.

Description/hazards: This is an easy run, being mostly class II-III (unless it's high). The river is very inaccessible, and even though it seems to be free of strainers, just one would be very bad. The Tug Hill Plateau has a number of gulfs; this is one of them, a long one. A gulf is a shale-y looking, sheer walled, diminutive gorge. For some reason they don't tend to be undercut. They're beautiful and otherworldly, but scary in their inescapability. With that being said, enjoy, this is a special place to be. The last couple of miles are a little steeper.

Notes

1

2

3

4

5

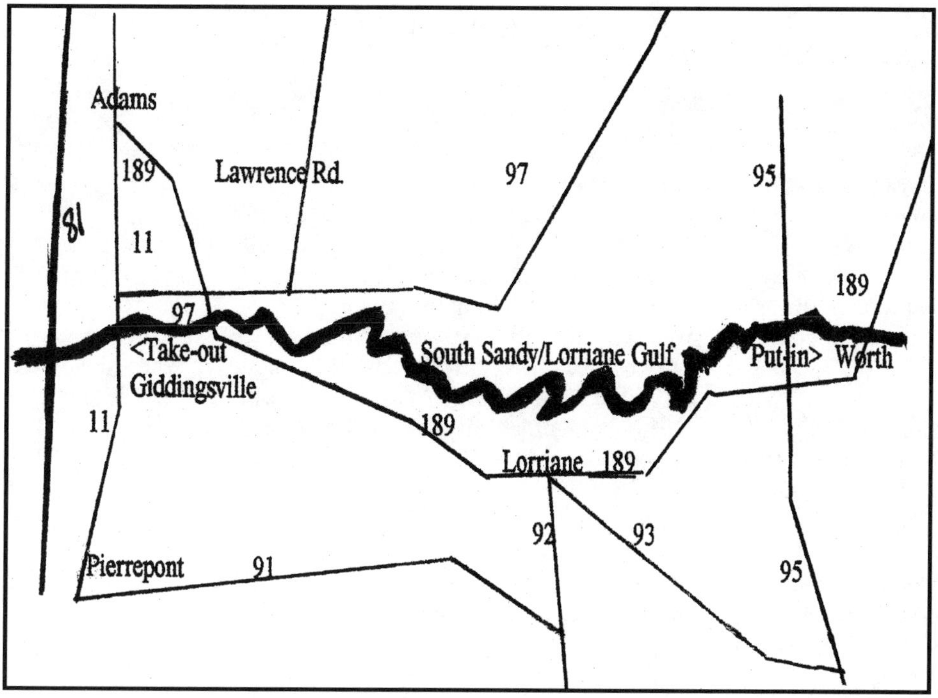
Adams
189
Lawrence Rd.
97
95
81
11
189
97
<Take-out
Giddingsville
South Sandy/Lorriane Gulf
Put-in> Worth
11
189
Lorriane 189
92
93
Pierrepont
91
95

River:	**Saranac**(Redford)**
Scenery:	Good-very good
Class:	II-IV+
Access:	.5-mile
Length:	6 or 10 miles
Average gradient:	40'/mile
Gauge:	Saranac 3.5'/600cfs is minimal / 6.5' is high
Water level:	This part of the river often stays up well into June, after everything else has gone away.
Best betting time:	April-May (try it in the summer too)
Other local runs:	We haven't done it but check out the North Branch. It's supposedly class II-III (even a little more when it's high) - from Mud Lake to Route 2 / West Ausable (IV-VI)***
Boogie time:	90% -- scout the falls -- it's rocky down there
Time to do first run:	3 hours
First known descent:	??
Raft:	Yes -- over 1000cfs
Ducky:	Yes
Food and gas:	Redford?
Camping:	Silver Lake Campground
Page in the Gazetteer:	102
County:	Clinton
Closest river store:	Adirondack Lakes and Trails in Saranac Lake

Directions: Take-out in Redford below the **play hole**. To get to the put-in head west on Route 2 and turn left on Silver Lake Road -- you can get in at the next bridge (if the dog is sleeping or dead). Or head up Casey Road and get in below the dam.

Description/hazards: Starting at the dam you'll have class III-III+ for a few hundred yards and then it's flat down to the next bridge. You'll find it flat for a ways below that bridge as well. The going is pretty easy until you spot the horizon line. Scout on the left. This drop is by far the hardest of the day. For the rest of the day a class III boater should have their selves a good time. There are a few big holes shortly after the falls. Take a quick look. This part of the river also has the best scenery -- enjoy. The rest of the trip is mixed, with moving water and frequent, easy to moderate rapids.

Extra: The first time I paddled this there was a loud nasty dog at the bridge so Kerry and I started up at the dam. The run was scenic and a great level for early May. Admittedly the most memorable spot on the river, for me, was the *play hole at Redford.* It's right next to the road and it's deep and bouncy. Alas, you won't find a great eddy but you'll have fun and get a good workout.

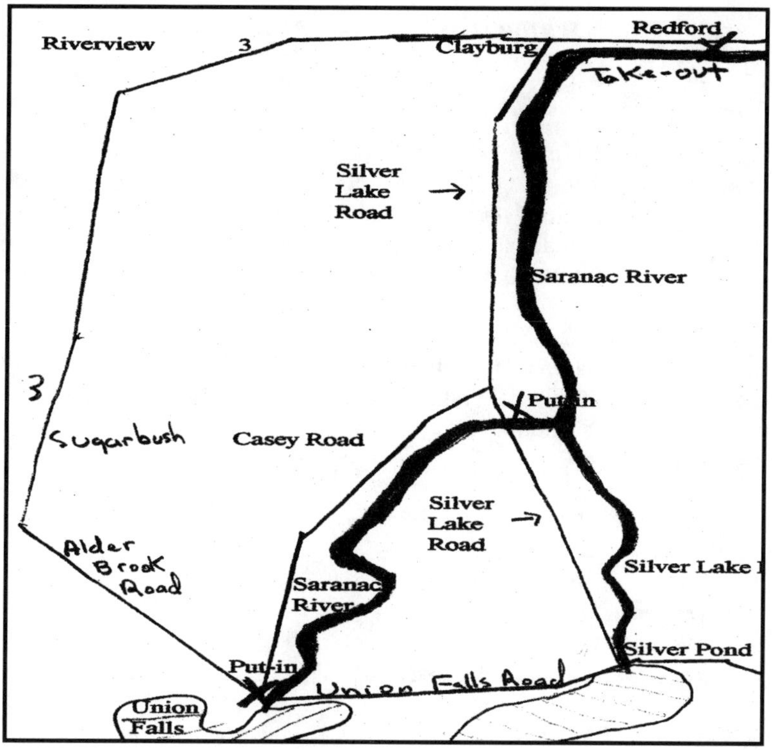

Notes

1
2
3
4
5

Save a puppy from the pound

River:	**Saranac/High Falls***(Wilmington)**
Scenery:	Good
Class:	V
Access:	.2-mile
Length:	1.6 miles
Average gradient:	The steepest part of this is over 300'/mile. What you're looking at drops nearly 200' in .75 of a mile
Gauge:	I understand that the best level is when the river is a bit low (600-800cfs on the gauge?)
Water levels:	This is a run on which you don't want much water
Best betting time:	June-October?
Other local runs:	Saranac/ Moody Falls (IV)** / Saranac / Redford (II-III-IV)**
Boogie time:	0% -- scout all of this first -- this is serious stuff
Time to do first run:	2-3 hours
First known descent:	?
Raft:	No
Ducky:	Maybe
Food and gas:	Wilmington
Camping:	The campground at Silver Lake
Page in the Gazetteer:	102
County:	Clinton
Closest river store:	Adirondack Lakes and Trails in Saranac Lake

Directions: Just west of Moffitsville on Route 3 is a dirt road that leads down to the put-in. The take-out is found by going across the bridge in town and taking the left, which is Soper Street. Go down about .5-mile and take-out by the power plant. There is a carry trail for canoeists along this whole stretch of river. As of this writing AMERICAN WHITEWATER is trying to secure releases for us on this section.

Description/hazards: This is a short and very intense run. There's a flume to start and then several waterfalls. All of this stuff is pretty nasty -- setting safety wouldn't hurt. A good scouting before you start will show you what you need to know. I hope you're feeling your oats and you're ready to go into the zone. I don't know of anybody running this yet; I hear it's been done though. If you're planning on it -- be sure to bring only the big bad dogs to chew on this bone.

Notes

1

2

3

4

5

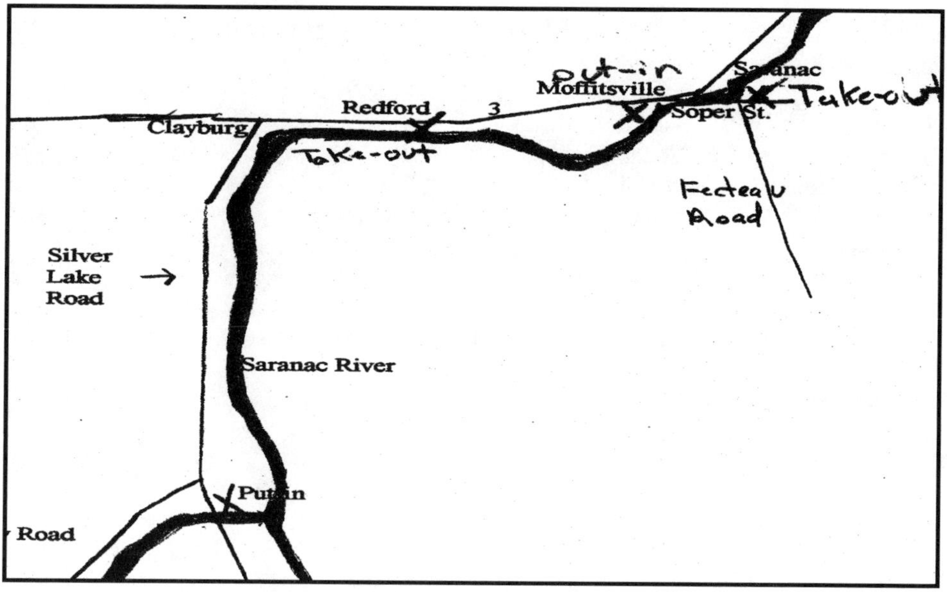
Redford
3
put-in
Moffitsville
Saranac
Take-out
Soper St.
Clayburg
Take-out
Fecteau
Road
Silver
Lake
Road
Saranac River
Put-in
Road

River: **Saranac/Moody Falls*(Oggyville)**
Scenery: Good
Class: IV
Access: .4-mile
Length: 2.1 mile
Average gradient: 80'/mile
Gauge: 800cfs at Plattsburg is the minimum
Water levels: This is a run to do when other things have dropped too low (late spring-early summer)
Best betting time: May-June
Other local runs: Saranac / High Falls (V)** / Saranac / Redford (II-III, IV)**
Boogie time: 50% -- scout the drops
Time to do first run: 2-3 hours
First known descent: ?
Raft: No
Ducky: Yes
Food and gas: Wilmington
Camping: The campground at Silver Lake
Page in the Gazetteer: 102
County: Clinton
Closest river store: Adirondack Lake and Trails in Saranac Lake

Directions: The take-out is at the Pete Sake Bridge. To get to the put-in drive west (take a right if you're facing the opposite of north). On Trumpet Road -- when you get to Route 98 turn right (north) and park by the bridge.

Description/hazards: This is a short and fun run. There's flat water and several waterfalls. All of this stuff is pretty straightforward. This could be just the run for that time of the year when spring creeking is finished and the summer releases haven't started yet. The run has long pools (flat water) and several drops (falls.) There's something for everybody. Elves and Fairies are often seen along the banks. I know of some swampland in this area that's for sale (practically free) if you're interested.

Notes

1

2

3

4

5

man Tam got spanked Hard!
Yeah-I guess the falls are in a bad mood!

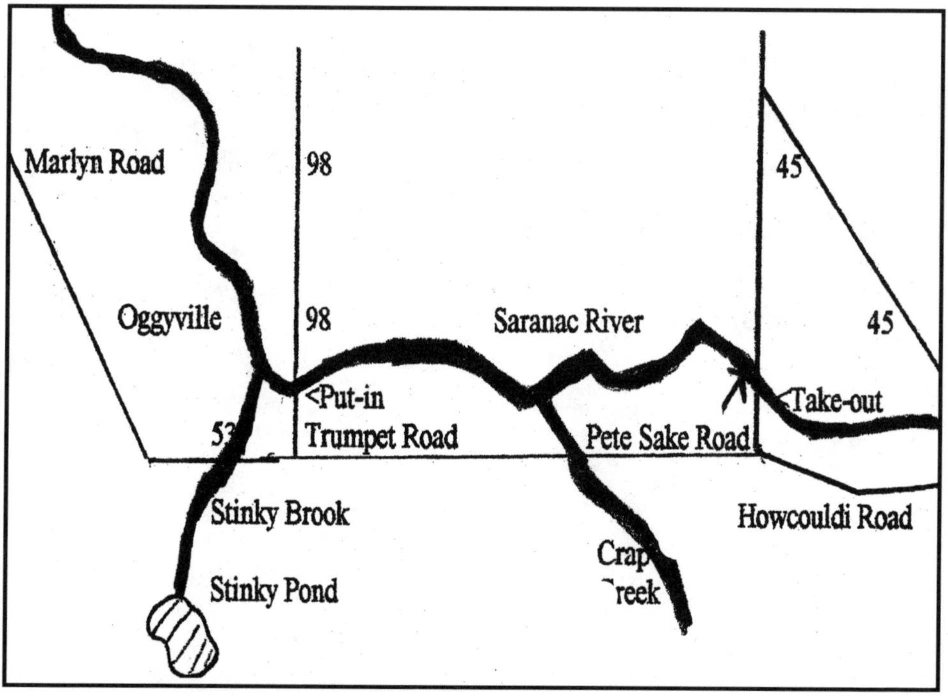
Marlyn Road
98
45
Oggyville
98
Saranac River
45
<Put-in
Trumpet Road
Pete Sake Road
Take-out
53
Stinky Brook
Howcouldi Road
Crap
Creek
Stinky Pond

River:	**Saranac/Permanent Rapids*** (Saranac Lake)**
Scenery:	Good
Class:	II
Access:	Roadside
Length:	1-mile
Average gradient:	40'/mile
Gauge:	No gauge, but it virtually always has water (Permanent Rapids).
Water levels:	This is a run to do when other things have dropped too low, but the last .25-mile of this gets scratchy if it's a dry summer
Best betting time:	Spring-mid summer / all fall
Other local runs:	West Ausable (IV-V, VI)*** / Ausable/ Lower (I-III)**
Boogie time:	100%
Time to do first run:	This is an easy play run -- take your time
First known descent:	?
Raft:	Yes -- in the springtime only
Ducky:	Yes
Food and gas:	Wilmington
Camping:	Both sides of the river are state land
Page in the Gazetteer:	96
County:	Essex
Closest river store:	Adirondack Lakes and Trails in Saranac Lake

Directions: If you are driving north on Route 3 out of Saranac you'll need to turn in St. Armand. Take a right and head up Route 18/River Road about 3 miles, you can put-in where you see the best spot. The road is right next to the river and pretty much stays that way down to the take-out. Just drive down River Road about a mile. The reservoir starts to back up where the bank sticks out from the road.

Description/hazards: You start off with class I for a ways. When you spot an island -- take the right side -- it's more interesting. The river narrows, even more as the river turns into class II. A little more and the river gets slightly harder (almost class III if you've got good water). This all lasts for 300' before the river widens and slows down. The last .25-mile will be bony at late summer levels. There's 200' of flat water and then the take-out is on the left, where the bank sticks out.

Notes

1
2
3
4
5

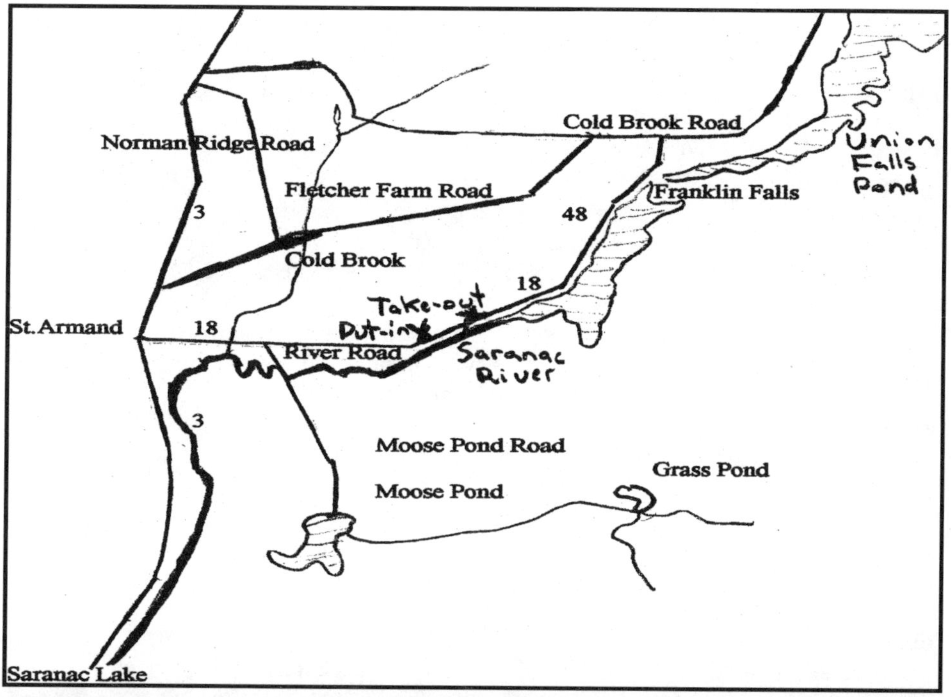

Dennis using 'that look' to get his Maypo. Photo by Sally Dewes.

River:	**The Branch***(Elizabethtown)**
Scenery:	Good
Class:	IV-IV+, VI
Access:	400 feet
Length:	3.5 miles
Average gradient:	140'/mile
Gauge:	The Hudson will have to be 7' or more
Water level:	It takes a lot of rain to make this run -- which is why I come here at the times when the other runs in the area are too high
Best betting time:	April -- while it's raining
Other local runs:	Boquet (IV-V)***** / Boquet/ Steele Woods (II-III)***
Boogie time:	80% -- be sure to walk around the huge unrunnable drop right below the bridge as you come into town
Time to do first run:	2-3 hours
First known descent:	Dennis, Tyler Maheu and Brian Conway in 1999
Raft:	No
Ducky:	Yes
Food and gas:	Elizabethtown
Camping:	At Split Rock Falls on the Boquet
Page in the Gazetteer:	96
County:	Essex
Closest river store:	Adirondack Lakes and Trails in Saranac Lake

Directions: Turn off I-87 and go west into Elizabethtown. We took out at a small park on your left side. Now drive up (west) 9N and check the level -- and keep looking for tree strainers (they're hiding -- but they're in there). Make sure you find the eddy above the class VI drop at the edge of town. Drive up and start where it looks good (we've been starting just above the little side road/bridge on the left side and running the culvert under the bridge to start the day). I don't swear to it -- but if you call this bridge #1, it should be bridge #4 that's just above the BIG drop.

Description/hazards: High up the river you'll find that it's very small. As you go around (and over and through) the trees you'll be looking forward to when it gets to be fun. It does -- quickly. The best part of the run feels like you're down in a magical ravine; flying over boulders, dodging wood and paddling some nice class IV-IV+ stuff. After that it opens up and eases up some. Just keep watching out for trees and walk around the BIG drop (which is probably unrunnable even without the trees wedged in there.) The BIG drop is 150' below the bridge you'll cross as you come down the hill into E-town. The drop also has rebar in it. Stay away. Get out well above it -- there are no easy eddies just above it. After portaging on the right you'll find that the river is still flinging you around. I hope that in your travels you looked at the river in town -- there is a huge tree all the way across the river not far below the big unrunable drop. There are no eddies above this tree. The usual line is to ski jump the thing. But then I've only been here when the water's high -- I don't know what you're going to do. After this things mellow quickly and you're at the park.

The Bad News First: - Who could stand this? "Too much rain?!" Arghhhhhh!!! Wasn't it bad enough that I couldn't paddle all spring? It had been poor water and the shoulder injury insured no aquatic fulfillment. Wasn't it bad enough that it barely rained all summer?

Now The Good News: - Hurricane Floyd in Sept. of 1999 was a blessing for whitewater withdrawal symptoms. The weatherman said it was only going to rain 1 inch in the Adirondacks. The rain was hammering the Catskills and Berkshires and we're thinking that they may be our best options. Brian and Tyler are super psyched for something great; it's up to me to help fulfill their fantasies (sorry... the girlfriend's always the last to find out). This is my curse for indulging my creekin' habit for so long, and now I'm leading others astray (hence this book).

Tyler had driven over the middle of last night from Boston. It was pouring and black as pitch, and naturally he has no windshield wipers. Now I'm riding north with Brian, and Tyler is driving his car. Tyler has no wipers, it's pouring and he's wearing sun glasses (!) All I can say is, I'm not the only one! We're amazed how much it's raining. The storm has turned north and slowed down. Everything is high and getting higher. We stop and look at Johns Brook. Unfortunately we can only look. It's in flood. Looking at a class V creek in flood (now class VI) is very sobering. We drive away planning on coming back tomorrow. As far as we know nobody has paddled the creek up in Elizabethtown, so we head there. It's high but looks like class IV-ish fun. It is -- try it -- you'll like it! I've got to save some stories so that I can tell you something new when we're eating dinner (after you come and paddle your brains out here in THE WHITEWATER STATE!)

And the next day: Talk about a letdown -- yesterday on The Branch had been fun -- but we were sure that Johns Brook would be good today. It had somehow done something so horrible and unthinkable during the night. It went poof! It was now too low to boat. So we went to Vermont (where I lost my wallet and the $850.00 therein). When you're buying dinner remind me to tell the rest of the story (that's Paul Harvey's thing isn't it?); Man I'm sorry -- I gotta' come up with my own stic....now about dinner....

Notes

1

2

3

4

5

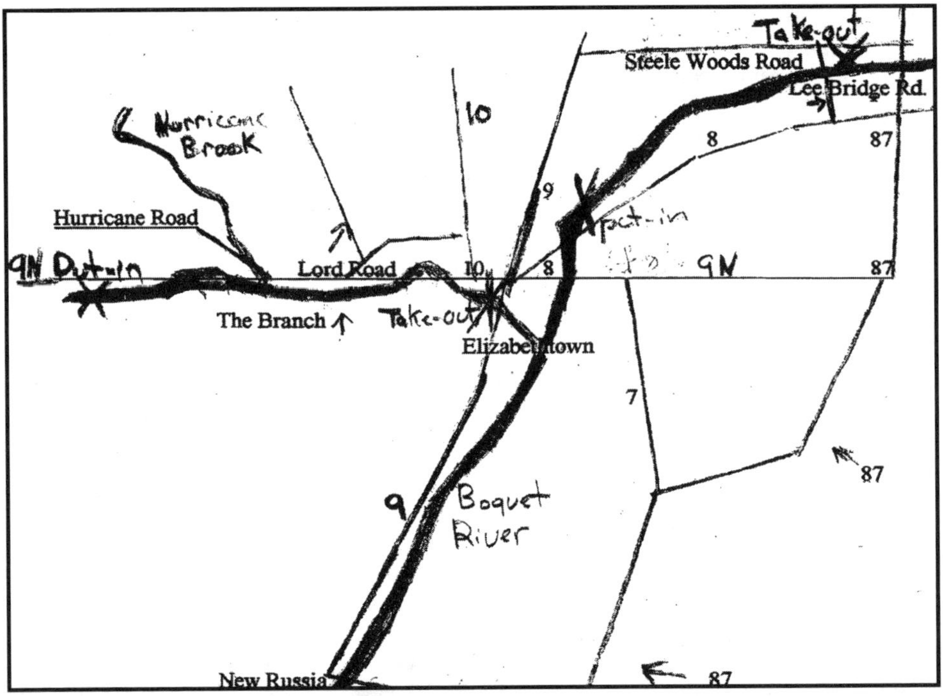

Caron Koll on the Funnel (Bottom Moose). Photo by Chris Koll.

The Secret is out!

In the late 1800's the Adirondacks were thee place to go for camping -- especially canoe camping. The good news is that the paddling in upstate New York is still: wild, beautiful and sees few paddlers on the creeks. Yes, it can be: cold (mostly from ice-out until mid-May) and there's a week in there in April called Mud season (this means stay off dirt roads). Yes, there are bugs (mostly from mid-May to mid-June). Yes, the water goes away (mostly from mid-June until the fall). And some times it doesn't rain in the fall. *

Much better news: the Adirondacks are part of a tremendous rock pile known as the Canadian shield -- between Nor'easters, lake effect storms and things that blow down from Canada, (besides kayakers from Toronto) we get a lot of rain and snow, (averaging 200+ inches of snow and sometimes getting up to 400 inches in the western Adirondacks and on the Tug Hill Plateau) -- and best of all, this area, which is larger than all of Vermont has been a "Forever Wild" park for over a century. This could be your personal playground, it's just waiting for you to come and paddle, you've obviously been lucky enough (or smart enough) to get your hands on the guidebook -- why aren't you here yet??????

If you show up in April or early May with a dry suit and a large cushy van (call me) -- you'll have a great time, this is a guarantee -- if you don't -- just call up Jody -- she's the Enforcer.

Because I like you (since you bought this book and told 2 friends) -- here's some insider info:
....the...rivers...............................
.....in...the...........western..........and.......................
northwestern...
....corner..
.....................................of...t
he...Adirondacks..
...stay..
.............up..............longer..they.....................................have...
................flatter.................................larger...............................swampier..................
....watersheds......(and lots and lots of ponds)..
these.........................include...the..........................Grass.........
..................................the.................................branches........................of........................
..............the...................Oswegatchie..the............................
St..Regis............the......Raquette..
....the Independence...............

When everything in the local area is **too high,** go check out: The Branch in Elizabethtown / Hudson / Cedar / Jimmy Creek / Elbow Creek / Doig Creek / Dunning Brook / Saranac (Union Falls) / Boquet (South Branch) / Grass (Lampson Falls) / (Lorriane Gulf) South Sandy / Otter / Bog / Steele Woods (Boquet) / Grass (Middle) / Grass (North) / Lake Ozonia Outlet.

When everything in your area seems to have **dropped too low,** go explore these: Round Lake Outlet / West Sacandaga Gorge / Middle Sacandaga / Lampson Falls / Upper Cedar / Ausable Chasm / Independence (last 1/4 mile) / Mettawee / Bottom Moose / Oswegatchie (Fine section often runs into June) / Raquette (Piercefield usually runs into June) / Raquette (Colton has a minimal flow release all summer , yes it's bony, but it's fun and you can walk back up either side to your car.) / Black (Watertown) / Black (Hawkinsville) / The Saranac has enough flow for a low water run most of the year, (this is especially so for Permanent Rapids.) /

In the fall after the leaves have changed: (their thirst, is seemingly endless in the spring and summer) the western Adirondack rivers come up easily, the Saranac is running and Ausable Chasm will likely have water.

There are lots of things that have releases on them; there are several more runs that we'll be getting releases on in the near future. Just check out the AW and keep track of what **www.h2oline.com** is doing. Keep watching **www.whitewateroutlaw.com** as well.

* This is here mostly (just so you don't worry too much) for the amusement of local paddlers. In reality this would be a horrible, worst case scenario that never happens. It just seems to be a paddlers' nature to worry too much, about some things anyway, like: where's the put-in, how high is it, where the hell is my lunch, where's my skirt and will my wife get mad (no sense worrying, you already know the answer) if I buy another boat?

FIRST DESCENTS TO BE HAD

(Do your parents know what you do for fun?)

I'd like to point out that when it really rains in N.Y. that there are probably 1000 brooks, creeks and rivers that could be run. They range from class II to class VI. Most have very short runnable stretches, lots of trees across the bed, barbed wire, high water bridges.... etc..... I've **played hooky a lot to distill this information** (long ago the family was told that water is thicker than blood -- and they know it's true), so enjoy the fruits of my questionable behavior -- read on!

Jimmy Creek - Wells - class V**** - 1.5 miles - check the description in book 2 (sections are over 400'/mile). The Hope gauge needs to be over 5000cfs, and still raining -- walk in 1 mile. See Book 2.

Elbow Creek - Wells - class V** - if it's running good - 2 mile run - (steep) - take-out in Wells -- start 2 miles up Gilmantown Road. The Hope gauge will be over 5000cfs. This has some wood on it. See Book 2.

Millbrook - Margaretville (this is posted and patrolled -- but check out the description in book 2 anyway) class III-V*** 3+ miles. N.Y. City is really touchy about their land right now - -don't.... iss them off (i.e. I don't know you).

Mill (no)/Lowville number 1 - Class 4-4+*** 1.25 miles -- this run ends on Cemetery Road in front of the cemetery (don't run the huge falls around the next corner) -- start 1.25 miles upstream in a big field (just above the second bridge that you'll cross). The first half of the run is non-stop (no eddies) big slides, be sure to scout all this part before getting in. The bridge at the bottom of the steep section has barbed wire on the upstream end.

Mill (no) Lowville number 2 - Class 5** 1.2 miles - this run also flows into Mill Creek in Lowville (just like number 1 does) -- the crux is about .5-mile long and is very busy (no eddies in the most extreme part). You must bank scout this first by strolling along behind the public safety building. This would be a good run to do in somebody else's boat or a quality inflatable -- there will be a very big hard and shallow landing.

Chasm Falls - Malone - (this is also posted) class V-VI**** - only .5-mile long - roadside, probably best from mid April-early May. This is extreme and non-stop- pool-drop. This is one of the hardest possible runs in N.Y. Several boaters are thinking about it -- but it hasn't been done, yet.

Spruce Creek - Dolgeville - class V-VI*** 4+ miles. Take a ducky, or somebody else's boat. See Book 2.

Platte kill Clove - West Saugerties - class IV-VI***** 2-4 miles. I'm running this in 2002 (walk up from the high fence in town). See Book 2.

Styles Brook - Jay - class V/V+*1-2 miles. In truth this is way too woody.

Jenny Creek - Harrisville - class III-VI** 3+ miles. See the description in this book.

Hamilton (outlet) Creek - Piseco Lake - class II-V*** 8+ miles. The lake is posted, so do the best you can. See Book 2.

Thorpe Brook - East Durham - class III-VI*** 4 miles. This looks promising -- if you like shallow landing zones. Ducks or kayaks are the preferred craft. See Book 2.

Mill Creek/Turin (South of Lowville - by the Snowy Ridge Ski Center) class V* 2+ miles, and everything lands on shallow rock (duckies only).

Bowery Brook - South Durham - class III-V* 1-2 miles. If you start on Bogardus Road when it's high the first stretch will be class V. It'll be 12' wide -- and have no eddies. This is a short run. See Book 2.

Book 2 will have a listing that greatly expands on this treasury. Oh, ya' -- check out parts of Trout and Orwell Brooks over in the southwest corner of the Tug Hill Plateau (north of Syracuse). There are also parts of the St. Regis above St. Regis Falls that have some good drops on them. I haven't got to them -- yet. I've been exploring much more obscure creeks and rivers. This has been done with only your best interest in mind. Ya', ya' that's it -- that's **why I did it!**

OVERNIGHT TRIPS*

Raquette (Piercefield)** (Flat, II-V+) / 16 miles / Piercefield gauge should be over 7.0'. There is no good access along the run. Has a long season -- check the Internet for levels. Rafts O.K.

Catskill*** (Preston Hollow – Catskill) - (Flat, II-III, V) / 33 miles / Cold Brook at 8.0' and rising or 10' and dropping. You have lots of road access and can stash stuff along the way. Rafts O.K. See BOOK 2

West Oswegatchie*** (Starting just above) Round Lake - Jerdan Falls Bridge) - (flat, IV-V, VI) / 18 miles / Harrisville at 1200cfs (holding steady or rising) is minimum. Walk in 3/10 mile at put-in. You have lots of access only in the first 8 miles. Rafting is possible only at high levels (of water and testosterone).

Middle Oswegatchie*** (At the upper end of Long Pond Extension Road) -(flat, III-VI) / 22 miles (to Bryants Bridge) or 26 miles (to Middle B1ranch) / Harrisville will have to be at least 1200cfs (and rising) or 2000cfs (or more) and dropping. There is no access in the upper 16 miles. Rafts are possible, down to Bryants Bridge anyway, but any portages will be brutal or worse.

S. Grass*** (Route 3 - Russell) - (flat, II-V, VI) / 35 miles / Harrisville at 900cfs is low. There is access at miles: 16, 18, 22, 24, 26.... check your map. Rafting would be a huge blast -- with huge drops and a lot of flat water.

S. Moose*** (Above Moose River flats - Route 28) - (I-IV) / 22+miles / Mckeever should be 3.0'. This has a long shuttle -- way out in the woods. Rafts are O.K. at higher levels. See the description in this book.

Independence* (Hike in from Stillwater Road 1.5-2 miles - Pine Grove Road) - (flat, III-V+) / 40+miles / Donattsburg needs to be 900cfs and rising or 1600cfs and dropping as a good level (to start really high up that is). There is no realistic access for the first 30 miles. Rafts are a possibility, but only for the last 3 miles or so.

Hudson*** (Henderson Lake or Newcomb to the Glen or points upstream) - (II-IV+) North Creek should be at least 5'. The longest run would be around 60 miles. The first two-dozen miles are mostly very easy and then there's lots of class II and a fair amount of class III and IV. This is a good rafting/fishing trip. See BOOK 2.

Cold River*** (Duck Hole - Long Lake) - (II-V) / 24+ miles / Hudson should be over 6'. There is no access. This is a long carry in, no rafts. See the description in this book.

* The number of stars (***) shows my rating of their desirability to do as overnight trips.

Cedar or Cedar-Hudson*** Starting at Wakely dam (if North Creek is 5.5'or more) will give you 30 miles before you even get to the Hudson -- the first 6 miles are class II-IV+ and then it's mostly class II down to the Hudson. The only access is in the middle of the run at Route 28 (a good rafting put-in). See BOOK 2. Rafting would be advised only from Route 28 down (watch out for the bridge in the middle of the golf course around the first bend -- you're going to have to get out). At high (7' or more) water you could start rafting even higher, but you'd better be bold and strong. See BOOK 2.

Rock-Cedar-Hudson*** (Starting at the state campground on Route 28) The Rock is mostly class I and II and has II nice hard drops (IV-IV+). After getting on this run there's no access for 30 miles (put-in to take-out). Rafts (Hudson has to be 7' or more) may have a few tough portages (it's small and there are trees) in the first couple of miles. See BOOK 2.

Moose*** (Singing Waters Campground or Route 28 to Fowlersville or more) - 3.0' (higher if rafting) at Mckeever is minimum. It's mostly class II down to Route 28, and then class II-III to the next bridge, then mixed flat and class IV-ish to Fowlersville Bridge. The next 4 drops are class IV+/V-, and if it's 4.5-5.5' you can run down the 4 drops after that (class IV+/V-). Good raft trip. These last 8 drops (which start at Folwersville Bridge) are not for the faint hearted and should be rafted only by pros. See the description in this book.

The Easiest Rivers in this guide

2a. Ausable (East) - Keene to Upper Jay (I-III) **
4. Ausable (West) - Upper (II-III, IV-)***
9. Black - Hawkinsville (II-III) **
11. Bog (I-V)**
13. Boquet - Steele Woods (II-III) ***
16a. Chazy - North (II-III) **
18a. Deer - Lower (I-III) **
19. Deer - New Boston (II-III)**
21a. Fish - Upper (II-III)****
24. Grass - Upper (I-III) ***
32. Little - Aldrich (II-III) ***
34. Little Trout - Burke (II, IV)**
42. Moose - Middle (II-III, IV-)***
43. Moose - South (I-III, IV) ***
51. Raquette - Piercefield (I-VI) **
57. Salmon - Malone (I-III, IV) **
58. Salmon - Pulaski (I-III) ***
62. South Sandy - Lorraine Gulf (II-III) ***

The Dirty Dozen

3. Ausable - West/Gorge (V-VI) ****
5. Beaver - Eagle (V) ***
30. Johns Brook (V) *****
39. Mill - Port Henry (IV-VI) **
40. Moose - Bottom (IV+/V) ****
45. Oswegatchie - Fine (IV-VI) ***
45a. Oswegatchie - Browns Bridge (V) ****
46. Oswegatchie - Middle (IV-V, VI) ****
46a. Oswegatchie - Sluice Falls (V-VI) ****
47. Oswegatchie - West (IV-V+) ***
52. Raquette - Colton (IV-V, VI) ***
64. Saranac - High Falls (V-VI) **

Some stuff in western New York

There are more runs in the western part of the state than what I've got here. If you'd like to know more than what is listed just check out the AMERICAN WHITEWATER INVENTORY. You'll find it at their website at American Whitewater. The list is pretty comprehensive; just realize that it's an inventory -- not a guide. It's not totally updated and many of the runs aren't really worthwhile whitewater runs, even though there is whitewater on them. I'm not knocking it -- it's a great resource, thank you AW!

Cattaraugus (Gowanda) II-III
Cattaraugus/South Branch (Otto) II-IV
Chautaugua (Lyon Road) III
Eighteen-mile Creek (Hamburg) II-V
Fall Creek (Ithaca) IV-V
Casidilla Creek (Ithaca) V
Keuka (Penn Yan) I-III
Twenty-mile Creek (South Ripley) II-IV
Sugar Creek (Canaseraga Creek) III-V
Six-mile Creek (Brooktondale) V
Rushford Lake Outlet (Rushford Lake) II-IV

If anybody has actually paddled these rivers or any of the other runs in the western part of the state please drop me a line…this state has too much stuff for one poor mortal to do himself (lord knows I've tried). You're input will go into a new edition in the future.

Glossary of Terms *

Eddy - A. a guy hiding on the river that nobody ever sees. B. name of a transvestite in Troy. C. a calm spot on the river.
Shuttle - A. that thing you swat playing badminton. B. U.S.A. spacecraft. C. driving between the put-in and the take-out.
Shuttle Bunny - A. a cute little animal that's been up in space. B. a female/male of the noblest kind. C. a dead fuzzy little rabbit used for playing badminton.
Eddy Wall - A. raised mound of water preventing escape into an eddy. B. the wall on Second Street that Eddy hangs out at. C. a trophy wall in Garcia's home.
Ducky - A. Old English slang, it means everything is fine. B. the thing your dad plays with in the tub. C. inflatable kayak.
Scouting - A. sneaking up on the enemy. B. an organization of little boys that grow up to be too nice. C. to inspect the river ahead (in your boat or out on shore).
Strainer - A. a kitchen utensil. B. a difficult bowel movement. C. an obstacle blocking the river
C.F.S. - A. cubic feet per second. B. "couldn't fly straight if you had to" (Eddy's father said this to him all the time when he was a child.
Cockpit - A. the big hole in top of a kayak. B. enclosed fighting area for roosters. C. hole at the bottom of a male chicken's beak.
Boof - A. noise Batman makes when punching out bad guys. B. sound made by a fat man landing in deep snow. C. the action (or sound made on landing flat on aerated water) of ski jumping off of boulders.
Bootie - A. adipose tissue in the gluteus maximus area of the posterior torso of a female. B. a pirate's treasure. C. rubber river wear for your feet.
Eddy Hopping - A. what Eddy does when he has trouble putting on his panty hose. B. to move from eddy to eddy as you paddle downstream. C. what (not too smart) Eddy does while wearing his Playboy bunny outfit.
Skirt - A. traditional female garment worn by Eddy. B. to go around a strainer.
C. rubber enclosure that fits around your cockpit (make sure it stays on).
Panties - A. breathing hard after surfing hard. B. type of undergarment most likely to be stained.
Suck - A. to blow something--badly. B. adjective for incompetent people (you suck). C. to inhale hard.
What people really mean when they say "Your boat looks like you paddle a lot" - A. get a life (and a job). B. you are a god to me. C. I'd never buy a used boat from you.
Tuber - A. a parsnip. B. people with funny tans and sore butts. C. a root like vegetable.
Ferry - A. 1960's term for somebody light in the loafers (i.e.-Eddy). B. a boat that takes people and cars across Lake Champlain in the summer. C. to paddle across the river without moving downstream.
Croakies - A. an eyeglass retaining strap. B. small New England tree frog preferred by Boston yuppies. C. a group of inexperienced paddlers very likely not to survive the day on the river.
Window shade - A. flipping around and around in a hydraulic. B. moveable window cover that prevents boys from looking at the girl next door. C. something you do at a

picnic (first you eat and drink too much): you hold your hands against your sides and roll down a steep hill--over and over until you puke.
Probe - A. the first boater down a difficult run. B. Eddy's favorite medical device. C. to skillfully distill personal information from an attractive paddler
Punch - A. a questionable drink from Eddy that you never ever swallow. B. to paddle through liquid obstacles. C. form of physical contact Eddy most often receives.
Bony - A. an overly excited male paddler. B. term for very low water. C. derogatory term for the gluteus maximus area of a skinny paddler.
Malfunction Junction - A. tangle of roads (built to handle the traffic for the Olympics) south of Lake Placid. B. the place in the brain that paddlers are wired incorrectly.

*This glossary is dedicated with the deepest respect (and humor) to the memory of William Nealy. His death in 2001 saddened me. His books and humor continue to be my best teachers.

Afterword

This book was more work than I ever thought possible (learning how to do word processing as I bumbled along didn't help I suppose). It was also more rewarding than I ever thought possible. There will be a BOOK 2 out there by the end of 2002. Book 2 will cover the south flowing rivers and creeks. It will be even bigger than this book and have more runs (possibly 100) than this one. By then I'll be able to spel beter, writ beter, carton beter and learn (hopefully) how to be funny. You'll notice that I've made a lot of mention to the second book. I didn't want you to have to wait to get the information you need to do overnight trips. And many of the first descents to be had in the state are in the south flowing rivers and creeks. If you want to do them first you'd better hurry --because they are on my priority list for 2002 and 2003. There will be other guides and related goodies coming down the pike, all of which will be available through the website: **www.whitewateroutlaw.com**. If you keep watching the site you'll see the developments. I'm not saying anything else, this outlaw finally has some good ideas and I'm not squealing until I'm ready. Paddle hard, laugh when in doubt (on and off the river) and enjoy simply being -- here and now.

P.S. for the book and for everybody who reads it.

Hopefully you've realized by now that whitewater paddling is an incredible sport. I think paddling/exploring is the ultimate: sport, way to enjoy the outdoors, to simply be.

Hopefully you've also realized that there is a certain element of risk involved in this path. There have been paddling deaths in N.Y. from rafting, canoeing and kayaking. It will happen again. I've had more than one close call. Some day, somebody that is reading this book will enjoy their last day of paddling as their luck runs out. I'm talking to everybody that is reading this page (since this subject is bumming you out I figure you're only going to read this page once) – **so pay attention!**

Guiding for 10 years didn't do it. Paddling/probing with others started to do it. Writing this guide did it even more. I'm talking about awareness and self-responsibility and even respect for nature and life. I hope you've got a clue what I'm talking about. My friend Larry has been saying all his life, "If you play you've got to pay." Larry has been in a wheelchair for over 20 years. I don't want anybody to have to pay the ultimate price. Explore with abandon and play with abandon, just do it intelligently. Live long and prosper! (The marching music starts again in the background, off to stage right.)

Another person that I feel deserves a special mention is my friend Denny who lives in Degrasse, N.Y. Denny is an independent, strong, friendly bear of a man -- a true Adirondacker. I hope he enjoys all the kayakers that are coming his way.

Suggested Reading and other books

William Nealy's - "Kayak: the animated manual of intermediate and advanced whitewater technique" (and any of his many other books).

AMERICAN WHITEWATER - Join the organization and get the magazine -- they do a huge and wonderful job of protecting and opening up new whitewater runs for **you!**

"New York Exposed : The Whitewater State : Volume 2" and any other book by **☯A White Water Outlaw ♋Publishing**

"Cadillac Desert" by Mark Reysner (you'll appreciate our water even more after reading this).

ADK (Adirondack Mountain Club) – They have tons of books that do a great job of covering all the awesome hiking in the state. There are even books that cover much of the infinite canoe runs along with a smattering of whitewater runs. The ADK does much to help us all explore, enjoy, protect and preserve the Adirondacks. Thanks ADK.

Any DeLorme State Gazetteer*

* In fact while I'm thinking about it I'll mention that AW is currently working on getting us all more summer releases. There are several dam controlled sections that we could get water on, these are on the: Raquette, Hoosic, Saranac and Oswegatchie. If you read the AW magazine you'll see what going on. For a relatively small organization the AW knows how to kick butt and get things done!

Whether you realize it or not, the reason that paddlers in N.Y. get to enjoy something to paddle all summer long even in a dry year is largely due to the dedication and commitment of Pete Skinner. I'd say more about him but he's getting a dedication in a future book, besides everybody knows how shy and modest he is.

And here's a formal thank you to Chris Koll. Between the Moose River Festival, the Beaver River Rendezvous and now Creek Week -- I'd say he sure knows how to throw some great parties. Thanks Chris.

I would like to also thank John Gangemi for ALL the stuff he's done the last few years. He's all over the country and making things happen. He couldn't possibly have time to paddle (talk about the ultimate sacrifice!)

About the Author

Dennis has been paddling New York rivers and creeks for 14 years; first in the Catskills, then in the Adirondacks, he went in a year's time from destroying a canoe to guiding and kayaking in the Adirondacks. He quickly knew his calling was there.

He's been a lot of things: salesman, carpenter, mason, cab driver, painter, guide, hypnotist, barbarian, ski lift operator, philosopher, etc. No longer on the path of the Renaissance man, he's content to be a seeker and a creeker. This is for all the people, even the ones who didn't know he paddled, that said, "You should write a book someday."

He's ignoring all those that said, "You should take a long walk on a short…"

In case you haven't realized it yet – Dennis isn't just right

☯A WHITEWATER OUTLAW ♋Publishing

NEW YORK EXPOSED : THE WHITEWATER STATE : Volume 1

#of-Books	Price/Book	S&H/Book
1 book	19.95/book	$3.00/book
2 books	18.95/book	$2.00/book
3-5 books	17.95/book	$1.50/book
6-9 books	14.95/book	$1.00/book
10-19 books	12.95/book	$0.75/book
20 or more	11.95/book	$0.60/book

__________Quantity
X
__________Price
='s
__________Sub Total
+
__________New York State residents add 7 % sales tax on **all** orders
+
__________Shipping and Handling (from the chart)
='S
__________Total

Please include your e-mail address
And feel free to ask about lessons and/or guided trips

Checks (or money orders) to:
A White Water Outlaw Publishing
PO box 1233
Margaretville, N.Y. 12455
www.whitewateroutlaw.com

AGMV Marquis
MEMBER OF SCABRINI MEDIA
Quebec, Canada
2002